Write
to Learn

Write to Learn

Donald M. Murray

Holt, Rinehart and Winston
New York   Chicago   San Francisco   Philadelphia
Montreal   Toronto   London   Sydney
Tokyo   Mexico City   Rio de Janeiro   Madrid

Publisher: Robert Rainier
Acquisitions Editor: Nedah Abbott
Project Editor: Melanie Miller
Production Manager: Annette Mayeski
Design Supervisor: Louis Scardino
Text Design: Caliber Graphics
Front Cover Photo: Helioptix © by Henry Ries
Back Cover Photo Credit: University of Wyoming Photo Services

Library of Congress Cataloging in Publication Data

Murray, Don, 1917-
  Write to learn.

  1. English language—Rhetoric.   I. Title.
PE1408.M79 1984   808'.042   83-12597

ISBN   0-03-061996-3

CBS COLLEGE PUBLISHING
Holt, Rinehart and Winston
The Dryden Press
Saunders College Publishing

for Minnie Mae
without her there would be no books

Contents

1 Writing as Process   1

The writing process and how it works is described in this chapter, which creates a foundation for the rest of the book.

2 Collect   14

Techniques for collecting the information that is essential for effective writing are introduced. These skills are demonstrated as the author collects information for a piece of writing.

3 Focus   50

The reader is given methods of finding a subject and then the techniques of giving that subject focus. The author demonstrates each focusing method in an evolving piece of writing.

4 Order   86

Strategies for ordering a piece of writing are presented and demonstrated as the author works toward a draft. The reader is also given tips for solving the problems of many different writing tasks.

5 Draft   130

The reader is given counsel on how to start writing and principles to keep in mind during the writing of the draft. Draft writing is demonstrated by the evolving essay written by the author.

6 Clarify   162

Methods of revising and editing are introduced and demonstrated on three evolving drafts of the author's essay, which is completed in this chapter.

7 The Writing Process at Work   210

The writing process is reintegrated. Solutions are presented to common writing problems, and the reader is shown one writer's log.

Preface

How to Make This Book Work for You

Writing isn't magic, but then magic isn't magic either. Magicians know their craft, and writers must also know their craft.

Study how effective writers write—writers of all kinds: science writers, novelists, business writers, critics, poets, journalists, technical writers, playwrights, historians, scholars, movie and TV writers, memo writers, essayists—and you will discover that there are more similarities than differences among those who practice the writer's trade.

This book is written in the faith that beginning students can understand the techniques used by effective writers in all fields and adapt them to their own needs. In these pages you watch a working writer—me—making a piece of writing. You will see all my false starts, the failures, the bad writing that is necessary to produce writing that works. Each technique of writing I suggest you try, you will see me trying. Unlike most books on writing, you will not just see the final game of the season, you will be beside me in the weight room and on the practice field.

There are many ways to make use of what you know and to make use of what this book reveals. There is no one way to write, and there is no one way to read. There are a number of ways you can make this book work for you.

1. Read the book as fast as possible; fly over its pages to get a glimpse of what is in the book so you will know where to look for help when you need it. Reading it this way, you will also get a feel for the way I wrote one piece of writing, an essay about my grandmother. You will see raw material shaped into a final essay. You will also see many writers' techniques defined and used. This backstage glance at the writing process will help you understand how writing is made, and you will be able to turn to it when you run into a problem in your own writing.

2. Read the notes and drafts I used to create a portrait of my grandmother. All these sections are printed in type like this. Don't worry, during this first reading, about anything except seeing how I discovered my grandmother by writing about her. Few of us have seen a piece of writing evolve from rough notes, through early drafts, to a final draft. Once you get a feel for the way my essay evolved you can go back and see what I said I was doing.

3. You can use this book to produce a piece of writing this week, and you may be able to do it in less than an hour a day. On Monday use the brainstorming technique on pages 19–25 to help you collect what you may have to say.

On Tuesday use the technique for finding meaning on pages 60–61 to help you discover focus. On Wednesday organize your material according to Outline 1 on page 100 so you have a sense of direction. On Thursday write a fast "discovery" draft according to the instructions on pages 140–144. On Friday edit it with the three quick readings described starting on page 166. You will have experienced in one week the basic writing process described in this book. Then you will be able to go back and use the book to develop other techniques on other pieces of writing.

4. Work through the book slowly, taking the time to try a number, or perhaps all, of the collecting activities in Chapter Two before moving on to the focusing techniques in Chapter Three. You can continue this process, spending a week or two on each chapter while slowly building an extended piece of writing about the same size as my grandmother piece.

5. Start writing and use the book as a resource. Work on your writing, and then read the sections that relate to what you're doing. The checklists, "Help for Your Writing Problems" and "Writing Techniques," at the front of the book are designed to help you find solutions to problems you face while writing. Use the book to reinforce the techniques you already know. Use the book to help you solve the writing problems you, your classmates, and your teacher discover in your writing.

You will see other ways to use the book, and so will your teacher. It is not a book of rules; it is not an instruction manual to be followed like a set of military orders; it is a toolbox, a book of choices, filled with techniques that you will learn to use as you face the demands of your own writing tasks.

This book will not teach you to write, and neither will your teacher teach you to write. This book, your classmates, and your teacher may help you to teach yourself to write.

There's not much that any of us can say in advance of your writing that will help you learn to write. If you read this book and do not write, nothing much will happen. But if you read this book while you write it may help you to do your own learning.

There are a number of other things you can do that will help you teach yourself to write. You should read the best writers of your own time who are illuminating your world with their language. Then read back to those writers who have developed a tradition that made it possible for the writers of your time to write. Read their language to hear its music and feel its strength. Explore the forms of writing to see how they keep reinventing and renewing themselves.

Most of all, through reading discover how much the human condition remains the same. As the contemporary poet Alan Dugan says, "I'm still doing business at the same old stand—love, work, war, death, what the world is like outside this window tonight." You, and Dugan, and Shakespeare, Toni Morrison, John Milton, Joan Didion, your classmates, and Keats are all writing the same basic themes.

Also read television and movies and plays and newspapers and magazines to see how the masters of these crafts use language to celebrate and comprehend life.

Read your classmates to see how they use language to make meaning evolve. Read their early drafts as well as their final ones to see how they discovered the writing problems they had to solve—and how they solved them.

Most of all, read your own writing—notes, scribbles, outlines, fragments, early drafts and late drafts—to discover from your own experience how your own writing is being made. That is the most important reading you can do.

Pay close attention to your own self, learn from your own learning. Richard Hugo was a fine poet and teacher who told his students, "You'll never be a poet until you realize that everything I say today and this quarter is wrong. It may be right for me, but it is wrong for you. Every moment, I am, without wanting or trying to, telling you to write like me. But I hope you learn to write like you. In a sense, I hope I don't teach you how to write but how to teach yourself how to write. At all times keep your crap detector on. If I say something that helps, good. If what I say is of no help, let it go. Don't start arguments. They are futile and take us away from our purpose. As Yeats noted, your important arguments are with yourself. If you don't agree with me don't listen."

Good advice. In the end, the writer at eighteen or eighty is alone with the writer's own experience and the writer's own language. The writer, in that loneliness, keeps learning to write. I learned by writing this book, and I will go on learning in writing the next one. "One thing that is always with the writer— no matter how long he has written or how good he is—is the continuing process of learning how to write," says Flannery O'Connor. "As soon as the writer 'learns to write,' as soon as he knows what he is going to find, and discovers a way to say what he knew all along, or worse still, a way to say nothing, he is finished."

You'll have to keep setting your own standards, putting the bar high enough so it trembles but does not fall when you jump over it. If your standards are too high you will choke and not write; if your standards are too low you will not learn and you will not be read. Those standards are always changing, and it is your job to keep inching the bar up, deciding what you can attempt this day at your desk.

Good luck.

Instructor's Preface

Learning while Writing

Can we teach writing?

Yes, but we can't teach writing in advance of our students writing. Our students do not learn to write, then write. Few students can listen to a lecture on writing or read a textbook on writing in advance of writing and understand the lessons they may need to learn. We are asking them to imagine and understand an experience they have not yet had.

Neither can our students learn to write with increasing effectiveness without instruction. Students need, just as professional writers need, response to their drafts in process. They need test readers who can help them see what is working and what needs work. Students also need to learn the principles and the techniques of their craft. We do know what good writing is, and with the research of the past two decades we better understand how effective writing is made.

The challenge is to combine experience with instruction. This textbook attempts to demonstrate that interplay as it reveals me writing while I am instructing. Each student should experience the same interaction between the act of writing and the process of learning about writing.

There is no one way to teach writing, but the most effective ways of teaching writing all combine a great deal of writing with instruction that is appropriate to what the student has experienced rather than what the student may experience. This textbook is designed to be used with both traditional and experimental curricula because it demonstrates the interaction between experience and instruction.

The book may be studied formally, with the student moving slowly through the stages of the writing process. It may be used quickly, with the student experiencing the writing process in a week, as described on page ix, then studied repeatedly as the student moves through the writing process again and again. The student may study how the writer wrote the grandmother piece, then study the techniques. The text may be used almost entirely as an individual resource, with the student depending heavily on the checklists on pages xvii–xx.

I believe in the diversity of writing, and I'm eager to learn how this book is being used, as well as to discover the strengths and weaknesses of this first edition. I would appreciate hearing from instructors—and students—who use this first edition so that I can make subsequent editions more effective. Please send responses to the English Editor, Holt, Rinehart and Winston, 383 Madison Avenue, New York, New York 10017.

Acknowledgments

It is traditional when acknowledging all those who have helped you with a book to place the name of one's spouse at the end. It would be totally inappropriate in this case. My wife, Minnie Mae, has been my closest colleague and strongest supporter on this writing project, as she has on every other one.

The lineage of this book goes back to the late Mortimer B. Howell of Tilton School, who turned my life around when he taught me Freshman English. When I first taught Freshman English he gave me my own Freshman English papers, which he had saved—a humbling gift. At the University of New Hampshire I have learned from and with many colleagues. Among those who deserve special mention is Lester A. Fisher. Our early shouted arguments in the corridors about the teaching of writing settled down to a relationship that underlies all my teaching and constantly reminds me of the importance of respect for the individual student. Thomas A. Carnicelli first got me involved in directing Freshman English, and he has been a constructive, tough-minded critic of my work through the years. Thomas R. Newkirk's scholarship has helped me keep my work in perspective. I've shared almost daily discussions of writing and the teaching of writing with Donald H. Graves. We have learned about writing and the teaching of writing together.

In writing this book I am particularly indebted to Brock Dethier, who has made especially perceptive comments on an early draft. He is one of the many master teachers of writing I've been able to work with on the staffs of the Freshman English and Advanced Composition courses at the University of New Hampshire. We have all shared our teaching and our learning, and I am indebted to all of them for contributing so much to my education. I've also enjoyed the chance to work with the writers who teach in our department, especially my colleague in nonfiction, Andrew H. Merton. I've learned most from the more than two thousand students with whom I've had weekly writing conferences at the University of New Hampshire.

I've also been fortunate in those away from Durham who have taught me about writing and the teaching of writing. A few who must be mentioned include Dr. Carol Berkenkotter of Michigan Technological University, for whom I was a laboratory rat who grew, I hope, into a research colleague; Susan Sowers, now at Harvard University, whose scholarly eye has scanned much of my work in process; Christopher Scanlan of the Providence *Journal-Bulletin*, who has been a stimulating writing colleague; John and Tilly Warnock, Stephen Kucer, and Stuart Greene, who made my residence at the University of Wyoming intellectually stimulating; and dozens of others who have influenced my thinking by their efforts to understand the process of writing.

I am indebted to the fifty students and twenty teachers from Idaho in the Whittenberger Foundation–State Department of Education Summer Program who read and attacked the first draft of this book and who are responsible for many improvements in the text.

I must also pay tribute to the officers of the Conference on College Composition and Communication, whose work has made it possible for those of us interested in studying writing to get together and exchange our views in print and in person.

And I owe special thanks to my editor, Nedah Abbott, the only editor I've ever let see incomplete drafts in process. I am also indebted to Melanie Miller, who supervised the production of this book with wit, intelligence and care, to Tessa DeCarlo, the copyeditor, who made certain I stayed within the boundaries of good sense and good taste, and to Lou Scardino, who supervised the design of this book so the graphic art supported my words and my meaning, and to all the people at Holt, Rinehart and Winston who gave me freedom and support.

Help for Your Writing Problems

▶ **When will I know I'm ready to write?**
▶ **What do I do if I can't get started writing?**
▶ **How do I get a draft written?**
▶ **Do I need to rewrite?**
▶ **How do I proofread my text?**
▶ **How do I edit for content?**
▶ **How do I edit for order?**
▶ **How do I edit for language?**
▶ **How do I find and use test readers?**
▶ **What else can I read about writing?**
▶ **How can I solve my writing problems?**
▶ **Why should I write?**

Writing Techniques

Write
to Learn

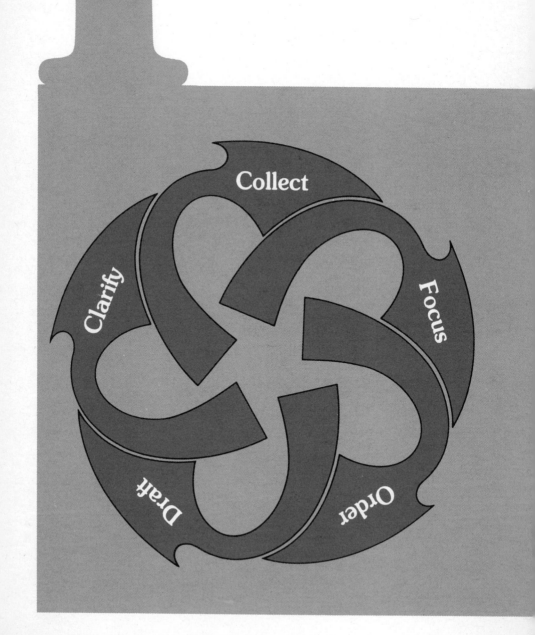

Writing as Process

I write to find out what I'm thinking about.
Edward Albee

How do I know what I think until I see what I say?
E. M. Forster

For me the initial delight is in the surprise of remembering something I didn't know I knew.
Robert Frost

When most people think of writing they see words on a page, all neatly ordered, marching towards a meaning. When writers think of writing they see a blank page, and they see what was before the blank page.

You are reading the finished process of writing. But before there was this page I stacked up 500 sheets of 8½-by-11, 20-weight blank paper. I was attracted to its blankness—and terrified by it. I didn't know if I had anything to say.

Before I could find words to put on the paper I had to go back. Staring out the window, beyond the pile of blank paper, I heard my uncle Will reciting poems as he carried me in his arms late at night. My grandmother, stern matriarch of our clan, stood approving in the shadows. Do I remember it, or was it something that was told me? No matter, I hear his voice, see Grandma's approving smile, and hear the music of those Scottish poems.

Looking out the window of my office I see myself, a small boy in bed, a lonely boy in a house of grownups with problems he couldn't understand. And I remember the stories that boy told himself about football, and fights in the street, and traveling across the ocean, and girls. There were more and more stories about girls.

Writing Is Discovering

What has this got to do with this book? Everything. That's where it started. The boy learned to read and to write, and the excitement in writing was that he didn't know exactly what he was going to say when he wrote. There were always surprises on the page. Sometimes the surprises were large, sometimes small, but there was always something unexpected. In writing, two and two may add up to five, or twelve, or seventy-seven.

This book is based on more than forty years, no, close to fifty years of published writing. I was first published in a newspaper printed on a strange gelatin substance in Miss Chapman's fourth grade at the Massachusetts Field School. And this book is based on years of teaching writing, teaching teachers about writing, and teaching professional writers to write. I have outlined and re-outlined, then outlined this book again. But these first pages are different than I expected them to be. I intended to be impersonal, to talk about other writers, and I found myself talking about myself, because I think you need to know that this book, and all books, start before there is a pile of 500 sheets of blank paper.

Writing begins with all that we have known since we were born, and perhaps with a lot of knowledge that was born in us. We write, first of all, to discover what we know and then what we need to know.

Words are the symbols for what we learn. They allow us to play with information, to make connections and patterns, to put together and take apart and put together again, to see what experience means. In other words, to think. "Writing a play is thinking, not thinking about thinking," according to Robert Bolt. Writing is thinking.

Writing, in fact, is the most disciplined form of thinking. It allows us to be precise, to stand back and examine what we have thought, to we see what our words really mean, to see if they stand up to our own critical eye, make sense, will be understood by someone else.

Why Write?

Sometimes we write just for ourselves, to record what we have seen or felt or thought. Sometimes we write to celebrate experience. Many times we write just to find out what it all means, for by writing we can stand back from ourselves and see significance in what is close to us.

Most of the time, however, writing is a private act with a public result. We write alone to discover meaning. But once that meaning is discovered, once we understand what we have to say, then we want or need to share it with other people.

Sometimes that need precedes the impulse to write. We receive an assignment and have to write a paper, an examination, a memo for the boss, a news story. We may have to report an experiment, turn in a poem, write a skit, send out fund-raising publicity, create a job résumé, complain about being badgered for a bill we've already paid. There are hundreds of writing tasks we may have to perform. We may have to write speeches, books, brochures, letters of sympathy, case histories on patients. But whatever writing we do, if it is to be done well we have to go back to gather information and make sense of it.

We can't write writing. Some readers think professionals who turn out political speeches or company reports can use language to weave a meaning without information. I've been hired as a ghostwriter and know we can't. First we have to understand what the candidate is trying to do, or why the company has made a profit or a loss. We have to do research and attempt to build a meaning from the product of our research that a reader can understand.

The writer may write to inform, to explain, to entertain, to persuade, but whatever the purpose there should be, first of all, the satisfaction of the writer's own learning, the joy and surprise of finding out what you have to say.

There are many side benefits to writing. Writing allows you to discover that you have a voice, a way of speaking that is individual and effective. It allows you to share with others and even to influence others.

Writing can bring attention to you or to your ideas. It can add to your job skills, and it can improve your grades. Writing can give you power, for we live in a complicated technological society, and those people who can collect information, order it into significant meaning and then communicate it to others will influence the course of events within the town or nation, school or university, company or corporation. Information is power.

If you have the ability to find specific, accurate information and fit it together in a meaningful pattern through language you will have the pleasure of making something that was not there before, of finding significance where others find confusion, of bringing order to chaos. If you can do this clearly and grace-

fully you will have readers, for people are hungry for specific information ordered into meaning.

And if you write, when you look out your window you will see what you
had forgotten and, by writing, you may discover what it means. My attention
turns from my uncle carrying me to my grandmother standing by the door of
the living room. She approves more by not frowning than by smiling. I study
the set of that stern mouth and begin to wonder how much her glance still
governs me. If I write about her I may find out.

We learn when we write. I hope you will learn about writing when you
read this book, but I know that when that pile of blank paper on my desk is
filled with the words you will read, I will have learned about writing by writing
about writing.

How We Write

Effective writing appears effortless. The words flow across the page, and we
hear as well as see them. We listen to the voice of the writer and have the
illusion an individual writer is speaking across time and space to each of us. It
seems magic.

But most of the time it isn't spontaneous. It was carefully made to appear
natural. A few moments ago the previous paragraph was typed, then edited by
me in this way:

> ~~When we read~~ | effective writing ~~it~~ appears effortless. The words
>
> flow across the page, and we hear ~~them~~ as well as see them. ~~The~~
>
> ~~music comes through, and we hear~~ the voice of the writer, ~~We~~ have
>
> the illusion that ~~the~~ writer is speaking to us ~~one individual speaking~~
>
> ~~across time and space~~ ~~to another individual.~~ It seems magic.

Writing is made. Writing is a logical, understandable process that we use
to move information around so that it makes sense. We use word as the symbols
for that information, and we follow a rational sequence in moving the words
around to make our evolving meaning come clear.

It is as hard to imagine how writing is made from reading a finished page
by a professional writer as it is to imagine a field of wheat from eating a slice
of bread.

Good writing does not reveal its making. The problems are solved, the
scaffolding has been removed, the discarded building materials have been hauled
away.

This book will take you back to the beginning, to the moment of terror
that every writer feels when there is a blank page or even before there is a
blank page, when there is an assignment to write and the writer feels empty,
without anything to say.

The writer never overcomes that feeling. Some writers get headaches, others get stomachaches; I get both. But I have learned, as all writers learn, that there are ways to work that will eventually fill the blank page with words that will make a meaning clear to the writer and the reader.

Writing Is a Process

Writing is, above all, a process. It is a logical sequence of activities that can be understood by everyone. You don't put on your overcoat, your pants, and then your underwear. We follow logical patterns in dressing, cooking, tuning a car engine, producing a draft. When we write, some steps precede others most of the time.

Of course writing is much more complicated than getting dressed in the morning. The writing process is one of the most complicated human activities. It varies according to the writing task. When we write of something we clearly understand to an audience we know, in a familiar form, we write differently than when we use writing to discover meaning, to reach a strange audience, or to explore a new form or subject.

Writing also varies with our thinking style. Some of us think out loud, and others work quietly. Some are long-distance runners, writing steadily and evenly day after day. Others of us are sprinters, and spend a lot of time sitting around between sudden spurts of writing. Some of us use a logic that is apparent, moving from A to B to C. Others use a logic that is less apparent, leaping to C and working back to B and then A. Or going to D, then B, E, F, C, G, A.

Most of us do not write—or think—the same way all the time. It varies according to the problems we have to solve, what we know about the subject, and how we feel. Our feelings are very important. Writing is a thinking activity, but our feelings create the environment in which we think. Terror, for example, can paralyze, so we have to know how to handle the feelings of terror before the blank page, or we would never write. Writing reveals us, and we know it. Yet we also know that we write best—just as we play tennis best—if we feel confident. We have to learn to write with confidence.

All of those factors affect the writing process, but no matter how much it changes from person to person and from task to task it is more similar than it is different. We usually follow the same process when we use language to make meaning of our experience.

A Model of the Writing Process

There are many models of the writing process. This book is built on one model. It is a way of introducing you to the process approach to writing, but you should pay as much attention to your own writing when the writing goes well as to my model. You should know how you made writing lead you to a meaning that others could understand. You should know what you did, how you did it, the order in which you did it, and how you felt before, during, and after you did it. You should develop your own models of the writing process so that when the writing doesn't go well you'll have those positive experiences to look back on. By following your own effective writing process you may be able to write well again.

Let us look closely at my model of the writing process. We have to start with what happens inside the writer's brain. Ernest Hemingway was once asked where he wrote, and he is supposed to have answered, "In my head." If we could open up a writer's head during the act of writing we might see an electro-chemical process that looks like this:

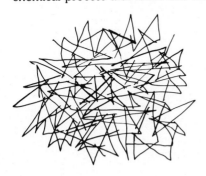

The Parts of the Process

If we could untangle that spaghetti we might find the following five primary activities taking place:

Collecting

The brain is constantly collecting and recollecting specific information that comes from all of the senses—seeing, hearing, smelling, tasting, touching. Some people believe that every piece of information delivered to the brain remains there in storage waiting to be called up, if only we know how. Writing is one of the best ways to recollect. We do not think we remember, but when we write we discover what we know.

Focusing

During the writing process we pay particular attention to certain scraps of information that have particular meaning for us. The poet Maxine Kumin says that the writer looks for information that "informs." This information may be a code word which has private meaning for us, a specific detail, or a combination of words and details that catches our attention.

Ordering

Our brain, as we write, keeps trying to fit the information that interests us with other information, so a meaning evolves. We keep lining up information and language, the way a baby builds with blocks, to see what it may mean.

Drafting

We talk to ourselves as we write, using our voices to tell us what we have to say. We say over and over again in our heads what we later say out loud.

Clarifying

Our brain is constantly trying to understand what we are learning, thinking, feeling. It tries to make it more sensible, sharper, more understandable. Our brain goes through a constant process of tuning and adjusting to make its signal from itself to itself clear.

The Parts Interact

All those activities take place simultaneously. It is indeed a complicated process.

▶ We clarify by ordering and reordering the information we are collecting and recollecting.

▶ We collect information by drafting what we have to say, reordering it trying to make it clear, and collecting new information to fill the holes we discover.

▶ We focus on a specific piece of information and then as we draft what we have to say about it we discover how it relates to other material. And as we collect that mateial we have to order and reorder to make it clear.

▶ We start drafting, not knowing what we are going to say, and find we are collecting material, and the order in which it begins to arrange itself on the page makes our focus clear.

I could go on making statement after statement about the writing process that would be true on a particular project at a particular time. Another way of looking at the primary activities in the writing process, to show how they take place simultaneously and also interact with each other at the same time, can be seen in the following chart.

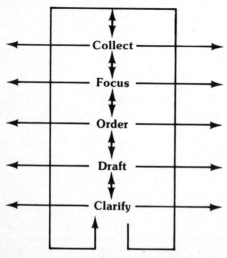

If we study those activities during the time that a piece of writing develops we begin to see a pattern of emphasis. We see that the writer continues to collect during the entire writing process, but does much more collecting at the beginning. We also see that there is clarification going on from the very beginning, but that the emphasis on clarity comes towards the end of the writing process. There is a natural sequence of emphasis during the writing, a process most of us follow most of the time; it is illustrated by the following chart.

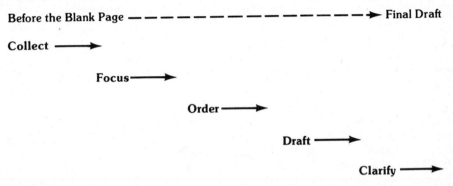

Before the Blank Page — — — — — — — — — — — — — — ➤ **Final Draft**

Collect ➜

    Focus ➜

       Order ➜

         Draft ➜

           Clarify ➜

The writing process, however, is recursive.. We move from an emphasis on collecting to focusing to ordering to drafting to clarifying, but it is not a neat, linear process. Often when we focus we find we have to go back and collect new information, and as we collect that information we have to refocus.

As we move down through the writing process to ordering what we may say, we often have to go back and collect and refocus and reorder.

When we draft what we are saying we may also have to go back to collect or focus or reorder or redraft.

And as we clarify what we have to say we may have to go back to any part of the process, or to the beginning. We may have to collect more information, focus again, or reorder, or redraft.

The following diagram attempts to show the writing process at work, how the principal parts of this system interact so that we write and learn.

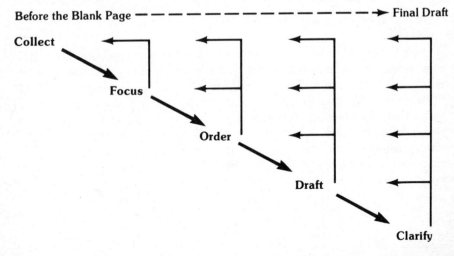

Before the Blank Page — — — — — — — — — — — — — ➤ **Final Draft**

Collect

    Focus

       Order

         Draft

           Clarify

How a Process Model Works

A mental picture of our writing process will help us solve many of the problems we run into in writing. If we don't have a model of the writing process we are more likely to try solutions that don't work. We may, for example, try to revise and edit the language when the problem is a lack of specific, meaningful information. If information is the problem, then we have to go back and research the subject. On the other hand the problem may be communication, and an inexperienced writer may go back and look for more and more examples, when the writer needs to prune and shape the language.

A model of a process that worked for us in the past may allow us, at any point in the writing process, to look back and understand what we have done and what we have left to do. It gives us a map, a way to study our voyage toward meaning and plot an efficient course. The model also takes the unnecessary mystery away from writing and makes it possible for us to see, and therefore improve, our craft.

A common model of the writing process, which will, of course, allow variations, helps us understand how our classmates are writing. We can begin to see how they are making language work, how they are producing drafts which are evolving towards a clear, documented meaning. We can learn more easily from other writers when we can understand their writing process.

The process view of writing also allows us to help other writers. We can respond more intelligently and constructively to their questions about their work. We can help them see where they are in the writing process and, therefore, suggest strategies and techniques which may help them solve their writing problems.

An understanding of the writing process makes us more perceptive readers of published authors. We will begin to understand what has gone on backstage that makes the published performance possible. We may begin to learn from the master writers of our language, for we will see that their writing wasn't magic, that it was craft before it became art.

The Process Log or Daybook

As you move forward and backward and forward again through the writing process you may find it helpful—and fun—to keep a log or daybook to record where you have been and, even more important, where you may go.

You will find that you do not march through the writing process hup, two, three, four. While researching a piece you suddenly may make a guess as to how the piece of writing will end—before you've even started it. While not consciously working on writing you may see a possible order of arguments you may want to use, or hear—in your head—a sentence or two that captures the voice or style in which you hope to write. You may hear a quotation or spot a fact in your reading that you can use later. You may get an idea for the piece of writing you will do after you finish this one. It will help if you have a way to capture all these guesses and fragments. The act of writing them down will help you remember them, and will lead to more ideas and productive connections.

The most valuable writing tool I have is my daybook, and the name is important to me. For years I tried to keep a journal. I imagined I was Gide or Camus. I wasn't, and what I wrote was not perceptive but pompous, full of hot air, hilarious to read, and utterly useless to me as a writer. At other times I tried to keep a diary, but then I found myself recording trivia—the temperature, or whom I met, or what I ate. It made a rather boring life seem even more boring.

I don't know where I heard the term "daybook," but a number of years ago I found myself using the term and writing every day—well, almost every day—in a ten-by-eight spiral notebook filled with greenish paper, narrow ruled, with a margin line down the left. This worked for me. I write in my lap, in the living room or on the porch, in the car or an airplane, in meetings at the university, in bed, or sitting down on a rock wall during a walk. A hardbound book doesn't work for me. I find a spiral book much more convenient, and since I write in all sorts of light, indoors and out, I find the greenish paper comfortable. I chose the size because it fits in the outside pocket of the canvas bag I have with me all the time.

The organization is simple day-by-day chronology. When I change the subject I write a code word in the margin. That way I can look back through the book and collect all the notes I've made on a single project or concern.

I usually write in the daybook the first fifteen minutes of the day before I eat breakfast. And then I have it near me all day long. If something occurs to me I make a note during a television commercial or in a meeting, or while walking, or in the car.

How I use my daybook varies from time to time. But it is always a form of talking to myself, a way of thinking on paper. And some of my writing that seems spontaneous has left tracks through years of daybooks.

If you look through my daybook here are some of the things you would see:

- Questions that need to be answered
- Fragments of writing seeking a voice
- Leads, hundreds of leads
- Titles, hundeds of titles
- Notes from which I have made lectures, talks, or speeches
- Notes I have made at lectures, talks, or speeches; also notes I have made at poetry readings, hockey games, and concerts
- Outlines
- Ideas for stories, articles, poems, books, papers
- Diagrams showing how a piece might be organized or, more likely, showing the relationships between parts of an idea
- Drafts
- Observations
- Quotations from writers or artists
- Newspaper clippings

▶ Titles of books to be read
▶ Notes on reading
▶ Pictures I've pasted in
▶ Writing schedules
▶ Pasted-in copies of letters I've written and want to save
▶ Lists, lots of lists
▶ Pasted-in handouts I've developed for classes or workshops.

I don't have any one way to use the daybook. Anything that will stimulate or record my thinking, anything that will move towards writing goes into the day-book. When a notebook is filled—usually in about six weeks—I go through and harvest a page or two or three of the most interesting material for the beginning of the next daybook. When I'm ready to work seriously on a project I go back through the daybooks for a year or more and photocopy those pages that relate to the subject I'm working on.

The daybook stimulates my thinking, helps me make use of those small fragments of time which on many days is all the time we have to write. It keeps my writing muscles in condition; it lets me know what I'm concerned with making into writing; it increases my productivity. In every way it is a helpful habit.

If you decide to keep a daybook, make it your own. Don't try to follow anyone else's formula. And don't write it for another audience. It's a private place where you can think and where you can be dumb, stupid, sloppy, silly; where you can do all the bad writing and bad thinking that are essential for those few moments of insight that produce good writing.

Make the Process Yours

The process log or daybook will help you make the process yours, will give you a chance to see how you write when the writing goes well. If you are to keep improving your writing you need to build on the procedures you used that have worked.

This book will provide you with the process as I see it now, based on my own study of other writers, writing process research, what my students have taught me, and my own writing experience. This is a model that you should adapt and change to fit your own thinking style, writing habits, and writing tasks.

You should learn how to write from how you write, as well as from how others write. The end does justify the means in this case. What works—writing that is meaningful, clear, and graceful—is the measure by which any writing process must be judged. As this book is being printed and published I will go on writing, learning more about the writing process. And as you read it, and write, you will go on learning from this book and from your own experience.

Keep Putting the Process Back Together

When the process works it is more than its parts. Dr. J., driving towards the basket, rising, hanging in midair, oh so gently twirling the ball into the basket, is much more than a simple description of dribbling, jumping, and shooting. I heard Jascha Heifetz warm up by playing the scales, and it was much more than playing the scales. Writing is produced by a process, but effective writing is not the simple following of steps in that process.

The main reason for this is that writing does not so much work from parts to a whole as evolve from a constant interaction of parts and whole.

Too many people think that if you teach spelling and vocabulary and punctuation and grammatical usage and rhetoric, then you have taught writing. But writing starts with a guess, a global idea of what may be said, and then as the writer collects information and starts putting words on paper the guess changes.

It is an incredibly complex, challenging, and difficult process. It wouldn't be any fun if it weren't. The global guess, at first vague and general, influences the writer's choice of facts, words, punctuation, spaces. And each fact, each word, each mark of punctuation, each space between words changes the guess or meaning of what is being said.

The writer constantly moves back and forth between part and whole, between word and meaning. Don't forget that as we study the writing process. We will concentrate on one part of the process at a time, showing all sorts of techniques that may be used in that stage of writing. But when you are writing keep trying to put it all together. Don't become so aware of the seam on the basketball that you can't shoot the basket, or so conscious of your manners you can't taste the food.

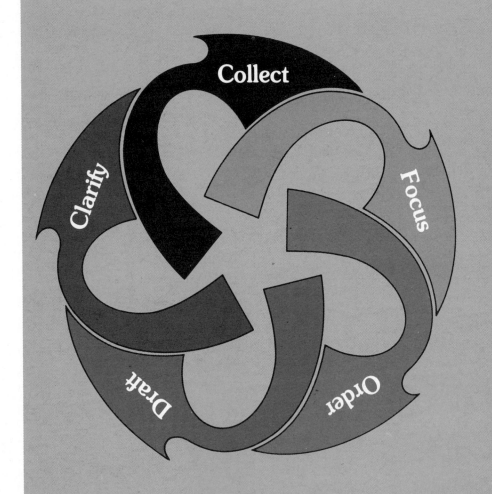

Collect

I could keep myself busy for months without moving from one spot, just by leaning now to the right, now to the left.

Paul Cézanne

I would want to tell my students of a point strongly pressed, if my memory serves, by Shaw. He once said that as he grew older, he became less and less interested in theory, more and more interested in information. The temptation in writing is just reversed. Nothing is so hard to come by as a new and interesting fact. Nothing so easy on the feet as a generalization.

John Kenneth Galbraith

The more particular, the more specific you are, the more universal you are.

Nancy Hale

Write with information, not words.

Effective writing is built from specific, accurate pieces of information. The reader wants, above all, to be informed. Whatever you are writing, you should try to make the reader an authority on your subject. The writer's greatest compliment may be when a reader turns from the page and says to someone else, "Did you know that . . .?"

Many students have the misconception tha writers write with words, language detached from information. They think that words are pretty balloons filled with air. But writing that is read has words that are firmly anchored to meaning. If you wrte a science report, a poem, a term paper, a business letter, a short story, an essay exam, a film script, an argument, a newspaper story, a personal letter, you will capture the reader if you give that reader writing that is filled with concrete details.

Words are the symbols for specific information. We use words so that we can arrange information into meaningful patterns. Words are a sort of shorthand by which we can capture, comprehend, and communicate experience. Man is the animal that uses words to think and share.

James Baldwin says, "The importance of a writer . . . is that he is here to describe things which other people are too busy to describe." Maxine Kumin adds, "What makes good poetry for me is a terrible specificity of detail, whether of object or of feeling. The poet names and particularizes and thus holds for a moment in time (and thus for all time, as long as time lasts for humanity) whatever elusive event he/she is drawn to. By terrible I mean unflinching. Honest and sometimes compassionate."

The Inventory of Information

The person who has a full inventory of detailed, significant information has the advantage over every other writer. It is more than an advantage, it is a necessity to have mental shelves stacked with information when you are writing. You must be able to select the statistic, the quotation, the descriptive detail, the anecdote at the moment of writing that will help you understand the subject you are exploring through writing, and will eventually help your reader understand it. You can't write nothing.

Beginning writers often misunderstand this. Young writers often become word drunk on their way to becoming good writers. They dance to the sound of their own voice. They try to substitute style for subject matter, tricks for content, ruffles and flourishes for information. It doesn't work.

Receiving Information

Writers learn to spend a large part of their writing time collecting information from which to build writing. Writers practice a wide-ranging receptivity to information, behaving like great dish antennas collecting signals to which they may decide to tune from satellites and from space. That collecting may be done in response to living or in response to an assignment, but collecting information is the beginning of the writing process.

This process seems random, and it may even feel random, but it is not. Most of the specifics are caught for a potential purpose. I almost always have my daybook or log with me, but if that notebook isn't handy 2½-by-3-inch cards in my wallet are.

I'm always receiving, as every writer is, specific information that can be connected with other information. Sometimes I have an assignment from an editor or from myself and I'm consciously looking for details that will fit that topic. But other times I'm just receiving the gift of details that will produce their own abundance, their own need to be related and understood.

The Process of Collection

We are all writers whether we know it or not. We collect information so that we can survive: What is that noise? What is that smell? Did that shadow move? We learn what brings punishment and what brings reward, what streets are dangerous, what behavior makes you popular. We learn how to dress and walk and talk and laugh. We learn how to make a dress, pass a basketball, make money, get through school. Our brain stores everything we see, feel, hear, taste, touch; and it also stores how we feel and think. Your brain has already collected enough information for thousands of books.

In addition to this spontaneous, unconscious collection process we also collect information when we are given an assignment to learn something or to write about it. This is usually a more formal, structured activity, but it shouldn't be too formal if it is to work. Even formal research depends on happy accidents, unexpected connections and insights. When we are collecting information the most significant specific is often caught in the corner of our eye.

Recollecting

We usually start the process of collection with ourselves. We begin not so much by collecting but recollecting, using techniques to remember what we know and what we don't know we know.

The term "research" itself means just what it says—RE-search. We start by searching through our memory bank to see what is there that we can make use of as we write. Don't worry if you think you have a poor memory. Most of us measure ourselves against those freaks on game shows who can remember every irrelevant detail about opera, football, politics, antique autos, or movies. That sort of memory is meaningless when you are writing. The writer needs to know relevant information, information that connects with other pieces of information, information that is available when the writer—and the reader—need it.

That is one of the most exciting things about writing: it makes it possible for us to remember what we didn't know we knew. We all know far more than we think we know. Our brain has recorded, through all of our senses, much more than we were aware of at any moment. Sometimes when we are in a terrifying situation—in a car that skids out of control, in a house that catches on fire—we become aware of how many things our brain is recording. Once in paratroop training my main chute didn't open. I seemed to have all the time in the world to consider and reconsider the problem. I had to make sure my parachute was not a streamer, a long tail of an open chute hopelessly wrapped around itself; then I had to open my reserve chute and feed it out. It wound around the legs of another paratrooper, and I became a pendulum dragging us both down dangerously fast. Then my main chute partially opened. I reached for the knife strapped to my right leg, cut free from the reserve chute, and managed to get into position to land.

Writing this I am back in the skies over Tennessee in 1943. I can feel the glasses strapped to my face with adhesive tape, the wind on my cheeks, see the blue southern sky, hear the planes and the silence as they disappear over the ridge, see the red clay earth rising fast, so fast. But somehow time slows down so I can prepare to absorb the jolt of the earth slamming up at me. I tumble over and over, and roll up on my feet. I could fill a book with the sensations of that one jump. I looked at my watch. It was only forty-seven seconds since I had stepped from the plane.

The material for writing is in your head. It will be recovered, relived, understood, and shared through writing. One of the principal reasons that writers write is to relive life.

Writing is also rethinking. When we write a personal experience we re-experience it and have the opportunity to give it a shape and meaning that may not have been apparent the first time around. This is just as true when we write an academic paper. We combine our living with what we heard in the lecture, what stuck in our notebook during the discussion, what we remember from the reading. All that we are learning is processed by our brain, so that when we write we often find out that we know more than we thought we knew. We can connect theory with practice, history with the present, our ideas with the ideas of others, facts from another course with facts from this course.

But to do all this we must collect the information—specific, accurate information—from which vigorous writing is constructed.

Brainstorming

One of the best ways to find out what you know is to *brainstorm*. When you brainstorm you put down everything that comes into your head as fast as you can. You don't want to be critical; you do want to be illogical, irrational, even silly. You just want to discover what is in your head. You want to be surprised.

After you have brainstormed, then you should look at what you've written down to see what surprises you or what connects. These surprises and connections remind you of what you know and will make you aware of meanings you hadn't seen before.

It is important not to worry about how the brainstorming list is written. It is not a time to worry about spelling or penmanship or sentences; it is a time to write in a sort of private language of code words that stand for particular meanings in your own mind. If the phrase "night jump" appeared on my brainstorming list it would remind me of another jump in Tennessee when I tumbled through the sky before my chute opened, when I had the feeling that I could reach out and touch the stars. If I were going to use that in an essay, a story, or a poem I would have to develop it, but for the moment "night jump" is enough.

I brainstorm before I write important letters or a memo. I brainstorm class lectures and novels. I brainstorm articles and poems and textbooks such as this. I also brainstorm before I decide to buy a car or take a job or choose a vacation. Brainstorming shows me what I know, what I need to know, and what the connections are between what I know and don't know.

In this book I am going to demonstrate every technique I introduce and every kind of writing I do with the same subject. I've chosen a powerful subject, the grandmother who brought me up. No, I've not chosen that subject, it's chosen me. When, on page 3, I relived the experience of my uncle's carrying me, I caught a glimpse of my grandmother in the corner of my eye. That image will not go away. I have to write about her, and in writing this book I felt that the reader could best be helped by seeing one writer at work on one piece of writing. I decided to write about grandmother because I had to and because I felt that in this way I could take the reader into the workshop and show that writing isn't magic, but that writing is crafted, carefully made. The reader will be able to see a mass of my raw material take shape and develop meaning. And the student will be able to second-guess a writer at work, to see what fails as well as what works.

I realized that the normal way to do this would be to take an academic subject and do a mock term paper or assignment or examination answer, but I am not a student, and that would be dishonest. I do write papers on specialized subjects, but I couldn't expect the reader to enter into that specialized world and understand what I was doing. I had to find an area to explore that could be shared by many readers. The more I thought about those blank pages and the possibility of making meaning for myself on them, the more my grandmother, the dominant figure of my childhood, came to mind.

Other subjects swirled through my mind as I used the techniques you will see on the pages ahead. Close to four decades after I marched into combat I am beginning to be ready to write about it. That might be a subject. So might be my childhood in the Great Depression. I might write about being a policeman in the army, and later a police reporter who observed policemen close up. I might write about the summers I spent in the New Hampshire woods, and I might write about Lee, the daughter who died at twenty. But at this time it was my grandmother who kept insisting herself upon my thoughts. And since all students have grandparents whom they knew or did not know, I thought they might be able to share my search for meaning.

My parents, my uncle, and I all lived as children in her home. She suffered a stroke—what they called a "shock" then and a cardiovascular accident today—when I was eight years old, and she was paralyzed for the rest of her life, but she still ran our lives from her bed. I've written very little about her, but this book will teach me a great deal about her while teaching you how one professional writer worked to develop one subject.

As I look out of my office window at New Hampshire woods filled with snow I do not know my grandmother as well as I will when I finish this draft and edit it under the hot summer sky of Wyoming. I am a bit apprehensive. I am drawn to my grandmother because she was such a strong woman. The family made her a saint and wrapped her in legend, but she was not a saint; she did harm as well as good. I know I will understand her better when this book is done, but I do not know if I will like her better.

You should brainstorm beside me in the margin of the text. There's plenty of white space. If you do that, you'll understand better what I'm saying—and you may discover a subject you want to explore through writing. My list will probably be personal; I'm writing about my grandmother. Your list doesn't have to be. Brainstorm any topic, personal or impersonal, with which you have some experience to see if there's something you wish to explore.

Now to brainstorm:

- back-scratcher on my desk
- left hand
- transparent skin
- soft, unused hand, curled
- wispy white hair
- had been auburn as girl in Scotland
- scissors up nose of bull
- no sense of time
- thought I was going to fight Napoleon
- go in to see if she was alive
- shawl, dark green and black
- thin but heavy
- Black Watch?
- named for my uncle; named for his uncle
- washed out my mouth
- broke her arm
- wood stove
- kidney soup. Thick.
- grape jelly
- dumped hot jelly on me
- forcing mouth open to eat eggs
- dining room rug
- underside of dining room table
- didn't like my father

▶ Father thought her a lady, feared her
▶ Mother always scared of her
▶ paper route—seeing if Grandmother was alive
▶ bedpan
▶ lifting her up in bed
▶ her talking to Jesus
▶ ringing bell for help
▶ warning of bridge collapse
▶ Islay
▶ London as a girl
▶ marrying widower in Glasgow hotel
▶ big house in North Grafton
▶ Newfoundland dog
▶ finding her on stairs
▶ trying to understand what she said. Family all around bed.
▶ canvas to carry her in
▶ Sunday dinners
▶ practical jokes. Cruelty.
▶ the uncles
▶ breaking robber's wrist
▶ maple trees outside her window
▶ her trunk
▶ my office in her closet
▶ playing imaginary games
▶ sitting in the gloaming
▶ tea

That took just under ten minutes. It's possible to brainstorm for a much longer time, but I find short spurts—fifteen minutes, ten minutes, five minutes—are more productive. You can also brainstorm together with another person, or a group of people. The important thing is not to censor what you say, not to judge it, not really to understand it—but to let it come.

This brainstorming list is printed simply as it came. I didn't prepare for it, except by living with my grandmother until I went off to school and in the army. I had to let it come.

How Brainstorming Leads to Writing

I don't know if it's a particularly good brainstorming list; that's not important. If I want to I can brainstorm again and again. The important thing is that it's a start. It is a jumble, but it may be a productive jumble. It jumps back and forth in time. The last time I saw her alive I was in uniform and she thought I was going off to fight Napoleon at Waterloo in 1814, as did her great-uncle for whom I was named. There are items from a house we left when I was four years old. Each of those things I mentioned are snapshots which I could devleop if I wanted to. I could, for example, become again the boy who got up for his paper route at 4:30 in the morning (I had one alarm by the bed, one on a chair further away, and a third on the chest of drawers in the narrow little porch room where I slept). I thumbtacked *National Geographic* maps to the ceiling, and I used to lie in bed looking at Africa or Asia or the west, dreaming of escaping this dull, unhappy home. (Note how my mind slides off the subject. Brainstorming has triggered memories, and all sorts of things from my past are coming back in a rush. I must decide whether to keep remembering or whether I should let my mind go on getting away from my grandmother. I will force myself back on track.) I used to walk from my room through the dark hall into her room, lit with a small night-light, a yellow light that was on the floor and cast shadows across the bed and up on the ceiling. I would stand and watch the covers to see if she was still breathing. When I knew she was then I would go further down the hall to the bathroom. I started each day contemplating death.

Looking for Surprises

It is too early for me to write, however, and I look back at the list to see what surprises me. Whatever you are brainstorming—an academic paper or job application letter—you should first go over the list to see what surprises you, to find out what discoveries you have made. Not too much on this list, but I am startled a bit by the abrupt "didn't like my father." I don't think I ever realized how she felt before, and writing it down makes it something I have to deal with. And "playing imaginary games" reminds me how good she was when I would tip a living room chair over, put an old black electric fan in front of it, line up a couple of wooden chairs, and take her on a airplane trip back to Scotland. If I made a tent from a blanket she would crawl in and visit me. If I painted the back steps with water she would admire my work and step carefully over the wet paint. A piece of writing could start from those surprises.

Looking for Connections

Next I look for connections. I see the legends that were built up about her: how a robber broke into the house when my grandfather was away, and she broke his wrist with a cane; how a bull attacked her on the way to school in Scotland, and she jabbed huge sewing scissors up his nostrils. This is how my brainstorm list looks as I circle the surprises and make connections:

- ▶ back-scratcher on my desk
- ▶ left hand
- ▶ transparent skin
- ▶ soft, unused hand, curled
- ▶ wispy white hair
- ▶ had been auburn as girl in Scotland
- ▶ scissors up nose of bull
- ▶ broke her arm

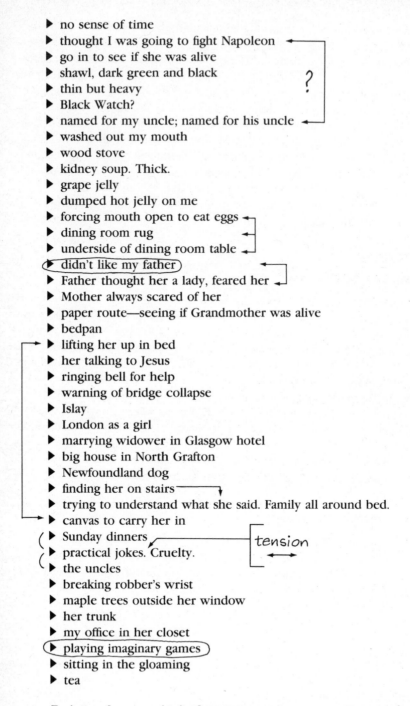

- ▶ no sense of time
- ▶ thought I was going to fight Napoleon
- ▶ go in to see if she was alive
- ▶ shawl, dark green and black
- ▶ thin but heavy
- ▶ Black Watch?
- ▶ named for my uncle; named for his uncle
- ▶ washed out my mouth
- ▶ wood stove
- ▶ kidney soup. Thick.
- ▶ grape jelly
- ▶ dumped hot jelly on me
- ▶ forcing mouth open to eat eggs
- ▶ dining room rug
- ▶ underside of dining room table
- ▶ didn't like my father
- ▶ Father thought her a lady, feared her
- ▶ Mother always scared of her
- ▶ paper route—seeing if Grandmother was alive
- ▶ bedpan
- ▶ lifting her up in bed
- ▶ her talking to Jesus
- ▶ ringing bell for help
- ▶ warning of bridge collapse
- ▶ Islay
- ▶ London as a girl
- ▶ marrying widower in Glasgow hotel
- ▶ big house in North Grafton
- ▶ Newfoundland dog
- ▶ finding her on stairs
- ▶ trying to understand what she said. Family all around bed.
- ▶ canvas to carry her in
- ▶ Sunday dinners
- ▶ practical jokes. Cruelty.
- ▶ the uncles
- ▶ breaking robber's wrist
- ▶ maple trees outside her window
- ▶ her trunk
- ▶ my office in her closet
- ▶ playing imaginary games
- ▶ sitting in the gloaming
- ▶ tea

tension

Each time I go over this list I see more tensions, connections, and surprises in it. It sparks memories, feelings, contradictions—the raw materials for other pieces of writing I could work on.

At the moment I am using brainstorming to explore my personal memory, but it is just as important a technique to use when you are deciding on what subject to explore in a term paper. Brainstorming will tell you the connections between memory or the connections between ideas. It is a way of developing theories, trends, concepts, a way of relating information. You can use brainstorming to develop a marketing plan for a new product, to start thinking about how to review a literary work, to plan a party, to decide what should be in a résumé for a job, to develop a legislative strategy, or to decide what to include in a report about a manufacturing plan that isn't making a profit. Brainstorming is a powerful thinking tool.

Mapping

Another form of brainstorming that may work when the traditional form doesn't is *mapping*. Many people think that brainstorming that works in lists is linear and tends to emphasize the kind of thinking that we do with the left side of our brain. The right side of the brain, supposedly, is less linear and doesn't work by listing. It circles the subject and makes unexpected leaps. It is certainly true that many of us think differently, by personality or training, and it is also true that we think differently when we have more experience with a subject or an intellectual task. What we need is tools that we can use when a tool with which we are familiar doesn't work. One such valuable tool is mapping. In mapping you put the subject or topic to be thought about in the center of the page, and then start drawing out lines from it when an idea occurs to you. These lines will branch off, and we can capture the fragments of information that we have in memory.

Again, I will demonstrate mapping by using it to see what it reminds me about my grandmother, since she is the topic on which I am going to be writing.

How Mapping Leads to Writing

The map on page 26 took only ten minutes, the same as the other brainstorm, but it produced different information. One thing that it emphasizes is her religion, and I've drawn arrows tying issues back to religion. For example, my mother had stones thrown at her going to school in Scotland because she was a Baptist and not a Presbyterian, and we didn't even have store-bought apple juice in our house in Massachusetts because that might become cider and give me a taste for booze. Again, I'm moving back and forth in history, but I have a lot more family in this outline. I've blacked out the name of one member of the family because I don't know if I want to get into that; that is private and might hurt family members who are still alive. You always have the choice of accepting or sharing what comes up from your subconscious. I remembered, while mapping, how delighted I was when I saw pictures of great black Watusi warriors in the *National Geographic*. I thought my African relatives looked like that. How disappointing when they turned out to be just pale, ordinary Scots.

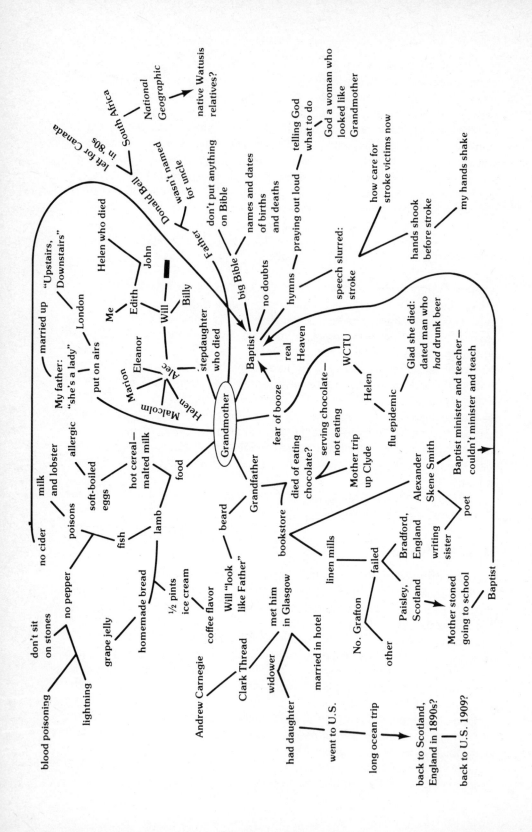

I can wander back and forth over this map and begin to catch the texture of my childhood. There was the fear my mother had that I would sit on stones; somehow that would give me bone aches when I grew up. I sat on stones; I don't think there's any connection, but I do have bone aches. I've never dealt with the fact that I had an aunt who died in the flu epidemic years before I was born, and that her mother—my grandmother—felt it was good she died because she had dated a man who had drunk beer. If I'm going to write about my grandmother I'm going to have to deal with the harshness of her faith.

It would take me pages, or perhaps books, to deal with all that is called up by that ten-minute mapping session. If I don't think I have anything to write I can brainstorm or map, or just sit down and use the third most successful technique I have to discover what I have to say.

Free Writing

Another technique I have found productive is *free writing*. When you free write you sit down and let the writing flow, seeing if language will carry you towards meaning. Sometimes this is called automatic writing. It is writing which seems to be writing without thinking. You have to suspend critical judgment, as you do when brainstorming or mapping, and hope that something will happen.

I'm never sure that anything will happen. In fact, right now I feel the fear in my stomach that nothing will come. It really doesn't matter. Some days the writing comes, and some days it doesn't. If free writing doesn't work I'll try brainstorming or mapping, or staring out the window, or turn to another project, or get a cup of tea, or take a walk, or otherwise create an interruption. But in a few minutes I'll be back, and something will work, most of the time.

Now I will free write:

I'm a bit afraid to write about Grandmother. Interesting I don't put in "my." Just Grandmother. Grandma. She was a frightening woman. I felt the fear in all the grownups around me. My mother was a big woman, even bigger than my grandmother, but she was afraid of Grandma. She wore her hair up in a knot on the top of her head like the queen of England. I'm interested in the fear. Yes, I guess it was physical. I said "darn" once and "bugger," and I was hauled down those wooden stairs in the Vassell Street house and she scrubbed my mouth out with Fels Naptha soap. When I came home with a tan from summer camp she tried to scrub it off with a big brush, the kind you use on the floor when you're on your hands and knees. When she fell in the dining room, I must have been in about the first grade, and broke her arm, she had a great big round welt, a big purple lump just rose right up. We were alone; I had to call Dr. Bartlett probably, I had to call someone. Dr. Bartlett always moved slowly and smelled like a pipe. Grandmother didn't let the pain bother her. What a strong woman she was. Some of the best time were when we sat in the gloaming. Harry Lauder had a song "In the Gloaming" she liked to sing. Sometimes we played it on the huge tall phonograph—the Victrola. You had to crank it up, and there were cactus needles you had to sharpen by hand. The gloaming was the time before you spent money to turn the lights on, but when it was too dark to do any housework. She sat in the shadows looking out the window. We spent a lot of time just sitting in those days, on porches, in the living room, during those awful Sundays or holidays when there were family dinners and I always felt like the poor relative. Maybe that was good, maybe I worked hard to show them. God, I hated those dark houses, dark woodwork, dark wallpaper, old lamps with yellow bulbs and heavy shades, and all the things that were not said. We never talked, I mean really talked. Silence was heavy. Loud? There was so much silence, so much not saying.

Again, that was ten minutes of following language. Note the threads that are woven through the piece of writing, and how the writing starts to develop its own form, working towards the silences. If I'm going to write about my grandmother I now know I've got to deal with the cruelty and with the silences.

You see, free writing isn't free. It starts to take you somewhere, to tell you what to say and how to say it. After you free write you have to look back and see whether you want to follow any of those paths, to fill them in so the writing stops being private and can go public. You have to decide whether you want to share what you are discovering with others. If you do you'll find that the more personal the writing, the more specific and private, the more it will spark memories and ideas in your readers.

Free writing is just as valuable a technique to use as a starting point for a term paper, a historical essay, or a review of scientific literature. It's a way of thinking in which you can preserve the flow of thought.

You should try brainstorming, mapping, and free writing. Good writing often begins when you find out what you know and what you need to learn. These techniques can also be effective when your head feels empty. Free write or map or brainstorm with no topic in mind, and things will start to happen on the page.

Do you have to do mapping or brainstorming or free writing every time? Of course not. Nothing in this book is absolute. There is no one way to write. These techniques, and all the other techniques in this book, are thinking and writing tools that should be in your intellectual toolbox. You don't have to use a Phillips screwdriver unless you have a screw with a Phillips head; you don't have to use these techniques unless you have the need to collect and recollect your thoughts, memories, observations, and information.

Making a Tree

Another helpful technique to discover what you know and need to know is to draw a *tree* that reveals all the branches that can grow from a single idea.

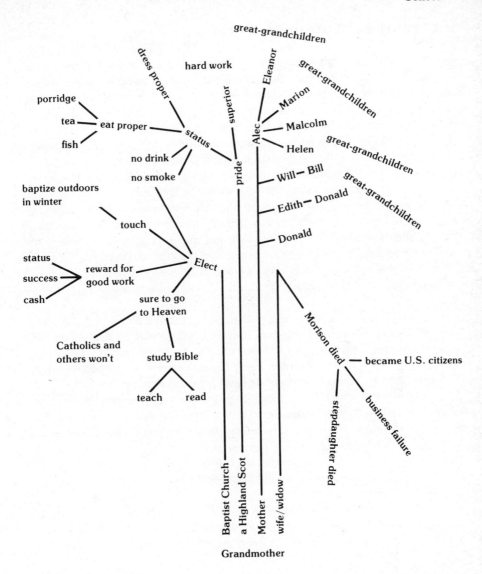

This is a way of breaking the subject down or a way of letting the subject expand. Some teachers who use trees successfully place the central idea at the top of the page and let the tree grow down; while others place the central idea at the left of the page and let the tree grow to the right. They both produce excellent results. But I am too literal; my trees grow up.

This tree took nine minutes, and, as you can see, it also produced some new insights. I see the tangle of Baptist and Highland beliefs in reward for hard work, and the certainty of being the elect, by God and by birth. But none of the techniques in this book will work the same way all of the time, and some may not work for you at all. They are tools that may help you solve a writing problem.

Increasing Awareness

As writers, it is important that we move out from that which is within us to what we see, feel, hear, smell, taste of the world around us. A writer is always making use of experience and extending experience. This is one of the most exciting things about writing: it increases your awareness of the world around you. To put it a different way, writers are receptive to the life they are living, prepared to receive what life brings so that material may lead to writing or be stored away in inventory, ready to be used when a writing project needs it.

I watch an old lady moving upstream against the students coming downtown for lunch. She has a stainless steel walker, a U-shaped contraption which she lifts and pushes eight inches ahead, then shuffles towards. What my grandmother could have done with such a gadget! She spent the last twelve years of her life in bed. Perhaps . . . The old lady has my grandmother's hair, a wispy halo of white, like the fine, white angel-hair that is sometimes used on Christmas trees. She also has my grandmother's jaw, tough, mean, determined. A friend stops and says, "You're looking good today." The old lady says, "I'd rather be seventy."

I don't know if I'll make use of that, but I received it and stored it away, the same way I clipped and read and stored away an article by William Stafford in which he talks of writer's block; I may use it in a scholarly piece. The scholar, the scientist, the lawyer, the writer, every thinking person keeps picking up bits of information that may fit into an evolving meaning now or later.

You do this every day without even knowing it. You pick up the latest slang, hear a joke and store it away to repeat it later, notice a jacket someone's wearing and decide you ought to have one, hear a song and think about buying a record. We all use our powers of observation so that we can survive. We receive messages that tell us how to live our lives.

The big difference between the writer and the nonwriter is in the number of messages that are received.

Each day we receive conscious and subconscious messages. I see the squirrels this winter madly searching for food in the snowy woods outside my window. I'm conscious of that. It's been a hard winter for squirrels, and there are stories of squirrels trying to get into houses. I can't tell you what I'm not conscious of, but I know those woods are stored away in my memory, and that this summer, or next, if I write about a snowy woods I will then see again, in my mind, the way snow has clung to the north side of a certain tree.

We can't write without seeing, and by writing we see better. A writer's life is at least twice lived, at the time of living and at the time of reliving.

Becoming a Camera

There are some specific things you can do to increase your awareness. The best is to go to one spot and sit for an hour and just write down the specific details you see. As Christopher Isherwood said, "I am a camera with its shutter open, quite passive, recording, not thinking. Recording the man shaving at the window opposite and the woman in the kimono washing her hair. Some day, all this will have to be developed, carefully fixed, printed." Make yourself a camera that is recording what it sees. Later you can edit the film to find out what it means. If you do this don't worry about sentences or spelling or neatness. Just record what you see.

It's amazing what happens when you go to a familiar place—the dormitory lounge, the dining hall, the basketball court an hour before the game, the student beer hall, a church, a hospital waiting room, a supermarket—and just write down what you see. It's easy to collect a hundred, two hundred, sometimes many more specifics than that in an hour. You will see things that you haven't seen before and make connections that you haven't made before.

But is this writing? It certainly is, because writing starts long before the first line of a finished draft. If you're going to write a book review you have to read the book, and possibly other articles and books about that particular book, that sort of book, or the author. You have to do the experiment before you write it up. You have to observe the game before you write the news story that tells who won, how, and why.

I can't go back and observe my grandmother, for she died many years ago. I'd like to go to the island off the coast of Scotland where she was born, but I can't afford that. I can't even take the time to go to the hospital and see stroke victims and how they are treated today, or go to a nursing home. But I can, on my way to school, stop in the supermarket, sit down or walk around with a notepad, and put down some of the things I see old people do.

This took me a few minutes. I had to wander through the supermarket until I found an old lady shopping. I stood at the end of the aisle where she couldn't see me, and then went and sat on a bench on the other side of the cash registers where I could see her shop and then check out. She wasn't at all like my grandmother. My grandmother was large, imposing; the woman I watched was birdlike. But just being a camera, watching her and her ostentatious manners, her obvious concern with what the neighbors thought, reminded me of the concern with propriety felt by my grandmother, who had been a farm girl from an island off the coast of Scotland sent when she was a teenager to live in a great house in London where she had to work and learn manners. She married an older man who was coming to this country to run a mill. The farm girl had to be a lady. It was terribly important to her to do the right thing. I was both amused by and very sympathetic to the efforts of the little old woman in the supermarket to be a lady.

As you look back through my notes you may see that I have the beginning of a piece about my grandmother, but I also have a character sketch, perhaps even a short story, about the lady I saw, or an essay or newspaper column about the little old ladies who live alone and dress up to go shopping: they make the trip last as long as possible, and the few lines of dialogue at the checkout counter may be their only conversation of the week.

I am never bored, for when I'm waiting in an airport or in a parking lot, for a meeting to begin or a movie to start, I am always receiving observations. I see how people dress, move close to or away from each other, walk, act when

Dressed up—camel's hair coat
rubbers make feet big—spindly legs
Hairdo—been to hairdressers
Dressed like lady
Moves slowly—make shopping last
Superior look on face
    Knowing
    Examines delicacies
No one to cook for but self
Acts as if someone were watching, judging
   her
Middle class
(See middle-aged man. I played football
   with him. I see the boy in the man. Same
   grin. Spraddle-legged walk.)
Others harried, hurried
Old lady wants to make time last
    (But you have a sense of time racing
    ahead as you get old)
Lifts up each foot separately and plants each one separately—scared of falling
Her awareness of others
Alone in aisle, I'm hidden behind display, she acts as if someone is watching (someone is)
Middle class—what will neighbors say
My grandmother's sense of propriety
    Keeps curtains half drawn
    Wear a hat when shopping
    Lace curtains
Does old lady buy "the right brands"?
  If anyone was in kitchen they'd see
  "right" brands. No one in her
  kitchen until she dies.
Wear clean underwear in case of an accident

Go back to what she was examining:
    Spanish olives
    olive butter
    sweet pickles
    piccalilli
_____

handbag hung on left arm
pushing cart as she pushed baby carriage?
_____

tiny, round-shouldered
_____

tips head up to read labels—bifocals
_____

large cart, few items
_____

pursed lips, raised eyebrows
critical lady
_____

small-boned, looks like bird
_____

Manners—she makes sure she has manners
Impatient in line but she has nowhere to go?

wrinkled stocking below neat coat
varicose veins
_____

walks flat-footed
_____

money from purse, carefully private

they don't think they are being seen. I'm a spy, or a sneak, enjoying the human comedy, and all that I observe is stored away ready to be called up when I'm writing.

The writer is always receiving revealing details—the way one teacher carries a pile of books to class and builds a little wall of books between himself and his students, the way another teacher uses the latest campus slang in precisely the wrong way.

Use Your Senses

All the writer's senses help the writer become aware of information that may become raw material for a piece of writing. The writer hears and overhears. The writer touches, tastes, and smells the world so the details can be used in writing that makes the reader experience the world through all of the reader's senses.

Practice Empathy

Another way to make yourself receive information that may be helpful to you as a writer is to practice empathy, the ability to put yourself in other people's skins. We can imagine what it might be like to be rich if we are poor or poor if we're rich, to be a policeman or to be arrested by a policeman, to be selling or buying.

These imaginings are not facts, but they can help us understand the factual elements in the world we observe, and they can let us know what questions we should ask when we investigate a topic. We may be shocked when we see an emergency ambulance attendant respond to an accident without apparent emotion, but if we imagine what it is like to respond to accident after accident, night after night, month after month, we may develop some perspective questions to ask him or her about the emotional price paid.

Searching for New Information

To collect enough information with which to write we usually have to search for new information. At first we know what we know and don't know by recollecting the information within ourselves. We might compare that to a base camp for an assault on an unknown mountain peak.

Then we make ourselves aware of the world around us and receive information that may extend our knowledge and our feelings. This is an advance camp part way up the peak.

Now we are ready to start the assault itself, and for most of the things we'll write the information is available if we can find where it is and how to get it.

Sources of Information

There are three principal sources of information: people, institutions, and libraries.

Too often in school we forget that people are authorities and fine sources of information. All of us are authorities on many things. You are an authority on being a student, and I am an authority on teaching. Neither of us is *the* authority, but you know something about being a student because you are one, and I am an authority on teaching because I've been teaching. I taught yesterday, I will teach this afternoon, and I will teach tomorrow.

Your Authority List

It may be helpful to take a moment and make an authority list. When we do this it helps us understand how other people are authorities, so that we can perceive their importance as resources. It also helps us discover things that we know which may provide us with topics to write on.

My authority list would include:

▶ My grandmother
▶ Starting college on a football scholarship
▶ Newspaper writing
▶ Snoring
▶ Being a paratrooper in World War II
▶ Teaching writing
▶ Eating
▶ Collecting records
▶ Avoiding working around the house and in the yard
▶ Being a kid in the Depression
▶ Being a husband, father, son, grandson
▶ Making the decision to let someone die—three times
▶ Serving on university committees
▶ Being a police reporter
▶ Yelling at hockey games
▶ Cultivating a beard

Those, and hundreds of other subjects, serious and frivolous, could provide topics for writing, or could be the basis for someone to interview me.

The Interview

The interview in which you ask a person questions is one of the basic tools of getting information. Most of us are shy about interviewing someone else, but we have to remember that the person who is being interviewed is being put in the position of being an authority, and most of us like to be an authority, to tell someone what we know. It is an ego trip for the interviewee.

Interviews can be informal—just a casual conversation—or formal—when we make an appointment and take a good deal of time.

You should prepare yourself for interviews by knowing as much as you can about the persons you are going to interview—who they are and what they do—and by preparing at least the four or five principal questions you have to ask if you are going to get the information you need. Those are usually the questions the reader would like to ask if he or she were there. Think of the reader; ask the reader's questions.

It's important to listen to what the person is saying so that you don't go on asking the potter about how he prepares the clay when he is telling you why he put his wife in the kiln. Many times the interviewee surprises us by what he or she says, and we have to decide on the spot which lead to follow.

Most interviewers take notes by hand, but it is more and more common to use a tape recorder. You should, however, practice taking notes by hand, capturing the essence of what people say, even if you use a tape recorder. Sometimes the tape doesn't work, and if you're not taking notes yourself you may become lazy and miss what's being said—that the wife was popped into the kiln.

It's always best to interview a subject in person so that you can see the expression on the face, the body language that emphasizes or contradicts what is being said, the environment in which the person lives or works, the way the person interacts with others. If you can't interview someone in person then you may have to do it on the telephone, or even by mail. But you lose a lot by doing it without seeing the person face to face.

For this piece I'm writing about my grandmother I will have to interview my Uncle Don, her only remaining child. I'm always a bit nervous about interviewing someone, even though I've done thousands of interviews, and I'm especially nervous about this one. There have been some family problems since my mother died, and I feel a bit uncomfortable about the interview. It will have to be done on the telephone, since he lives in another state and I don't have the time to visit him, but I realize I've got to talk to him. He's the only firsthand authority I have on my grandmother.

As I started to think what I could ask him about my grandmother, I realized that I knew nothing—or very little—about my grandfather, who died long before I was born. All I have is a few family myths. I have to talk to my uncle about his father, who must have died about seventy years ago.

I think I'll start by asking him what my grandfather looked like. I like to get an interview started on very specific ground, and I'll try to ask questions that get specific information and can't be answered yes or no. I won't ask, Was he a nice man or a good father? I will ask, What do you remember doing with him? and How did he punish you?

The interview went well but it was different than I expected. Here are some of the notes I recorded of what my uncle said:

"I don't remember too much about him either. I remember his mustache and his side-whiskers, and so forth. He wasn't particularly my pal. Alec, you know, my brother, was ten years older than me and was really my pal when I was a youngster. I didn't see too much of my father. He had a fiddle foot; he went from job to job.

"All I can remember was that he had a pretty good job for his day representing the thread company, and he was quite a boy in North Grafton, had his own coach, buggy, and so forth, servants, and all that. But that wasn't enough for him, he wanted to be in business for himself. He went into business for himself in Clinton and flubbed that, and then he went into business in Worcester. That's when I was born. And he went over to England to do some business, and his partner sold out, or something, and so we eventually went to England, and he was there alright, but he decided to go into business for himself again. For a while he decided to make chocolates because he had heard of the Cadbury Company, you know. And he was always in something like that. Poor Mother was having to hold the family together. He was making candy at home in the kitchen and boxing it up in the hopes of making a reputation, you know. He'd read of the Coates people [a successful thread business] starting small and becoming big, and the Cadbury people starting small and becoming big, and so on, and so he was trying to do that himself.

"He died when I was sixteen in high school, he died in, let's see, 1911.

"We came back in 1909 [to the U.S.].

"Well, he was disgusted because the people he worked for, the Peytons in Paisley, had promised to take him into partnership there, and like everything else they had some relatives they wanted to put in. They put the relative in and [he] got disgusted and decided to come back here, thank God, he did come back, but he never had much of a job here. He went to Philadelphia as a bookkeeper, or something. He didn't get a job very easily. And that's the last job I know he had.

"For a while Mother was making bread and selling it . . . that's how we got by.

" . . . I can remember being in bed and feeling very badly about some quarrel between my father and my mother."

How the Interview Can Lead to Writing

I found out I knew things about my grandfather my eighty-eight-year-old uncle didn't, but I found out some other things, too. I never knew my grandfather went into business in Clinton and Worcester. I'd never heard about the chocolates, and I never knew he'd gone to Philadelphia, because the family never moved there, and they were in Boston when he died. I'd never heard of Grandmother making bread to sell. She would be too ashamed to tell me about that.

My grandfather faded into an even more ephemeral ghost as I talked to my uncle, but how significant that was. I had thought of him as a substantial man, a man of authority and success. My grandmother and mother had told me only of the good moments, the times of success when he had a buggy of his own and they had servant girls. Now I met a grandfather who was rarely home, whose youngest son hardly knew him, who had a "fiddle foot."

In doing research, what you don't find out can be as significant as what you do find out, and each piece of information, or noninformation, can fit into patterns. I've often wondered what my mother saw in my father, and I wondered about the tensions that made their marriage unhappy for forty-nine years. My mother was terribly attracted to her father and felt very close to him. She talked of trips on the River Clyde and how he loved chocolate, and how they ate chocolate together. She never mentioned the making of chocolate—and his failing at it. And she married my father. I'd never heard the expression before, but if anyone ever had a fiddle foot it was my father, who kept leaving jobs to go into business for himself. And Mother always supported him and destroyed him at the same time. The pattern was repeated over and over again.

In collecting this material I have all sorts of pieces I could write—a poem called "Fiddle Foot" or an essay with the same title about my father and my grandfather, an article about interviewing relatives—and I have more material about my grandmother for this piece I'm writing. I can remember the taste of her bread cooked on a wood stove in our kitchen before she collapsed with a stroke—a shock, they called it then—when I was eight years old. That bread tastes differently in my memory now that I know the former mill owner's wife had cooked it to sell.

My uncle also said in the interview about my grandmother, "I guess she was working as a housemaid, or something. I don't know, I think she was a servant of some sort, and he met her that way." And now I know more about my grandmother's airs and why she was so unpleasant to my father's mother, who'd been a factory girl. It was important to that farm-girl-turned-servant-girl who had married up at the age of twenty-seven, listed in the marriage record as "a spinster," that she not be identified with my Grandmother Murray, who did not put on airs and spoke with an honest Scottish burr.

When you are doing research on any topic, from criminal justice to World War II to urban blight to environmental hazard, don't forget to use live sources, and talk to the people who are involved. They will not tell you the truth, they will tell you their own truths, and then you will have the challenge of weaving all the contradictions together into a meaning.

Using Organizations to Find Information

Another source of information when you are searching for material is organizations. The library has directories of organizations that will help you find groups that have come together, and one of those organizations' main functions is to educate the public or to serve the public. They will often send you pamphlets or brochures or reports and answer questions you have. Most of the time it's free, although I had to pay the Scots Ancestry Research Society in Edinburgh, Scotland, to have them get information on my family.

Here are a few excerpts from pages of reports:

The birth of Mary Bell was next found to have been recorded as follows:

> Mary Bell was born 8th November 1855 at Gearrach, Kilchoman. The daughter of Donald Bell, farmer, aged forty, born in Kilchearan, Kilchoman, married in Kilchoman in 1850, with two boys living one boy deceased, aged thirty-four, born in Kendrochit, Kilchoman, her fourth child.

The marriage of Mary Bell and Morison Smith was found to have been recorded thus:

> 17th August 1883 at St. Enoch's Station Hotel. After Banns according to the Baptist Church. Morison Smith, flax mill clerk, widower, aged 37, of Hagg Crescent, Johnstone. The son of Alexander Skene Smith, flax mill clerk, and Jane Thomas [*sic*] deceased.
>
> AND
>
> *Mary Bell,* aged 27, spinster, of Newton Bridgend, Kilarrow, Islay. The daughter of Donald Bell, retired farmer, and Mary McCannell.

Ten years ago when I was in Scotland I found that birth record myself and saw my great-grandfather's fine steady hand recording the birth of his daughter, my grandmother. I don't know what the term "retired farmer" in the wedding record means. The family legend is that the Bells had farmed the same land for years. I do have records that show that Duncan Bell, "tenant," was farming in the area in the 1700s, but they never did manage to own the land. My grandmother, when she was a teenager, was taken by the wife of the absentee landlord to work in her house in London. And I also know that Donald Bell, in his eighties, either disgusted with the system or desperate to survive, went to Canada to find land he could own.

Each of these fragmentary pieces of information gives off echoes of half-understood family legends heard in my childhood, makes possible connections, sparks questions. Grace Paley once said, "We don't write about what we know so much as we write what we don't know about what we know." The writer is challenged to make a meaning where there isn't a meaning. The writer is a connector, a person who tries to weave coherence where there has only been confusion, and organizations can help us collect the bits of information from which we can construct a meaning.

Using the Library

One of the greatest sources of material, of course, is those attics that exist in almost every town, city, and state in the country, as well as in schools, universities, and the nation's capital itself. These attics collect books, magazines, newspapers, pamphlets, phonograph records, films, TV tapes and audio tapes, photographs, maps, letters, journals—all the kinds of documents that record our past—and we call them libraries.

Every library has a card catalog that shows what is in the library and gives the location where you or the librarian can find it. The wise writer always makes sure to have a good working relationship with a library and its librarian. When I was free-lancing in New Jersey I found it a good investment to pay to have cards in four library systems. Libraries are an elemental source for a writer, as important as wind is to a sailor.

If you are going to write it is vital that you become familiar with your library. Most college libraries have tours that will show you how the library works. Take the tour. Most libraries also have mimeographed sheets or pamphlets that will help you find what you need to know. Study such materials. And most of all, use the library. Browse. Wander. Let the library reveal its resources to you. And if you need help, ask for it. Librarians are trained to be of service, and all of us who write are indebted to their patience and skills in finding information for us.

It's important when you find a reference in the library to make a note of all the essential information about the book so that you can use the library easily the next time, and so that you can use the book in footnotes or bibliographies. Even if you write something that doesn't have footnotes or a bibliography you should know exactly where you got the material so that you can respond to questions from editors or readers.

Usually you record the author's last name first, then the first name, then the middle initial, the title of the work, underlined if it is a book, put within quotation marks if it is an article, the publisher, the place published, the date, the number of pages, and, for your own use, the library reference number together with the name of the library.

Here are a few of the many books I have used to help me catch a glimpse of my grandmother:

> Murray, W. H. *The Hebrides,* A. S. Barnes & Co. Inc., New York 1966, pp 248. In personal library.
>
> Turnock, David. *Scotland's Highlands and Islands,* Oxford Univ. Press, London 1974, pp 48. HC/257/.S4/T87–UNH library.
>
> Campbell, R. H. *Scotland Since 1707—The Rise of an Industrial Society,* Barnes & Noble, Inc., New York 1965, pp 354. HC/257/.S4/C3–UNH library.
>
> Lenman, Bruce. *An Economic History of Modern Scotland, 1660–1976,* Archon Books, Hamden, Conn. 1977, pp 288. HC/257/.S4/L39/1977–UNH library.

I can look up many topics to try to understand my grandmother's world. There are guidebooks to Scotland, accounts of travelers in Scotland at the time she was a girl, social histories of Scotland and the United States which tell how people ate and dressed and decorated their houses. There are histories of the textile industry, to which her life was tied, and in which my other grandparents came to this country as indentured workers. There are history books that re-create the background of their time and books that tell about the ships that brought my grandparents to this country. I could read the newspapers of the time, and I could explore the history of the Baptist Church, which was central to my family's life. Whenever I take a note I must record not only the book or other document from which it came, but its location, so I can check it easily if I need to. There are few horrors worse than having exactly the right note and no idea of its source.

Here are some notes I have taken to help me find my grandmother:

> "The islands of Argyll are the most exposed of the Inner Hebrides. Un-shielded from the Atlantic Ocean, which stretches 2000 miles to Labrador, they are, like the Outer Hebrides, outer isles. There comparison ends. Strange though it may seem, the Islay group are the palm-tree islands of the west, and Islay (pronounced Ila) is the greenest of them all—like a slice out of Ireland, which lies in full view twenty-three miles to its south...."
>
> Murray, *The Hebrides,* p. 22

> "The gulf between the landlord and the tenant was repeated between the tenant and the farm labourer. A tenant, no matter how lowly, was at least on the ladder of social promotion, even if he might never ascend

far. Though the structure of land ownership, and the provision of credit facilities, offered the prospects of social and economic progress to the farm labourer, he was regarded by the tenant farmer as belonging to a different group until he made the first move. Some tenant farmers drew a social distinction between themselves and their workers as rigid as that drawn by the landlords between themselves and their tenants. Neither was easily breached. The more responsible farm worker, the grieve or manager, was normally employed only by the larger tenant farmers and was himself likely to become at best a small-scale, rather struggling tenant farmer."

Campbell, Scotland Since 1707, p. 163–4

Those were notes recording direct quotes that I might want to use in something I would write. It's also possible to paraphrase or make a note for future reference, as follows:

Good account of conditions that forced all grandparents to leave Scotland in Chapter 6 of Lenman.

The purpose of such notes is to tell you where the information is and isn't. It's important to keep a record of the books you found worthless, so you won't go over them again, as well as the ones that are particularly valuable. Most research doesn't result in big breakthroughs, but a slowly growing understanding of the subject. I do not have a clear picture of my grandmother's world, but I am beginning to understand it better. I had visualized Islay, the island of her childhood, as bleak, and I have discovered that it was not. I begin to understand a little more of that tension between grandmothers that ran through my childhood. Partly it was the strong prejudice of my maternal grandmother, a Highlander, against my paternal grandmother, a Lowlander. As much as that, however, it was the fact that my father's family had been laborers and my grandmother's family had been tenants. Neither owned land; both lived in poverty; but one felt superior to the other and lived in fear they would slide back across that thin line and lose the status that meant so much to them.

Disciplines for Writing

All this collecting—remembering, receiving, searching, and researching—produces the mass of material that is essential for effective writing. It also produces a need for discipline, a habit, a way of working that will allow the writer to turn a jungle of raw material into publishable copy.

"There is no one right way. Each of us finds a way that works for him," says Robert B. Parker. "But there is a wrong way. The wrong way is to finish your writing day with no more words on paper than when you began. Writers write."

Sounds simple, doesn't it? But it isn't. Getting the writing done day in and day out, despite interruptions, other demands, obligations, duties, responsibilities, inertia, exhaustion, poor health, bad weather, invited and uninvited guests, too much drinking, too much eating, too little eating, wars, storms, births, deaths, marriages, divorces, travel, letters that come and letters that don't come, and a million other problems, is what separates the writer from the hope-to-be writer.

There are three elements in every writer's discipline—time, tools, places. There are variations among writers, and a writer's discipline may change over a lifetime of work. But if you are to get the writing done this semester, and in the years ahead, you should pay some attention to the following counsel.

Time

We have two kinds of writing times—fragmentary and insulated. We obviously have much more fragmentary time than we have insulated time, and it is important that we make use of both kinds of time.

As I mentioned earlier in the book, 60 percent or more of my time is spent planning, and most of this work is done in small fragments of time that can be measured only in minutes, sometimes in seconds.

I can write in small chunks of time. Try it yourself; see how long it takes to brainstorm five titles, or write a lead paragraph, or do a test description, or try a definition, or sketch out an anecdote, or even outline an article. I suspect you will find that when you thought you worked ten, or fifteen, or twenty minutes, you've worked two minutes, or four, or ninety seconds.

If you make good use of those fragments of time then you'll be able to write when you have a stretch of uninterrupted time. For most writers an hour is good, but not good enough. Two hours is plenty; three hours heroic. During those times unplug the phone, lock the door; do not read, create interruptions, plan, edit, nap, or eat—just write.

The time of day is important. Most young writers start out writing late at night and end up writing in the morning—the early morning—when their mind is fresh and the world is less likely to intrude. Goethe said, "Use the day before the day. Early morning hours have gold in their mouth."

The time of day, however, is not as important as habit. Most productive writers—there are exceptions—establish a routine and write at the same time every day. They know it and the people around them know it. "When I sit down to write—that's between 9 and 12 every morning, and I have never, incidentally, written a line in the afternoon or at night—when I sit down at my table to write, I never know what it's going to be until I'm under way. I trust in inspiration, which sometimes comes and sometimes doesn't. But I don't sit back waiting for it. I work every day," says Alberto Moravia. And Flannery O'Connor explains, "Every morning between 9 and 12 I go to my room and sit before a piece of paper. Many times I just sit for three hours with no ideas coming to me. but I know one thing: if an idea does come between 9 and 12, I am there ready for it."

Do not try for long, exhausting writing sessions. Few writers are productive in that way. Most writers write regularly for one to three hours every day. Philip

Larkin says, "I don't think you can write a poem for more than two hours. After that you're going round in circles, and it's much better to leave it for twenty-four hours . . ." Some days it goes, and some days it doesn't go. But over weeks and months I am productive.

And then once you have produced a draft, fragmentary time can serve you again. I find it better to edit in short bursts. If I edit more than fifteen minutes at a run I tend to be kind, far too kind. In these slivers of time, early and late in the day, I can cut, insert, reorder, and perhaps decide that I need another draft when I have a few hours of insulated time.

Tools

Every writer knows there is magic in tools. Writing comes from the ink, the pen, the typewriter, the paper, even the word processor, as much as the brain.

I have a huge closet full of once-favorite tools, and when I travel it is with a reserve of favorite pens, and paper that has the right tint and texture.

It's possible, of course, to be self-indulgent about tools. If the need for a special instrument or type of paper keeps you from writing, then make sure you break that habit. Many writers write on whatever is handy. Lorus and Margery Milne use the back side of correspondence, memos, notices, press releases, or any other kind of paper, and they are enormously prolific nature writers. Other writers grab whatever pen or pencil is nearby. Fine. But most writers do have a productive relationship with the tools of their trade.

Consider some of the aspects of writers' tools:

▶ Try to have rehearsal tools—pens or pencils, notebooks or file cards—that you can keep with you at all times so that you can use fragments of time and work when you are away from the writer's desk.

▶ Have some device, usually a typewriter or a word processor, but sometimes a technique, such as calligraphy, that allows you to see your work at a distance, in print, so that you can be more objective about it.

▶ If you don't type, learn.

▶ Make sure that the tools you use work easily. A pen should flow—there *is* such a thing as writer's cramp.

▶ Consider using a lap desk, either a small piece of board mounted on a beanbag or a piece of wood that will go from one arm of the chair to the other, with a stomach circle cut out (mine larger than yours). This allows you to work in hotel rooms, mountain cabins, automobiles, a sailboat, a dormitory lounge.

▶ Pick those tools—the 0.3 penpoint, the grainy mimeograph paper, the light plastic clipboard, the green eye-ease notebook paper, the portable electric typewriter, the jet black fountain pen ink, the soft lead pencil, the satisfying legal pad—that do not just feel good, but give you joy. Writing is a physical act of craft, and you should have fun using the tools that make writing.

Places

It helps to have a place where you go to write. It should be a place where you can leave your work lying out and come back to it later. You have your tools at hand and you have the climate that you prefer.

Ross Macdonald tells us, "I took my lifelong tenancy in the bare muffled room of the professional writer where I am sitting now, with my back to the window, writing longhand in a Spiral notebook." I like to look up from my writing at a view. Other writers, such as Ross Macdonald, turn their backs to the view. I need music when I write; other writers have to have silence. Create a place of your own where you can shut the door and be by yourself.

That's the ideal most students can never achieve. Joyce Carol Oates says, however, "If you are a writer, you locate yourself behind a wall of silence and no matter what you are doing, driving a car or walking or doing housework, which I love, you can still be writing, because you have that space."

It isn't easy to create that internal space, and women writers in particular have difficulty achieving Virginia Woolf's "room of one's own." But it can be done, as Lois Duncan points out: "Now I keep a typewriter with a sheet of paper in it on the end of the kitchen table. When I have a five-minute lull and the children are playing quietly, I sit down and knock out a paragraph. I have learned that I can write, if necessary, with a TV set blaring on one side of me and a child banging a toy piano on the other. I've even typed out a story with a colicky baby draped across my lap. It is not ideal—but it is possible." Donald Graves has been able to write in a dormitory room with pneumatic drill construction going on next door or in a small summer cottage filled with family, friends, and dogs by using earphones and Beethoven at top volume.

You have to find ways to detach yourself from the world and go to that place where you can hear the writing. Depending on our personalities, those places may not be the ideal artist's cabin high in the Rockies. I wrote most of one novel in a park, either sitting in the car or at a picnic table far out of the range of my mother-in-law's voice. I like to write in coffee shops and diners where no one knows me, and where there is a stimulating but unobtrusive background life that I can observe or ignore.

When I was an undergraduate my favorite writing places included the top row of the empty football stadium, a pleasing assortment of rocks on the Atlantic coast, a special table in the library, an empty classroom late at night. Find your own place where the writing comes.

Collecting for the Reader

Throughout the collecting process you've certainly been aware of one reader—yourself. You have found information that interested you and other information that didn't. You have seen things that relate to other things and things that had no apparent relation. In all this process you have been role-playing, consciously or unconsciously, the reader. Writing is not writing until it is read, and so throughout the writing process there is a continual attention to audience.

Many times this audience is specific. We are writing something that will be read by a teacher, a classmate, an employer, a friend, someone who needs to know the information, someone we want to persuade or educate or entertain. In some modes of writing the audience is paramount. This is true when we're writing a memo asking for financial support from a college administrator, or when we're writing an examination for a teacher. In other forms of writing, the personal essay or the poem, we may be at first writing for ourselves, and later realize that others would be interested.

The reader should help us write. Being aware of who may read what we write gives us additional eyes with which to see the subject. The reader's eyes help us collect and select, and they will be with us throughout the writing process.

Being aware of the reader does not mean that we change what we see, avoid what we think is important, or in any other way pander to the reader. Our job as writers is, above all, to be truthful, accurate, fair, even if the message we deliver does not please the reader.

When collecting I generally work from inside myself out, from childhood memories of my grandmother to books on Scotland. I realize I will remember more as I write, but I have stimulated my memory, and each day I am remembering more things. I have reached out from myself to collect those bits of information that I can find around me, and I've worked outward using books and documents from other times and other places.

What I have are fragments: facts, quotes, memories, images, pictures, notes, lines, phrases, and questions, many, many questions. It's a mess, a great, big, glorious, confusing mess. This is usually what happens in the collecting stage of the writing process. We don't get all the information we want, and we often get much information that we don't want. There are contradictions, vagueness when there should be concise accuracy, fragments instead of completeness, disorder and chaos.

That's the writer's raw material. Most people think the writer works with neatly organized material. That hardly ever happens, and it wouldn't be any fun to be a writer if that were true. It's not the job of the writer to write what the writer already knows and what the reader probably knows. Writing is thinking. As Joyce Cary says, "The work of art as completely realized is the result of a long and complex process of exploration." The writer's challenge is to think about the material, to select from the chaos what is significant, and to order it in such a way that a meaning is created for the writer, and therefore for the reader. The writer writes to learn first and then to teach by sharing that learning.

Remember that the process of collecting material continues all during the writing, but when there is a wonderful stew of raw and contradictory information it's time for the writer to begin to see how to discover a way to focus it, to catch a glimpse of meaning in that challenging mess.

Questions about Collecting

When do I know that my research is finished?

You'll never know. You'll always feel there will be a new and wonderful piece of information in the next book you read or the next interview you do—if only you had the time. Some writers get so involved in research that they never become writers. Most professionals stop when they know the answers they will hear as they ask the questions. In other words, they aren't finding much new. When that happens it's time to write.

And of course, there's the deadline. You have to figure back from when the writing is due and allow enough time for clarifying, drafting, ordering, and focusing if you're going to have a good piece of work.

I don't like what I'm finding out.

That often happens. We don't write *what* we know, we write *to know*—to learn. What we discover may not be what we want to discover—the football hero writing about what it's like to play big-time football may confront the fear of injury he's never admitted before.

A lot of the stuff I'm coming up with is personal, about me. Who would be interested in that anyway?

If it's too personal you don't have to put it down and share it with anyone, but if you are willing to share it, the more specific and personal the information, the more readers will be interested.

I feel funny writing about my grandmother, and I wonder if anyone will be interested. But I know as a professional writer that the more I talk about my Scottish grandmother and the more specific I am, the more universal I will become, and the more readers will think of their Lithuanian, Australian, Italian, Japanese, Russian, Chinese, Jewish, Mexican, French, Nigerian, or Indian grandmothers, and the more they read about grandmothers the more they will think about grandfathers and mothers and fathers and aunts and uncles and brothers and sisters. As E. B. White said, "Don't write about Man, write about *a* man."

Who is an authority?

The best way to find out the authority you should interview is to ask the people in that business who's the best. Ask nurses in the hospital, policemen on the force, teachers in the school, scientists in the lab who you should talk to to find out about your subject. They work with all the authorities. The ones you want to interview are those whom the people in the trade turn to when they have a problem.

How do I know who's telling the truth? If a fact is a fact?

By checking. It's a good idea to have three sources for any important fact or piece of information. It's not so much that people lie as that they're uninformed;

they believe what they're telling you, but it may not be true. As a researcher you have to keep your common sense in good working order. When you are suspicious about a statement or a detail, pay attention to that hunch and check it out.

I'm shy; I don't like talking to people.

Most reporters are shy. I used to hide in the closet when I was a kid and company came to the house, but it got uncomfortable sitting on a pile of shoes. I still get a funny feeling in my stomach when I go out to interview people. I was just reading an article about the most famous reporters in the country and they all shared a common difficulty—making the first phone call.

What you have to realize is that interviewing someone is very flattering for the person being interviewed. If you come in saying, "You're the greatest living authority on cockroaches," you won't be able to shut the delighted authority up.

What if people won't give me information?

You have to give them a reason to give information to you. Flattery, as above, is a good reason. If that doesn't work then you have to find out what is a good reason for them—they want to educate the uneducated (you); they want to persuade; they want to raise money. There are many reasons people will give out information, and you have to find the reason that will unlock the information you need.

I've got too much information; I've got more notes than I've got dirty socks. It's a mess.

Good. Strong pieces of writing come from an abundance of information. Walk away from your notes. Take a pad of paper and sit down somewhere quiet and put down what you've learned from your research, the things that have surprised you the most or that seemed the most significant or that connect. What you remember will usually be what is most important.

And read the next chapter. It tells you what to do with a mess of contradictory, interesting, confusing information.

Collecting Activities

1. Brainstorm, as described on page 19, by thinking of an important event in your life, when you were scared or happy or unhappy or angry, or brainstorm by thinking of an issue, argument, or opinion you want to develop, and put down every detail you can think of as fast as possible.
2. Map, as described on page 25, using the same event or topic to see what different things are recalled. But don't worry if the same things come up at first. Just go as fast as you can. Some things will be the same, and some may be different.

3. Free write: write as hard and fast as you can without worrying about grammar, spelling, mechanics, penmanship or typemanship. The important thing is to get a flow. You may even want to tape-record to hear what you have written. The important thing is to let language lead you to discover what you know and what you need to know.

4. Work to make yourself more aware. Go to a familiar place and list as fast as possible fifty specific details, or a hundred, or two hundred. The more you list the more things you'll see you haven't seen before. It may be fun to take a frame or cardboard tube and see what you can see in a small framed area. It may be profitable to take one sense at a time and record what you can smell, hear, taste, and touch as well as see.

5. Make an authority inventory, listing all the things you're an expert on—the jobs you can do, the things you can repair, the places you've lived or visited, the problems you can solve, the hobbies you enjoy, the people you know, the family background you have. Each of us is an authority on many things, and our best writing usually comes from what we know and care about. There is a significant relationship between the word "author" and the word "authority."

6. Interview someone else to find out what the other person is an authority on. Dig in to find out how the person became an authority on the subject. What makes the person angry, satisfied, happy, interested, sad, laugh when they talk about their subject?

7. Go to the library and find out what sources exist on a subject that interests you. The people who work at reference desks are very helpful in showing you all the places in the library that there might be information on a specific subject.

8. Practice scanning—quick reading—to find out what interests you by taking a book that covers the subject in its broadest terms. For example, if you're interested in one variety of seagull, take out a book about birds and go through it fast to see what you can find out about your seagull.

9. Practice making quick notes by watching television news and taking down the essential details.

10. Collaborate with one or two other classmates to research a limited topic. It's interesting to learn from others how they approach a subject differently from you. Each of us has our own researching style and tricks, as well as a different background that changes our angle of vision on a subject.

11. Look up a piece of writing on a subject you want to research and try to figure out where the writer got the information. Some books have interesting appendices in which the authors talk about the problems of research and how they solved them.

12. Try to apply the research techniques in this chapter to a problem in your own field so that you can see how these techniques can be adapted to a problem in social work or hotel administration or physics or history. Ask a professor in your major field to share some of his research techniques with you, and report on these to the class.

13. Role-play. Watch a situation—a crowd growing unruly, a person making a speech, an ambulance responding to an accident, a person being hired or fired—and imagine yourself in that situation. Figure out how you would act and react, think and feel. This will give you some interesting questions to ask. Go to a person who is involved in the situation and ask them.
14. Practice looking for the detail that reveals—how the doctor walks calmly when there is a crisis, how the expert teacher uses silence to control a class, how a politician uses first names, how an expert programmer plays with the computer. Try to catch the action in a few words that reveal.
15. Write down as fast as you can a list of all the details you remember from last week's activities. Use all your senses. Doing this you'll be surprised at what you remember, and you may find things you want to explore more. Doing this kind of collecting will also make you more aware in the week ahead. And the more you see, the more you'll have to learn by writing.

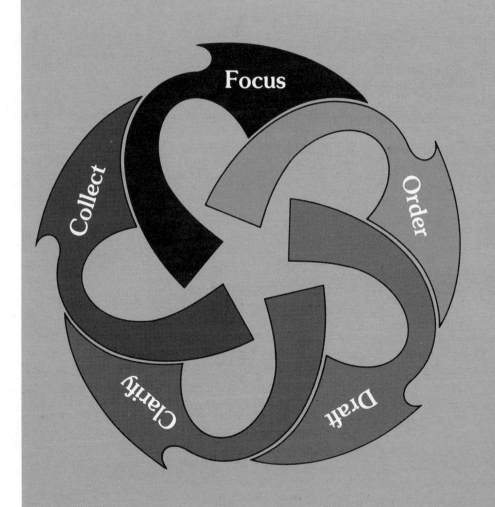

Focus

Collect

Order

Clarify

Draft

Focus

The writer . . . sees what he did not expect to see. . . .
Inattentive learner in the schoolroom of life, he
keeps some faculty free to hear and wonder. His is
the roving eye. By that roving eye is his subject
found. The glance, at first only vaguely caught, goes
on to concentrate, deepen; becomes the vision.

Elizabeth Bowen

That could almost be cited as the definition of a
poet: Someone who notices and is enormously taken
by things that somebody else would walk by.

James Dickey

That's what a writer is: someone who sees problems
a little more clearly than others.

Eugene Ionesco

The photographer using a zoom lens first selects a territory to be explored, then zooms in close. The photographer sees a meadow of wild flowers, a gang hanging around on a city corner, a series of waves exploding against a rocky coast, and then selects the three wild flowers, the hood leaning so carefully and casually against the telephone pole, the seventh wave to catch, print, and develop.

The writer works much the same way, and the following techniques are designed to help you find a territory that you may want to explore with language. Later in the chapter there are other techniques that will help you move in close and concentrate your vision.

Find Your Own Subject

Listen to John McPhee, my candidate for the best nonfiction writer working today, as he tells how he got the idea that led to his *New Yorker* magazine piece that ended up as a book called, simply, *Oranges*. "What started me on the 'Oranges' piece was a daily glass of orange juice I would have at a stand in Pennsylvania Station when I worked in New York. I noticed over the course of the year that the juice's color would change depending on the season. I wondered about that. Then I saw an ad for the Florida Citrus Commission that had a picture of six oranges. They looked almost exactly the same, but had six different names. I decided it might be interesting to understand the differences, so I went to Florida, intending to do a short piece."

You can work to develop an insatiable nosiness, such as John McPhee's. Everything that you see, hear, feel, touch, overhear, read, dream, imagine, remember is a potential subject.

Be Nosy

The way that subject comes clear is by collecting concrete specifics about it, and you can collect the specifics by observing and by asking why, who, what, when, where, how. The most ordinary things—oranges—can be a subject.

You go to a football game and see the player with the ball tackled again and again. Nothing extraordinary in that—or is there? Talk to the best tackler on the team and you'll find out that tackling can be a complex craft.

How do you tackle a runner moving outside the end of the line of scrimmage? How do you tackle a player coming through the line? When do you tackle low? When do you tackle high? How do you tackle a player who may pass? How do you catch up with a player and tackle from behind? How do you get an angle on a player and use the sidelines to help you tackle? What's a legal tackle? Is there such a thing as an illegal tackle that's okay to do? Is there such a thing as a legal tackle that isn't okay to do, that's a cheap shot? Have you seriously hurt anybody tackling them? Did you mean to do it? How do you feel about doing it? How did you feel when you did it? What are you afraid of in tackling? Have you been hurt seriously? How did you feel about that? How do you tackle to keep a runner from making a few inches for a first down? How do you tackle to cause a fumble? Where do you place your weight to be most effective? How do you use your arms when tackling? How do you tackle without using your arms? What different steps do you take before tackling?

That's just the beginning. Each answer will bring new questions, and you can ask other players and coaches and read books and articles. You could write a book on tackling. A writer has a license to explore both the familiar and unfamiliar.

There are good pieces of writing in bread, diesel motors, word processors, tea, trees, highway pavement, grass, snow removal, desert reclamation, dormitory design, wood stoves, deer hunting, vegetarianism, sewing, taking photographs, gardening, driving a truck, work habits, passing laws, water, weather—anything that is part of your world.

Mine Daily Experience

Make use of your personal experiences. You have to go to the dentist to have a cavity filled. What new equipment are dentists using to drill teeth? Are people having fewer cavities? Do most people lose their teeth because of cavities? (No, gum disease. I had a problem with my gums: I wrote an article on that.) What materials are they using to fill teeth? Why do they use different materials? Are people allergic to certain materials? How does the price of gold affect dental care? Can different kinds of metal used as fillings react badly to each other? Do dentists do unnecessary fillings? How do dentists describe a good filling? How do you find a good dentist?

Look Backwards

We get good subjects by digging out the history of an event—a law, an institution, or a place. Why did your hometown become a town? How has it changed and moved in response to changes in economics or geography or population? What's the history of your street or your house or the field or alley in which you used to play? How does that history affect the way you think and behave? How are your parents the product of their history? Your grandparents? What are you doing and thinking and seeing today that will become history? What will today look like through the telescope of history?

Look Forward

Speculate about the future. Where will you be in five years, ten years, twenty-five years, fifty years? What will your world be like? How is your hometown going to change? How is your school going to change? How does the past predict the future of your neighborhood? How will changes in transportation or the economy or a new discovery, such as plastics, affect your hometown? What change do you fear the most? What would you like to have remain the same? How will people think differently twenty-five years from now? How will they think the same?

Watch People

People are one of the primary sources for good pieces of writing. Watch how people behave, how they speak with their bodies, how they say what they say, what they don't say, what uniforms they wear, what masks. How do they look when they don't think anyone is watching? Role-play the person you're observing. What is it like to be a policeman or a nurse, a factory worker or an executive, a salesman or a politician, a soldier or a professor? What do they fear? What do they like doing? What are they good at? What qualities do they try to develop in themselves? What is the reason they act the way they do? What rewards do they hope for? What are the limits of their world? Talk to the people who interest you. Listen, and they will reveal themselves to you.

Observe Process

Readers are forever interested in process. How do you arrest a drunk in a college bar? Decide what injury is most important in a hospital emergency room? Tip a slapshot into the net? Sell a used car? Write a news story on deadline? Decide who deserves a bank loan? Keep an assembly line going? Place groceries on the supermarket shelves so people will buy high-profit items? Laws are passed by a process; children are adopted by a process; planes take off and land by a process; plays are rehearsed by a process; and games are won by a process. Readers like to get inside a story—backstage, into the emergency room, behind the banker's desk—to see the process that makes each part of our world go.

Find the Problem

Problems make good subjects. Define a problem so the reader can understand its importance and then see the alternatives. Problem: how to make an icy New England road safe for driving. One solution is to dump salt on the road, but salt gets into the plants and tree roots and water supply along the road. New problem: how much salt to use. When is it important to use it and when not? One of my students wrote a fine piece on this subject. He came from Idaho, where the problems of snow removal are different from those in New Hampshire, and he saw a good story in what was obvious to us. He taught me that I didn't know as much as I thought I knew about my world.

You can reverse this one; if you see a solution—an attractive nursing home, a successful business, a tax, a popular resort, almost anything that works in our society—you may be able to find a good subject by discovering the problem that sparked the solution.

Read to Write

A text—or a movie, television show, or play—can provide a subject for writing. We can examine the text internally. How do the parts of the text work with and against each other? What does it mean? How is the meaning supported? Is it supported well? How could it be improved? We can look at the text externally. How does it compare with other texts? What tradition does it belong to? How does it fit into that tradition? How is it in conflict with the tradition? We can compare the text with our own personal experience. How does the text fit with our reality? How does it disagree with our reality? We can look at a text from the point of view of a writer. What was the writer trying to do? How did the writer try to do it? What did the writer do that made it work? Or not work? What could be changed, and why?

The text can supply us with information that we can use in any form of writing. Or it can simply spark an idea. We read, for example, George Orwell's *Down and Out in Paris and London* and realize there is a story in the kitchen at the resort we worked in last summer. Or we read his "Shooting an Elephant" and it makes us think of a story about a gang fight in our neighborhood.

Use What You Know

Look into yourself to discover what you know that might interest or help other people. What you consider ordinary may be extraordinary to someone else: how to track a deer, bicycle in Europe, tune a car, get a tip from a stingy diner, sail a boat, lasso a calf, repair a roof, develop a picture, survive in a subway, light a play, save money by buying used clothes, cook on a hot plate or a camp stove. You are an adult who has had many experiences and performed many jobs that would interest other people. List them, or team up with someone else. Interview the other person and have that person interview you, so each of you will discover what interests the other.

What Do Readers Need to Know?

Imagine what readers outside of the class need to know. If you can answer a reader's need you will have an effective piece of writing. Readers off the campus may need to know how many students have to work to pay their way through school, that some parents don't want their children to go to college, that all jocks aren't dumb, that undergraduates often work on important research projects, that some students have to drop out of college because of increasing costs, that alcohol—the drug adults approve of—is the biggest problem on campus. A good way of looking for a subject is to look first for a reader.

What Would You Like to Know?

Writing is a marvelous way to satisfy your curiosity. When I was a freshman I wondered what college was like from the point of view of a night watchman, so I got permission to go around with him, and ended up with a fine feature for the school paper. Think what you're nosy about: What's it like to watch a football game from the sidelines, or with the coaches watching the film on

Sunday? Who cooks the rolls for breakfast and when do they come in? How do they audition for the play? How do they set up the equipment for a rock concert? How can a student rule be appealed or changed? What are the best-paying or most unusual summer jobs? How do foreign students see the school? What happens to shoplifters when they are caught downtown? Look at the world around you and question it.

Use Your Emotions

The way you feel can lead you to a good piece of writing. A while back someone grilled me about my combat time in World War II. I became very agitated; I didn't want to talk about the killing. But afterwards I wondered why I was so agitated, why I had hidden my feelings for so long and hidden them so deeply, why I was afraid to face the complicated feelings of war. My feelings have led me to write paragraphs that are leading me to a book. Your fears, your anger, your sadness, your happiness, your discomfort, your comfort, your reactions to people and situations may produce powerful pieces of writing. The more you face your emotions honestly the more you will touch the emotions of readers.

Use Your Mind

Writing is, of course, an intellectual activity. Use writing to think about your world. Observe what you see, and ask why, what if, how come, what's the alternative, what's going to happen, what should be changed, how can it be changed?—all the questions that do just that: question. Doubt, be critical, speculate, connect, create, make up answers and look for their questions. Create theories and examine their consequences. Look for the roots and the branches of what you see in the world around you.

Making an Assignment Your Own

An assignment may produce a good subject, but the problem of many assignments is that they seem to be owned by the editor or teacher who gives them out, and therefore the assignment seems to contain a preconceived solution—like the "cookbook" science experiment in which the student has to get the right answer. The trick of getting a good subject from someone else's assignment is to turn it around so that you can write about the subject on your own turf, using your own knowledge and experience and point of view to develop and document the piece. You have to make the assignment your own idea, take it away from the editor or teacher so you can discover your own meaning in what you're writing.

Subjects Lead to Subjects

The more you become aware of potential subjects the more pieces of writing you will begin to see. Awareness multiplies awareness. Paint all the colors you find studying the bark of a single tree and you will see all the colors in the grass, on the hill, in the stream, on the rocks.

Your increased awareness will make the world a more interesting place. An experienced basketball fan watches how the good players move without the ball. As you record and explore your world through writing you'll begin to hear what isn't said, notice problems that are not solved, find the ordinary people around you interesting, discover meaning where you saw no meaning before. The writer is never bored, for where others see dull monotony the writer sees potential subjects.

Find Your Own Focus

Sometimes a writer finds a focus for a piece to be written before the process of collecting information begins or while the process of collecting is taking place, but most of the time the writer has collected information that is contradictory, confusing—a mess.

The inexperienced writer panics, and either quits or tries to fit the information into a preconceived meaning, which is usually like trying to put mashed potatoes through a keyhole: it doesn't work.

Experienced writers recognize that the feelings of confusion and despair are normal. In fact, the richer their material the more likely writers will imagine they are going down for the third time. It is the normal challenge of the writer to find a way to control and utilize the flood of material.

Circle Back

To find the focus, the key that will unlock the meaning in the mess, the writer circles the raw material. Often the writer circles back through the collecting process, gathering more information, since the sheer abundance of information may point towards its meaning, or uses brainstorming, mapping, interviewing, library research, and other methods of collection to see the meaning that lies within the material. The writer knows from experience that good writing can not be produced unless there is a full inventory of accurate, interesting material.

The effective writer also knows that there is no point in pushing ahead until a potential way of focusing the information comes into view. And so the writer circles, trying first one focusing technique, then another, until one works.

Circle Forward

The chart on page 60 shows some of the ways an experienced writer may bring a subject into focus. You can start at the top and work around clockwise or counterclockwise, start at a point that has worked for you before, or just move around in random order. The important thing is to keep seeing the material anew.

The techniques we use to circle the material may vary according to the way we think. Some of us who are very orderly may always start with a sequence. Those who have been successful at one form of writing—argument, narrative, exposition, whatever—may start with a genre or familiar form of writing and try to see the subject through that form. I have found that my engineering students and my poetry students both tend to start at the same place—with images, visualizing a subject.

There is no right or wrong way to do this. The important thing is to realize that there are many techniques of focusing that you can use, so that you have them on call when the ones with which you are most familiar don't work.

The techniques may vary according to the writing task. Argument will start with a purpose more often than not. A narrative may start with a face, exposition with a reader. But you will discover that almost all of these techniques are appropriate ways to focus on information you have collected.

I will describe each of these techniques and demonstrate them at work as I continue to try to write a piece about my grandmother. But while you are reading my list, see if you can add techniques of your own. Ask your teacher and your classmates to share the tricks they have used to focus a piece of writing.

Use a Reader

As writers circle their material they may be aware of a reader at their side. Sometimes that makes them nervous and they have to tell the reader to go away and come back later, maybe as late as the clarifying stage of the writing process. Many times, however, writers find that the reader is a helpful colleague, and they will even carry on a conversation with this reader as they look at the raw material of the writing together.

"What do you think? Would it help you to undersand what I have to say if I used a narrative approach?"

"You mean story?"

"Yeah."

"I always liked stories, but . . ."

"But what?"

"Well, I don't see how this is a story. Sometimes making something a story makes it sound like you're talking down to me. I don't like that."

"Yeah. I can understand how you feel. Maybe it isn't a narrative. Let's move along a little bit here. Perhaps we could try . . ."

If you find it's helpful to take a reader along, do it. If not, tell the reader to go away and come back later.

Now that you have focused on a territory that is yours you are ready to learn techniques that will help you sharpen your vision, intensify your focus. Remember the photographer with the zoom lens. First the area of the picture was chosen; then the photographer moved the lens to tighten and sharpen the vision. The following techniques will help you bring your subject into focus.

Eighteen Ways to Find Your Own Focus

Work along beside me, using the margins or your own notebook. Work on your material while I work on mine. Often you'll find you're working in a different way than I am. Fine. There's no right or wrong in this. The purpose is to help you see how to make use of your own material in your own way.

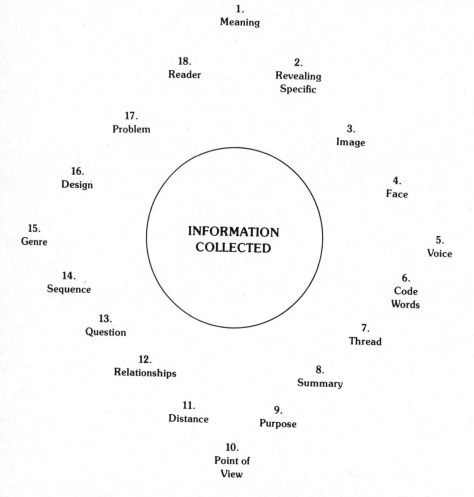

1. Meaning   The writer looks for a single, dominant meaning in the material. Writing is thinking, and the writer's primary function is to find significance in an apparently confusing and contradictory mass of information.

Sometimes this meaning is clear. The information provides news that the reader needs to know—for example, that tuition is going up. There may be a great deal of information about state and federal politics, trustee and administrative decisions, but the reader of the student newspaper is best served by a story built around the fact that tuition is increasing. There may be "news" in a new critical interpretation of a poem, a laboratory experiment, a memo on factory productivity, a letter of resignation.

Another way that a writer often finds information is by a meaning that surprises the writer—the hockey player admits he is afraid of being hurt, the majority of battered wives return to their husbands. The writer's surprise may be a signal that there is a meaning that will interest readers and that needs to be told about this particular batch of information.

The meaning is sometime revealed by applying the "so what" test. I used to have an agent who sat behind a glass desk, and when I talked with enthusiasm about a potential book, he would simply say, "So what?" It made me mad, but it was a pretty good question. In a good piece of writing that quesion has to be answered.

At the moment I'm circling the information I have about my grandmother, making notes in my daybook that may become a meaning and give me a way of making use of the material.

▶ Grandma spent her life trying not to be the farm girl from Islay.

▶ Grandma was surrounded by men with fiddle feet. Her father left Scotland for Canada in his eighties. Husband back and forth across the Atlantic. Lived with son-in-law who kept moving from job to job.

▶ Grandma born before our Civil War, hearing uncles talk of fighting Napoleon, and died when I was overseas fighting Hitler.

▶ Grandma was always a tenant farmer's daughter, defending that thin line between tenant and laborer.

I don't see the meaning that clicks for me, that reveals a piece of writing I'd like to develop. I'll keep moving around the circle.

2. Revealing specific A piece may come into focus when you can zoom in on a revealing or organizing detail. I remember that the Vietnam war first came home for me when I was told that a helicopter crew rammed Vicks up their noses when going out to pick up our dead. In many stories there is a fragment of information—a quotation, a statistic, a bit of description, an action (or a lack of action—the people who didn't call the police when the woman was being raped)—that will bring the entire piece into focus. The writer can use that piece of information as a North Star to guide the trail through the writing.

▶ **Great sewing scissors**
▶ **Black Watch shawl**
▶ **Chinese back-scratcher**
▶ **Singing hymns**
▶ **Bedpan**

Each of those specifics has a particular meaning for me. I don't suppose that my grandmother's huge sewing scissors, almost a foot long, were the same ones she was supposed to have jammed up a bull's nose in Scotland, but I remember how frightened I was whenever I found those scissors. They were a symbol of her vigor and courage and, perhaps, a righteous meanness.

When she wasn't wearing it on her shoulders, she kept her shawl, a thin ragged square of black and dark green wool with fringed edges, at the foot of her bed. I can feel it in my fingers now, and I wish I had it. I think it was the Black Watch tartan, that famous Highland regiment. My mother probably gave it away. When I came home from the war I opened my closet and saw nothing but empty hangers: my mother had gotten rid of all my clothes. But that's another piece of writing. Once you become open to the specifics that give off meaning to you, more and more of them keep exploding with meaning in your head.

On my desk is the Chinese back-scratcher my grandmother used when she was an invalid, to extend the reach of her good right arm. With it she could pull the shawl up around her. I can hear her singing hymns, and I can remember the indignity of this proper Victorian lady needing to call her grandson to bring a bedpan.

One of the most effective ways to focus on a mass of material is to look for the specifics that spark a meaning in your mind. These specifics, for example, point me towards a piece of writing that would reveal the sadness in a strong, powerful woman being imprisoned in her bed for the last twelve years of her life. That's a piece I could write, but I don't know if it's the one I want to write now. I'll keep circling.

3. Image Writers are constantly seeing images, little pictures that have a particular meaning for them, what William Faulkner called "a mental picture." In a famous interview in *The Paris Review* he told about how his novel, *The Sound and the Fury,* began.

> "It began with a mental picture. I didn't realize at the time it was symbolical. The picture was of the muddy seat of a little girl's drawers in a pear tree, where she could see through a window where her grandmother's funeral was taking place and report what was happening to her brothers on the ground below. By the time I explained who they were and what they were doing and how her pants got muddy, I realized it would be impossible to get all of it into a short story and that it would have to be a book. And then I realized the symbolism of the soiled pants, and that image was replaced by the one of the fatherless and motherless girl climbing down the rainpipe to escape from the only home she had, where she had never been offered love or affection or understanding."

We all tend to see in images, those mental snapshots that we remember from our past: the time we saw Father cry when his mother died, our dog at the side of the road not moving, our girlfriend on a date with someone else.

Television commercials use images because they are so powerful, to manipulate us into buying or voting or avoiding or committing. Movies are, of course, full of calculated images, and writing that has an impact on the reader summons images in the reader's mind.

▶ The transparent, shiny skin on the back of my grandmother's curled, useless left hand. It was the kind of shininess you see on the inside of a seashell. Translucent.

▶ Grandma curled on the stairs grunting, trying to crawl.

▶ Later that night. I was eight years old. The doctor had left. Mother, Father, Uncle Will, everyone around the bed terrified for this powerful person, and for themselves. One side of her face was torn loose from the other side, pulled downward as if a giant had yanked at it. Animal sounds came out of her throat, and her left arm twitched. I knew what she was trying to say, and I shouted, "Sunday dinner—she's trying to tell you what to cook for Sunday dinner." Grandma nodded, and grabbed me with her good hand. We got paper and a pad and she scrawled instructions for Sunday dinner. It was Saturday night, and she was still in charge, and I had been the first one to understand her.

As I study that moment in my mind I realize that many of my emotions then did not involve sympathy for Grandmother. I don't think I was glad to see this terribly powerful woman grow weak, but I don't think I was scared either. It was something different. I had found her. That made me important. This was a matter of life and death, and I was involved in it. And later in that bedroom I was the first one who understood her. At least, I remember it that way. Eight years old, I was equal for the moment with all the grownups in the room.

Images are such a strong way of focusing on the subject. I may want to start writing with the images from that night, but I'm not sure yet. It's become my habit and the habit of most writers to keep circling the material. I can always go back to these notes, but I wonder what other ways I can see the subject.

4. Face *Time* magazine made the cover story famous. What *Time* did was to develop a well-known journalistic technique: take a complex subject—the World Bank, nuclear power, a new tax bill—and put a face on it. The cover would portray a person who was responsible for the story, deeply involved in it, or affected by it, and inside the story would be told through that person.

People like to read about people, and by following a person (after all, readers are familiar with people) readers can begin to understand the information they need to know about a complicated subject.

It is always a good idea to look for the people involved in the subject and to consider telling the story in terms of one particular person: the assistant coach who recruited the player who won the game, the former drug addict who is working to help drug addicts, the teenage father who is not married but who is trying to adopt his daughter. When we put a face on a story we are forced to tell it in terms that the reader can understand.

The piece of writing I am doing is a biography, or a form of biography called a profile. It is a short piece about my grandmother, and therefore the story has a face. That helps me focus the story, but it isn't enough. Still, I will spend some time in my daybook seeing my grandmother.

I look at the drawing of my grandmother that my daughter did. Anne was born eleven years after my grandmother died, but the drawing, made from a photograph, is more like my grandmother than the photograph itself. It's spooky to see how she caught that stern, determined jaw, the set of the mouth that could be so disapproving and speak with such a powerful silence, the eyes that so often seemed to be focused on some other world back in Scotland, or in Heaven, the place where Morison lived and that was as specific to my grandmother as Boston.

I felt that writing start to draw me along. I could go with it, and perhaps I should, but I still want to hold back a bit to make sure that I have found the best way of focusing on the subject.

There's nothing wrong with grabbing hold of the first way that you see into the subject. There's no virtue in circling the subject and delaying the writing just to make sure you've seen the subject from every angle, although I find myself doing more and more of that. With experience I'm like the photographer who moves around, taking hundreds of shots with his mind's camera before squeezing the shutter. And I have set myself the task of showing how, in this book, many of these focusing techniques work, and so I must keep moving around the circle.

5. Voice A good word for what we are doing in this chapter and the next, before we get to the first draft, is rehearsing. When we rehearse a play we practice our speeches, speaking them silently and aloud, changing the emphasis, the rhythm, the pace. In writing we do the same thing, but we can also change the words. We rehearse what we are going to say or what we might say the same way you rehearse what you plan to say in asking for a date, an extension on a term paper, a loan to buy a car, a summer job.

Some of this rehearsing is silent, and in some cases we speak out loud. Often this rehearsal takes place on paper, but in every case we must hear language as if it were spoken. Effective writing almost always creates the illusion of an individual writer speaking to an individual reader.

Writing is not speech written down, but lively, effective writing does create the illusion of speech. And one important way of discovering meaning in a subject is to hear the way our voice begins to write about that subject. The lines we write in our notebooks have their own music, their own intensity. They reveal our feelings to us. The sound of our own voices beginning to write about a subject will tell us the meaning we feel in the subject. We will hear our caring in our voice—anger, humor, nostalgia, sadness, happiness, defensiveness, nastiness, objectivity. We can hear in our voice the whole range of our feelings, and our feelings often tell us what we are thinking. In fact, in some subjects our feelings provide us with the way of handling the subject. It may be important, for example, to communicate the subject in terms of anger, happiness, concern, or humor.

Our language also tells us what we think about a subject. Our voice may be scholarly or argumentative, scientifically detached or poetically involved. This is the fun of writing. We may write a poem and hear our voice being scientifically detached and write a laboratory report and hear a poetic voice.

I spend a great deal of time in my daybook and in my head listening to what I say. In this case I am listening very carefully to how I am writing, or beginning to write, about my grandmother.

▶ Grandma died in a letter when I was overseas.
▶ I can hear my grandmother working in the kitchen and singing that hymn, "When the roll is called up yonder I'll be there." She sang it in a

firm voice, a voice used to singing hymns, a voice that learned to sing long before radio, the phonograph, or TV. And I used to join in, singing along with her, but I was never as confident as she was. It was clear that we would both be there when the roll was called and it was clear her name would be on the roll, but it was not at all clear mine would be. I tried to feel good about the fact we would be in, or at least some of us would, but I spent a lot of time thinking about those people who would be out. Some of them would be out simply because they were Catholics or Presbyterians, or Christian Scientists, like my other grandmother, and I worried about the fact there were people who were pretty nice but couldn't get on the roll unless they were Baptists. And then as I grew older it became clear that only a few Baptists could get on the roll. I joined a liberal Baptist church (relatively liberal—they allowed dances on Saturday night in the church hall) and it was clear none of those Baptists, including Pastor Tatum, were on the roll.

▶ I was a twitcher, a jiggler, a twister, a scratcher. I probably had a fiddle foot, but if I ever sat still when I was a little boy it was probably in the gloaming, that time in the afternoon when it was not yet time to turn on the lamps but already too dark to continue with household chores. Grandma would sit in the shadows behind the living room window with the half-drawn green blind and the lace curtain and slowly become a shadow herself. It was always a time of sadness for me, but not a scary sadness, a natural kind of Scottish melancholy that seemed to go with the moors I had never seen, a barren landscape and long northern nights.

▶ I could hear myself laughing, a high-pitched, unpleasant, screaming kind of laughter. It was shrill, and there wasn't any humor in it. It was Sunday dinner and the guest tried to put sugar in the tea, but her spoon had a hinge in it and the sugar fell on the table. She drank from a cut-glass drinking glass that was embellished with fake leaves and fruits, like our other glasses, but her glass had a hole near the top and water dribbled down her front. When she went to cut her meat her plate would rise up and fall: there was a bladder under the plate and a secret hose that connected with a pump between an uncle's knees.

The guest would try to be polite at first, and everyone would try to avoid laughing, until finally the laughter would come, whoops and gales of laughter, and I would shriek along with the rest, trying to find the humor in it, trying to hide myself in their laughter, for I could still feel the shame when the tricks had been played on me, and the cruelty was so sharp that I had to join in with the others.

Years later when I went into fine German middle-class homes looking for evidence of war crimes and found the evidence, I often thought of those Sunday dinners and how hard I laughed at the discomfort of our guests.

In writing each of these I hear a voice. Try it yourself: write and listen to the variations in voice as you report on the subject, or try to write on the same subject in a voice that is angry, sad, questioning, humorous, nostalgic, objective, personal.

The line "died in a letter" came to me in a poem. That's where I first heard that voice. The poem has never quite worked, but there seems to be some kind of pertinent surprise in that line. People do die in letters—or on the telephone—and someday I think a piece of writing will spin off from that line.

If I write about the roll being called up yonder I'll have to communicate the military nature of that hymn, its marching beat, but I hear a voice there of uncertainty, questioning, and doubt that plays against the certainty and lack of doubt I heard in my grandmother's voice. The fragment about the gloaming has a nostalgic tone, a sort of quiet and comfortable sadness about it. I like that word "melancholy," and as soon as I say that I hear another Scottish word, "dour." We Scots seem to enjoy our sadness and inflict it on the others around us. There's another piece coming.

I don't think the Sunday dinner piece works at all—yet. But it could—there's anger in it, and guilt. I'd have to set the dinner up differently, but my voice tells me a lot about the cruelty of that kind of family fun, and reveals my own guilt about joining in it. There is a voice in the piece that I will have to listen to and develop, but the meaning of those Sunday dinners will first come to me in the voice I hear as I tell myself about them.

6. Code Words   There are words that have special meanings for us. When we say "picnic" we may think of a happy time, but the person we speak to may think of being lost at Jones Beach. "Championship game" means one thing to the winners and another to the losers. The name of a person may conjure up a whole time and place. When I say "Butler Mitchell" I see a happy boy who lived around the corner, and I see the long black hearse backing out of the driveway to carry him away. He was the first person I knew of my own age who died.

Code words are private, and if we are going to write so that readers will feel what we feel and understand what we understand we have to develop those code words, by writing an entire piece that makes the reader feel as we feel when we say those few words.

This private language can be very helpful at this stage in the writing process. It can help us talk to ourselves in a quick shorthand. I put "prayer meeting" down in my daybook and I don't have to, at this time, recreate those Wednesday night meetings when old men got up and confessed brief sins with long testimony. I am there, sitting beside my grandmother, who smelled like lavender. I remember worrying that she would hear something she shouldn't. She didn't, and after my first few prayer meetings I was bored. I knew better sins than the ones being confessed.

Since I think I may write about my grandmother, my notebook has a lot of code words related to her and to my childhood. I'm talking to myself in a private shorthand. Some of them are in lists, others stand by themselves, and still others jump out of a paragraph.

- ▶ Wood stove
- ▶ Tim's car
- ▶ Loch Lomond
- ▶ Harry Lauder

▶ Mr. Titus

▶ High road/low road

Each of these code words is a piece of writing—for me. I don't need to expand unless I'm writing for someone else. Looking at these code words, I may find a key to writing about my grandmother.

For example, when Tim, a friend who had recently come over from Scotland, bought a car our flat filled up with resentment. I can remember the strange bitter remarks about anyone who had good fortune. It was resented. There was so much resentment of anyone who saved their money, or made it: it had to be luck, or lack of character. I wonder if I knew that if you were successful, whatever that meant, your reward would be resentment. It makes me unhappy to write that. Why? I guess I knew how hard I would have to work to try to earn love, and that what I would get would be resentment.

Mr. Titus sold fish, and I can remember the wonderful strong odor of fresh fish in his narrow store and the terribly sharp knives ground down so often they were thin as a stiletto, knives that could fillet a fish in one swift cut. He was *our* fish man; we talked as if my grandmother owned him. She had her fish man, her druggist, and S. S. Pierce with their special collapsing boxes, who delivered groceries ordered by phone to the houses on the hill, and still delivered to us in the tenement behind the gas station, while our neighbors smirked, until S. S. Pierce would give us no more credit.

Notice how language starts to carry me away. A few words and I remember what I didn't know I remembered. I have details, names, places, feelings. Any of these code words—Mr. Titus, S. S. Pierce, Tim's car—could get me started. But I still want to keep circling the subject. I could come back to these code words and let the private language of my own history tell me what I might write. The language is there, a fire ready to start whenever I put a match to it.

7. Thread   As you circle the raw material for a piece of writing—notes, articles, memories, feelings, facts, references, interviews, descriptions—that exists in your notes and in your head you may see a thread that runs through a number of parts of the raw material.

I remember one story I did in which a grandmother made great sacrifices for a child, but she was motivated not by love, but by hate of the child's parents. Hate was the fuel that kept her going, and it was the thread that held the story together.

The writer is always looking for a thread in a story, the way a quarterback looks for a receiver who moves through a confusion of bodies into the open.

A thread is a common element in the story, or something that each element of the story can react against. I could write about my grandmother in terms of a proud Scottishness, our militant, almost hateful Christianity, our love and resentment of money or food. I have tried to write a poem about how we could never say "I love you" in our house, but we could bring each other food: bakery pies, Fanny Farmer chocolates, Howard Johnson ice cream. When we needed to talk we ate. There were myths about food; fish was good for you and pork was lower class. I was a man when I could eat as much—the drumstick and more—of the Thanksgiving turkey as Uncle Donald. All my bad food habits were learned, carefully, at home. We ate to celebrate, we ate to battle boredom, we ate to communicate, and we ate to console ourselves. I could tie together a story about my family's religion, lack of money, Scottish heritage, or any number of other subjects by using the thread of food, showing us buying, preparing, and eating.

8. Summary   Often it helps to write out a short statement of what will be written as if it were already written. This can be called an executive summary, an abstract, a scenario, a thesis statement. Whatever it is called, at this stage it should not be considered a contract or a firm plan. It is a good way to gain distance on a subject and see how you might focus on it.

In my daybook, you might find such statements as:

▶ This article shows how a young boy's vision of his grandmother changes as he grows up, leaves home, and becomes a parent himself.

▶ In this article the writer explores the ties that bound family members, himself included, to his grandmother, and shows how those ties can be cut.

▶ This personal essay uses the author's relationship with a powerful grandmother to show how we can struggle to get free of our family connections only to realize we are never free.

▶ This is an unusual case history that shows how a stroke victim was cared for in the 1930s.

▶ This investigation of the role of the Baptist Church in Scotland in the late nineteenth and early twentieth centuries reveals its theological lessons by the examination of one family, and in particular the role of a matriarch in a Scottish immigrant family.

9. Purpose   Sometimes a piece of writing has a clear purpose: we write to get a job interview, to appeal a parking ticket, to earn an A, to tell someone else the directions to a party. When the purpose is that clear it may make the writing easier. I find it helps to write the purpose down and then to make sure that everything I do in the writing advances that purpose. Purpose is a powerful driving force in writing.

I will go to my notebook to see if I can find the purpose for writing about my grandmother. My technique is to put down any purpose that might come into my head, whether it makes me uncomfortable or not. I have to be honest with myself, because when I write I don't want to have a high-level, conscious purpose being attacked by a low-level and probably more powerful secret purpose. For example, many times we say we are making art when we're really writing to make money. I free-lanced for seven years, and there's nothing wrong with writing for money. It may, in fact, be a cleaner purpose than trying to make art, or trying to become famous and impress people. But the writer must know what's going on.

What's purpose of grandmother piece?

▶ To get back at my grandmother?
▶ To record some family history for my children?
▶ To find out how I feel about my grandmother?

▶ To write examples for my Freshman English text?
▶ To scratch an itch—if I write about my grandmother maybe I'll stop thinking about her so much.
▶ To preserve a portrait of a powerful woman?
▶ To try to understand a family saint who really wasn't?
▶ To explore another time, another place?
▶ To find out why I'm like I am?
▶ To use some good rich raw material for writing?
▶ To celebrate the life of a powerful woman?

That list interests me, but it doesn't tell me of a single clear purpose that makes me want to write. It does give me insight into the fact that I probably have many reasons, some of them contradictory, for writing about this strong person in my life. I may need to understand some of those purposes, or the very practical purpose may be enough. I have assigned myself to write about my grandmother for this text, in the same way that you have self-given or teacher-given assignments to write. "I have a paper due Monday" may be purpose enough to produce a good piece of writing, but usually we need more than that, and my purpose may become clear through the process of writing if it isn't clear now.

10. Point of View   Think of a photographer at a wedding, continually circling the subject, catching the bride with her father, the couple before the clergyman, the shot down the aisle, the cutting of the cake, the bride's mother, the car with the Just Married sign pulling away. Almost every story can be told from a dozen points of view.

The battle can be described in terms of one side or the other, by the general or the private, the wounded or the dead, the farmer on whose land it is fought or the pilot who flies five miles above that plot of earth.

One of the most helpful tricks for finding a focus for a story is to move around and take quick notes of the place from which the story can be observed.

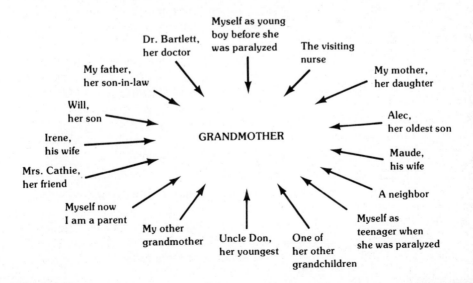

Dr. Bartlett, her doctor

Myself as young boy before she was paralyzed

The visiting nurse

My father, her son-in-law

My mother, her daughter

Will, her son

Alec, her oldest son

Irene, his wife

GRANDMOTHER

Maude, his wife

Mrs. Cathie, her friend

A neighbor

Myself now I am a parent

My other grandmother

Uncle Don, her youngest

One of her other grandchildren

Myself as teenager when she was paralyzed

Let's reverse it. Look at it from her point of view:

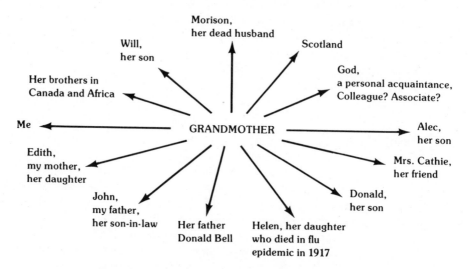

It doesn't take much time to circle a subject in this way. You can do it physically by going out to a scene or a place that you might write about, or you can do it in your mind, as I did. But it helps to see all of the different spots from which you might help the reader see the subject. I'm not sure of the point of view I'll choose yet, but I know that it's important for me to think of the places from which I may view the subject. Each quick glance educates me about the subject.

I remember, for example, that those grandchildren who only saw Grandmother on ceremonial occasions viewed her differently than I, who had to bring her a bedpan. I remember that her son-in-law, my father, saw her differently than her children, who were of her blood. Writing down these points of view made me remember Mrs. Cathie, one of her friends, and then I remembered that Grandmother did have friends. I'd been concentrating too much on family, and looking at Grandma from outside the family made me see her, for a moment, in a different perspective.

If I find a point of view—if I decide to write about my grandmother from my point of view when I was a small boy and she was a tall, vigorous, powerful woman—then I have simplified the writing task, for everything about her illness and what I know now has to be left out. Point of view is one of the best techniques for clarifying a complicated subject. You see the subject through a single camera lens, seeing everything in that lens with clarity, but leaving out all that doesn't belong there, that can't be seen from that point of view.

11. Distance   When we are trying to focus on a subject we have to adjust the distance. Sometimes we want to stand way back, and other times we want to zoom in close. Most of us get into the habit of always writing at the same distance, the same way that poor photographers always line the family up and take their picture in front of the Grand Canyon, the Capitol, Niagara Falls, the bison herd at the zoo. We should choose a distance that makes the

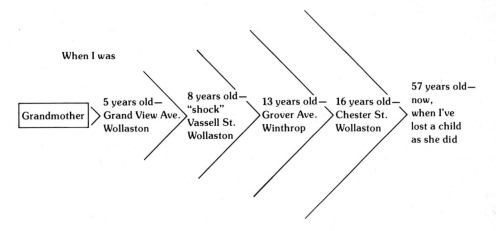

meaning of what we want to say come clear to the reader. And adjusting the distance, of course, is a way of making the meaning come clear to the writer.

I go back to my daybook:

▶ My grandmother's bed. A piece that describes the hills and valleys, the whole landscape in which she lived for a dozen years.

▶ I could stand back a bit from the bed and follow a whole day, circling around her as Mother and I waited on her, as a neighbor came in to sit with her when Mother went out, as the doctor visited.

▶ I could stand back a bit and look at the tenement we lived in against the memory of the great house in North Grafton she once lived in. I could show all of us living in this flat that we all had come to feel was a mark of our failure.

At each point I could write at a different distance from my grandmother. At five years old I see her as an enormous woman, God herself. At eight years old I see her when she is first paralyzed. The strong has become dependent. At thirteen I spend most time on the streets plotting my escape. I begin to see, for the first time, Grandmother as a tyrant, running the family from her bed. At sixteen I still admire her strength, but I have begun to escape it, to have my own life, a secret life away from her and the family. At fifty-seven I find I have not escaped. Grandma is in how I think and how I act, and we share many things now, including, tragically, the death of a child.

Wherever I would place the camera the lens would include different information. Each position has its own advantage and disadvantage. I should choose the one that serves the reader best. At the moment I'm drawn to the last one. I feel a need to explore the fact that we don't escape the family we flee. But I won't stop here. That may be a good point from which to start, but I want to continue moving around the material to see what other things I learn, what other ways I may bring the raw material into focus.

12. Relationships   One of the most helpful ways to examine the raw material for what may become writing is to look at the relationships between the pieces of information. Which pieces of information

- ▶ Connect?
- ▶ Attract?
- ▶ Repel?
- ▶ Contradict?
- ▶ Balance out?
- ▶ Qualify?

The connections between pieces of information often produce both the skeleton or design of the piece of writing and the energy for it. Usually I see these connectons in a fragmentary way in my daybook. I'm dealing with raw information or the symbols for that information, and the writing I do doesn't yet look like writing. That's on purpose. I want to strip down to the bare bones of meaning to see the connections and relationships that lie behind the writing I may do. Too many formal sentences and paragraphs at this stage may hide the meaning.

And notice that by relationships I don't mean just those things that neatly fit together. The attraction of two people in a marriage may make a good story, but the attraction plus the forces that push them apart may make a better story. Our best material is complicated; the pieces of information are drawn together and pulled apart, both at the same time. There are surprises, contradictions, and ironies—the difference between what is and what should be.

Here are some ways I play with the relationships in the raw material I have about my grandmother.

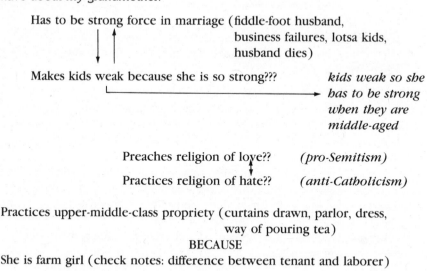

Has to be strong force in marriage (fiddle-foot husband, business failures, lotsa kids, husband dies)

Makes kids weak because she is so strong???   *kids weak so she has to be strong when they are middle-aged*

Preaches religion of love??   *(pro-Semitism)*

Practices religion of hate??   *(anti-Catholicism)*

Practices upper-middle-class propriety (curtains drawn, parlor, dress, way of pouring tea)

BECAUSE

She is farm girl (check notes: difference between tenant and laborer)

My father tries to measure up to dead mill owner father-in-law   But mill owner isn't. Makes candy in kitchen, dies as bookkeeper in Philly. Did my father ever learn this in 49 years of marriage?

Grandma doesn't like (respect) my father.
1. He's Lowlander—true
2. He comes from laborer class—true
   (but tenants not far off)
3. My father and I think because he
   is unlike her husband

Really because he is so like him
   Both have fiddle feet:
   keep changing jobs, failing,
   planning great new successes

> Did my mother marry
> my father because he was
> like her father, and was the
> marriage bad because he was
> like her father?

Note the number of question marks. That doesn't disturb me, that excites me. One thing I'm looking for when I write is a good question that may be answered by the writing.

13. Question   "I start my work by asking a question and then trying to answer it," says Mary Lee Settle. Her technique is an excellent way to find a focus. Often a confusion of raw material is brought to heel when you discover a question that must be answered, a question that keeps tickling your intellect, a question that will intrigue a reader.

I write some questions about my grandmother that I might explore through writing:

▶ Where did she get the strength to keep the family together married to a husband with a fiddle foot and a track record of failure?
▶ How much did her Scottish tradition help to keep her going? What were the most important of those traditions?
▶ Did she ever doubt her religion?
▶ What really was her religion?
▶ Is there any way to avoid the familiar pattern of a strong leader in one generation—usually a father or a mother—making the next generation weak?
▶ Did she know what she was doing to her children?
▶ Did she make herself, consciously, into a legend? Why? How?
▶ Is there a book on immigrant matriarchs and the effect on their families? A biography? A series of biographical portraits? A novel?
▶ Did her children love or fear her?

As you keep going over the raw material you may see a question that has to be answered, or answers to a question that hasn't yet been asked—then you can ask it. I had never thought, for example, that my mother might have married my father because she saw her father in him. Her father was always presented to me as a strong man, and she always spoke of my father as a weak man, but now I have an interesting question that might result in a short story, an essay, a fragment of autobiography, a movie, a novel—depending how far and in which form I want to pursue it.

Sometimes the reader will be directly confronted with the question, as a title, a lead, or a point of focus early on in the text. But most of the time the question is only implied. The question is what impels the writer towards the material, or what the writer uses to choose what is significant and insignificant in the raw material of the writing.

14. Sequence   As you examine the raw material you have collected you may see an order in it. There are many forms of order or sequence that can cause pieces of information to snap together and lock in place. Some of the most common sequences of information are:

▶ Logic: a series of pieces of information lead to a conclusion or lead from a conclusion, supporting it, or lead from a hypothesis to a proof
▶ Cause and effect
▶ Time
▶ Travel: movement through time and place

It's productive to play around with these sequences, to put down some pieces of information and see where they may lead.

Mother admires her father, ignores his faults.

Mother marries my father, can't ignore his faults.

Mother becomes bitter, those who don't fail in business must be corrupt. Refuses to face his (her) faults.

Father marries my mother because she has higher social status that will help him in business.

Father discovers my mother has higher social tastes that take more money than he has and help him fail in business.

Father blames mother for his failures but they were his own.

I work hard to be the success my father feels he wasn't.

He works hard to be the success his father was becoming when he died young.

His father worked hard to escape being a farm laborer and then to escape being a mill worker in this country.

His father worked hard to eat.

(How "polished" was my father before he married my mother? Did he learn his "airs" from his wife's family, or as department store floorwalker, or from deacons in church?)

*(When can a family afford ambition?)

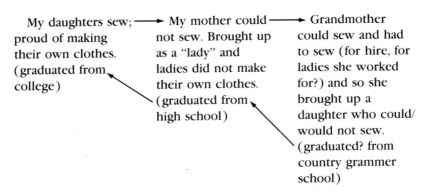

My daughters sew; ——► My mother could ——► Grandmother
proud of making   not sew. Brought up   could sew and had
their own clothes.   as a "lady" and   to sew (for hire, for
(graduated from   ladies did not make   ladies she worked
college)   their own clothes.   for?) and so she
                         (graduated from   brought up a
                         high school)   daughter who could/
                                                  would not sew.
                                                  (graduated? from
                                                  country grammer
                                                  school)

I don't think that any of these sequences will work for me today. In other words, I don't think that any of them were breakthroughs. But they each provided an insight into the subject, a new way of looking at it. I was able to work back and forth through the material, and I may find traces of this work popping up later.

15. Genre   Genre is a term we use for the forms of writing, such as poetry, drama, fiction, and nonfiction. Then we break writing down within those categories. Nonfiction, for example, may be biography, in which we write about others, and autobiography, in which we write about ourselves; a news story, in which we tell readers what happened today, and history, which reports what happened a long time ago; argument, in which we attempt to persuade, and humor, in which we try to entertain. There are many more categories, of course, and these forms of writing do overlap. We can write a historical biography to persuade, for example. Still, it is helpful to know something about the customs and traditions of the form in which we are writing. These aren't laws that must be followed, they are a record of what has worked for other writers. In Chapter 4, I will show in some detail how the writing process fits the principal forms of writing that you are likely to use.

At this stage of the writing process, when we are still circling the raw material, it's helpful to use genre as a lens. Poets keep seeing poems, novelists stories, reporters news. We can train ourselves to look at the material to see it in terms of different genres.

As the photographer changes from a wide-angle lens to a telephoto lens the scene changes before the photographer's eye. Each lens has its own limits and its own perspective. Any piece of raw material can be looked at to see if the reader will be best served by a poem or an essay, or an argument, or an explanation. Any form of writing can be used as a lens, and the lens may help us see what needs to be told about the subject.

As I turn to my daybook I will make quick notes to myself about how I may see my grandmother if I use different genres.

> *Biography:* Profile of Grandmother .... *New Yorker* type? What's hook? ... Does it need any? Just an interesting person in a time and a place. "Upstairs, Downstairs" ... *Reader's Digest* "Most Unforgettable"? Don't think so.

Autobiography: Don't have any letters or journals, diaries of hers. Would have to be made up.

Novel: Grandma is in her bed, paralyzed. Her life recreated in her head. How to show her reality versus the realities of others.

Short story: From point of view of grandson who sees her every morning to make sure she's alive. What's conflict?

Argument: In favor of being brought up by a grandmother ... sense of history, racial identity. Argument for or against religion that gave her strong faith, but also gave her stern limitations, maybe hate.

Magazine article: Check with sociologist to see what we know about effect of strong grandparents, especially grandmothers, on children and grandchildren. Is there an alternating pattern of strong and weak?

Short story: Recreate moment when Grandfather has fiddle foot and Grandmother has to hold things together, baking bread while he dreams of building mills.

Poem(s):

▶ Grandmother singing hymns
▶ Grandmother being carried to Thanksgiving couch in living room in canvas sling
▶ Grandmother's paralyzed left arm
▶ Grandmother slipping back and forth over eighty years in time in her bed
▶ Grandmother talking to Jesus from her bed; he is close associate, perhaps administrative assistant to her.

Feature article: Use experiences with Grandmother as a hook for an article revealing the price on a family of caring for someone at home when a family member is chronically ill.

None of these notes are particularly exciting to me this morning. No matter, each of them made me take a quick glimpse at my subject—my grandmother—and helped me to see familiar material in a slightly new way.

16. Design   Many writers see what they may write in shapes or forms that reveal the pattern of the meaning. The novelist John Updike says, "I really begin with some kind of solid, coherent image, some notion of the shape of the book and even of its texture. *The Poorhouse Fair* was meant to have a sort of Y shape. *Rabbit, Run* was a kind of zig-zag. *The Centaur* was sort of a sandwich."

My daybooks are filled with such diagrams. I couldn't imagine how to organize a text I wrote, *A Writer Teaches Writing,* until I saw it as a pebble thrown into a clear pond. The first chapter on the writing process was the pebble, the next chapter on teaching was the first ripple or concentric circle around it, and so on. A novel of mine was a crisscrossing series of records from a fever chart. The characters move up and down in their fortunes and feelings. Where they cross each other are important scenes in the book. Sometimes I

Father   Grandma   Mother   Me

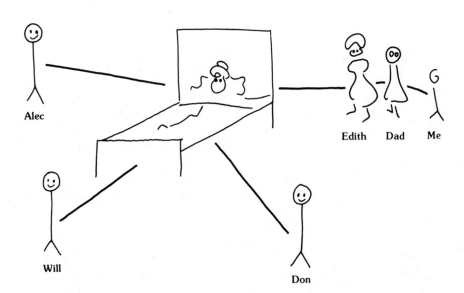

Alec

Edith   Dad   Me

Will   Don

see an article as a series of stair steps, or a cone funneling down to the main point. I don't always see what I write in terms of visual diagrams, but I do more often than not. And most of the time they are helpful. Here are some diagrams from my daybook that help me visualize what I might write about my grandmother.

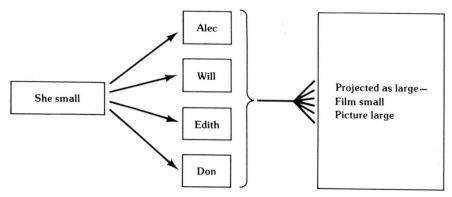

Protestant Saint
Mother (and the others) couldn't measure up to her
Focus on mother (no room for uncles)
     No matter if she was
         really extraordinary ⎫
         or a family legend ⎬ mother was measured daily by that

In each of the diagrams I was surprised to see how important my grandmother's size was. She was a big woman, but it was her psychological size that came clear on the page. I found myself using terms like "measure up to her." That may be how I will write about her, as a Protestant saint. There's a nice irony there, because she hated the idea of saints—they were Catholic—but she was made into one herself by her family.

17. Problem   Some studies of the creative process have shown that creative people see problems where others don't. Writing might be defined as a solution to a problem, and so one of the things I look for as I circle the raw material that may become a piece of writing is a problem that I can solve through writing.

It's a very different thing to know there are problems in writing and to define a specific problem. The definition of a specific problem often makes a solution, or a range of possible solutions, clear. For example, if I see that it might be a problem to write about my grandmother in the first person—to use "I"—then I have a simple choice. I use the third person—"he" or "she." The second person—"you"—simply never works well enough to carry a piece, for the reader will identify with the third person, becoming the "he" or "she" on the page, or the first person, becoming the "I," but will not identify with the "you," which somehow keeps the reader at arm's length from the writer.

Often I look for the problems in a piece of writing, not just as problems, but as opportunities. I can often turn that problem to my advantage.

The problems that I foresee in writing often break down into three categories:

1. *Problems of content*
   ▶ Where can I get enough information?
   ▶ How can I tell if the information is true?
   ▶ How can I get information on *every* side of the subject?
   ▶ How can I make the complicated information clear?
2. *Problems of order*
   ▶ How do I limit the subject?
   ▶ How much background information does the reader need? Where do I fit in?
   ▶ How can I keep the parts of the story in proportion?
   ▶ How long—or short—should the piece be?
   ▶ What is the sequence in which the reader needs the information?
3. *Problems of language*
   ▶ What voice is appropriate to this subject?
   ▶ How can I give the illusion that an individual writer is speaking to an individual reader?
   ▶ Are there other voices which need to be heard in the piece?

In my daybook I'll talk to myself, attempting to foresee some of the problems that may give me a way of writing about my grandmother.

Grandmother as Saint   How to be fair?
Grandmother as Tyrant

                                        Read Orwell's
                                        essay on saints?

How show her weakness, her strength?   Imaginary monologue—
                                        Grandma talking to
                                        herself in bed.
                                  To Jesus (no, she'd deal
                                        directly with God)

Can I make reader see Grandma as I saw her when I was young and as I see her now?

          Familiar Essay (nostalgia?)
            Grandma   then or now
                       then—when I was a child
                          —later, when I was young, rebelling
                       now—when I'm trying to add it up

> How do I write about Grandma—what I think she did to her children—without hurting feelings of family

Fiction—Short story	Don't want problem I had in
—Novel	MWHE—main char paralyzed,
—Play	in bed

| She was almost 90. How compress? | Focus on remembering scene on stairs when I found her?? If I remember that I can weave in what happens in future if I look from now. |
| | Do first person? (might solve problem of family truth— this is only my truth) |

Again, this is a kind of playing around. The more I mess around with a subject this way the more I see ways of dealing with it. Here, for example, I see a real problem: how to be fair. Grandmother was a saint, and Grandmother was a tyrant. That's not only a problem, however, it's an opportunity, for there is dramatic tension between these two forces, and dramatic tension is a marvelous force to use in writing.

I have a real problem being fair in another way. My grandmother is not the same person to her other grandchildren. They did not live with her. This may make it necessary for me to write in the first person so I don't seem to be saying *the* truth—or their truth—about her, but simply *my* truth.

When you are working in your daybook or journal, in your head or on scraps of paper that are predrafts, you'll find yourself writing in shorthand. For example, I say "don't want problem I had in MWHE." That stands for a novel— *The Man Who Had Everything*—I wrote and published. The hero was paralyzed, a quadraplegic who could not use his arms or legs. I can write in code to myself and don't have to spell it out at this stage of the game. So can you.

18. Reader   The writer, of course, is the writer's first reader. But the experienced writer has an eye on the person who will be reading the finished product. Looking at the raw material, the writer may choose to be greatly concerned with the reader or may choose not to.

This concern with the reader changes with the form. If you are writing an argument and trying to change a reader's mind, then you are very concerned with the reader at the earliest stages of the writing process. If you are writing a short story, you may want to get the story right first and only think consciously of the reader when you are in the final stages of the process, trying to make the story clear.

No matter what form you are writing in, however, it may be helpful to look at the raw material to see if there is information that will serve the reader.

In writing we try to deliver information to the reader that the reader needs or wants. If we look through the raw material and find such information we may have a way of writing the piece.

What does reader need to know about my grandmother that can help the reader?

▶ Grandma immigrant. Behavior appropriate to young immigrant widow may not be appropriate later on.
▶ Racial/religious values may not fit new time, new place.
▶ When you're older you may understand why grandparents or parent acted the way he or she did.
(But I don't yet understand my parents. Would I if I wrote about them? Understanding doesn't mean approval. Understanding may not help.)
▶ Understanding may not help—may make an essay.
▶ Reader might like to know something about another time, another place.
▶ An essay might work that would show me beginning to understand my grandmother, and might show reader how to come to terms with saint/tyrant.

Looking back at that daybook page I realize there's something underlying it. Young writers feel that they have nothing interesting to say, that no one would be interested in them or their lives. But experienced writers know that each of us has the raw material of significant writing in us. One editor said, "A good reporter is forever astonished at the obvious." I know that if I am specific and honest about my grandmother, other people will be interested. The more specific I am the more universal I will become. And people reading about the particulars of my grandmother will remember the particulars of their own lives and see significance in them. A good, honest, specific piece of writing will have what we call resonance; its meaning will echo and re-echo in the reader's mind.

These are eighteen ways to circle raw material and discover a focus that we may want to develop through writing. There may be other ways that work for you, and some of these ways may not work for you. They certainly don't work for me all of the time. The important thing is to have a lot of different ways of looking at material that may become an effective piece of writing. The writer, after all, is an explorer, and each writing act is a voyage of discovery. We don't write what we know as much as we write to know. That's what keeps the excitement of writing fresh. There's always something new to find out. We know, through writing, what we did not know we knew. We write to learn.

Questions about Focusing

What if what I want to say has been said before?

It probably has, but don't worry about it. It hasn't been said by you. Your own particular background and way of thinking and speaking may make it different.

But difference isn't the important thing. The important thing is to have a well-explored subject, a piece of writing that is so well made it will stand up and speak to a reader.

And remember that at this stage you can't be sure just what you're going to say. You may have a focus—you know the island you want to explore—but you haven't done the exploration yet. A good piece of writing will almost always be different when it is finished than what the writer thought it would be when the writing process began.

What's most important?

What the reader needs to know or what you would need to know if you were the reader.

What if what I think is most important isn't what the teacher thinks is most important?

You have to be able to support your idea of what's important with convincing evidence. That evidence will be lined up and presented to the reader during the next stages of the writing process. But, of course, this depends on the teacher. Some teachers believe there is only one right answer, and you may have to find that answer to pass the course, but most college teachers are willing to be persuaded if you have a specific focus supported by concrete evidence.

Everything seems equally important.

Ah, that's the challenge. You have to find the key, or just decide arbitrarily for this piece of writing that one element is most important. You can write about two or three things that are equally important, but then you have to find a way of making the combination of them most important: for example, "Most law school professors agree that there are three qualities an effective courtroom lawyer needs," or, "There are four equal forces that came together and led us into the Vietnam war."

My focus seems too personal.

Most good writing does start from a personal point of view. The writer thinks and cares. The writing, however, shouldn't sound too personal. You need to get out of the way and let the evidence speak for itself.

The reader is persuaded by information, not by being told what to think (remember how long it was since you really enjoyed a sermon?). As you move from focusing to clarifying you will be providing the information for the reader. The starting point may be personal, but in many cases the final draft will be written in such a way that the reader will be convinced by the objectivity and the fairness of the prose.

I think I'm too close to the subject.

Then stand back. Role-play someone who doesn't know the subject. The most obvious things about the subject may be the most important.

I'm too far away from the subject, I guess. I don't care about it.

Then find a new subject that you do care about, or at least want to explore.

But it's an assignment—I don't have any choice.

You have to find a way to make the assignment your own. Get in and do the research, root around in the information, see what connections you can make with your own experience. Professional writers learn how to take assignments and adjust them so that they write on their own territory. For example, a football player faced with an abstract assignment on ethics may be able to write a strong essay about the issues he faced when a coach taught him, as one of my coaches taught me, how to make illegal blocks and get away with it.

What if my focus isn't the right one?

There isn't usually a right one, and that's something that's hard for most beginning college students to accept. William Perry of Harvard has done studies that show college freshmen want to find an absolute right or wrong. That's natural, but college is not a place where you get precise answers; it's where you discover how to ask good questions. We live in a complicated and complex world, and although for some of us there are absolute wrongs (if I were president I would make it a capital offense for anyone to eat a smelly, gooey, soft-boiled, poached, or sunnyside-up egg in a public place—but I would face pressure from egg lovers, the police and courts who would have to enforce the law, and the egg lobby), most issues are complex.

In writing there ain't nothing that is absolutely right or wrong. I just used incorrect English, on purpose, to make a point and get attention, and therefore it became correct. In writing what works is right. You can write correctly and produce unreadable prose. You can write incorrectly and communicate. This is one of the things that makes writing hard—and fun.

Focusing Activities

1. Circle your subject, performing each of the activities listed in the chapter, or picking out those that spark your interest.
2. Go back to Chapter 2 and look over the collecting techniques to see if there are one or two you want to try to help you find a focus.
3. Collaborate with another student to see if he or she can help you find the focus. You can, for example, try out a potential focus or describe your subject to see what interests that test reader.
4. Think back to the techniques you've used in other areas of your life—on a job, playing a sport, resolving problems with people, studying a subject—to find out what methods you used to focus on what was important. Try that method to develop a focus on your subject.
5. If you've kept a process log or daybook, go back through it to see those words, facts, or ideas that keep recurring. They may tell you where the

focus of the subject is. I find that certain ideas will keep coming up, sort of like a whale that surfaces from time to time. When I spot that recurring information or thought it may become the focus for the piece I'm going to write.

6. Make lists in answer to the following questions about the area you are exploring through writing:
   ▶ What surprised you?
   ▶ What made you mad?
   ▶ What made you laugh?
   ▶ What made you curious?
   ▶ What information could you make use of?
   ▶ What information could the reader make use of?
   ▶ What would you like to know more about?
   ▶ What forces are in the material?
   ▶ Where do those forces intersect?
   ▶ Where do they work together?
   ▶ Where do they work against each other?
   Make up your own questions, and ask them of yourself.

7. Put your notes away and write in one sentence the most important thing about the subject you're exploring. Be specific. Nail it down.

8. Make believe you're the reader. Tell you, the writer, what you'd like to know about the subject.

9. Tell someone about your subject. Listen to what you say to see if you reveal the focus.

10. Imagine the piece you are going to write after it has been published in a journal or magazine or book or newspaper. Describe it to yourself. What would the title be like? The ending? The length? The approach?

11. Take a football game or a scientific experiment or a legislative decision and talk with the people involved to discover the most important moment in the series of actions, discoveries, and decisions that occurred. Practice looking for such key moments as you watch a game, a movie, or a governmental hearing, or work on an experiment.

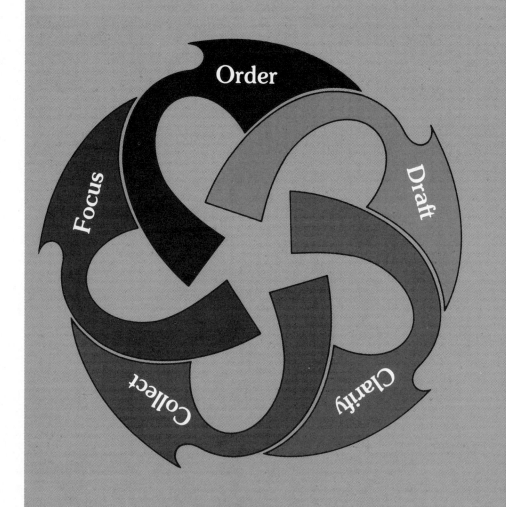

Order

Has a drinking song ever been written by a drunken man? It is wrong to think that feeling is everything. In the arts, it is nothing without form.

Gustave Flaubert

Prose is architecture, not interior decoration.

Ernest Hemingway

Because I'm interested in structure, I must sound mechanistic. But it's just the opposite. I want to get the structural problems out of the way first, so I can get to what matters more. After they're solved, the only thing left for me to do is tell the story as well as possible.

John McPhee

Wait. Don't write yet.

Well, sometimes it may be time to write. You have collected a pile of information, found a focus, and feel you're ready to plunge ahead. Try it if you want. It may work. You may write so fast you will feel you're on automatic pilot, with everything falling into place without conscious effort. The writing seems to be writing itself.

It's wonderful when that happens. But sometimes we find we have flown into the side of a mountain, smiling with confidence right up to the moment of impact. Other times the plane suddenly starts to wobble and then heads into a nosedive.

Most of the time we write too soon, and run into problems that could have been solved in advance, or lose our way and have to waste time starting over again and again and again, hoping that by shooting in the dark we'll hit the target. Virginia Woolf told herself in her diary, "As for my next book, I am going to hold myself from writing it until I have it impending in me: grown heavy in my mind like a ripe pear; pendant, gravid, asking to be cut or it will fall."

As you move through the writing process you move closer to the reader, and it may be appropriate to become more aware of the reader's needs. You'll feel most comfortable doing this if collecting and focusing have made you feel confident of your material and its significance. You may feel less comfortable confronting the reader if you're still deeply in the process of discovery. There is no right or wrong to this: sometimes you'll want to be aware of the reader, and that awareness will help you order the piece; other times you'll have to ignore any reader but yourself and use the ordering techniques to help you understand the pattern of meaning within your subject.

Many a battle is lost because the general follows the plan regardless of what happens on the battlefield. A writing plan is not an order or a binding contract. It is a sketch, a guess, a hunch, a suggestion—"Hey, let's head for the beach." When you write you may not get to the beach; you may stop along the way, decide to go to a lake, meet some interesting people and spend time with them. The picnic may be eaten in a restaurant or the restaurant food taken out on the rocks. But it helps to have a plan, to have a sense of destination, and that is what planning writing gives you. And most of the time you do go to the beach.

Titles

Most writers don't write titles. They let editors do that, and then complain that the title doesn't fit the article. I never wrote titles until, as a junior editorial writer, I got to work by myself on Sunday. I was my own editor, and I was able to write my own titles. Then I started writing the titles first, and found it greatly improved my writing.

In writing the title I captured the direction of the story, a glimpse of its limitations and pace. Most of all, I discovered its tone. Now when I write an article I take the time to brainstorm many titles. I average about a hundred and fifty titles before I settle on one. The one may be the second or third or thirteenth title, but I don't know it's the right one until I see the others that don't work.

It doesn't take much time to write a title. In fact, it's something that can be best done in small chunks of time, while waiting for a class to begin or for a friend to come out of the store, or sitting in a car when the drawbridge is up, or waiting for a string of commercials to get off the tube. As in all brainstorming, you have to be willing to come up with silly titles, even stupid ones, to get to those that may work.

When I begin to brainstorm titles some are just labels—"Grandmother" or "My grandmother." Others are too long or vague or weak. A good title has a strong sense of voice; it's specific; it catches the reader and draws the reader into the article. But to find those good titles I have to write a lot of bad ones. I don't like doing it, but it seems to be part of the process for me, and I know that the time spent fishing for titles will make it possible for me to write a draft that works in a much shorter period of time than if I didn't mess around with titles first.

Grandmother	Grandma died in a letter
My grandmother	Every morning I went in to see if
A saint to her children	Grandma died
A Protestant saint	Was Grandma alive?
She wasn't a saint	The strongest woman in the world
A saint with a topknot	Lady in a tenement
Grandmother was God	Behind the lace curtains
God with a Scottish accent	I was going to fight Napoleon
She's still keeping score	She never had a doubt
Grandma scrubbed off my tan	For her there was no in-between
She was strong; her children	A cup of tea, a prayer, and no re-
weak	grets
Married to a fiddle foot	Her strength was her weakness
Hymns and Fels Naptha soap	Good Christian hate
She ran the house from her bed	Cambric tea, sugar on toast, and
"She was a lady"	fear
She gossiped with Jesus	Fear, guilt, and hate
"In the gloaming"	My grandmother's faith: hate
	Catholics and fear the Lord

When I finish brainstorming titles—I've reproduced about ten minutes' worth—I usually feel, as I do now, a sense of disappointment, even failure. Sometimes a really exciting title leaps off the page, but usually I have a rather ordinary list, as I do this morning, and I have to look back to see if anything is happening.

I notice how much God comes into this, and maybe that's what I'll be writing about. These titles are less sympathetic than I would have expected, and I have to pay attention to that.

I'll keep coming back to these titles and putting new ones into my day-book. The title I'll end with may look spontaneous, but it probably will be worried into place. As Phyllis McGinley said, "There *is* such a thing as inspiration (lower case) but it is no miracle. It is the reward handed to a writer for hard work and good conduct. It is the felicitous word sliding, after hours of evasion, obediently into place. It is a sudden comprehension of how to manufacture an effect, finish off a line or a stanza. At the triumphant moment this gift may seem like magic but actually it is the result of effort, practice, and the slight temperature a sulky brain is apt to run when it is pushed beyond its usual exertions."

When the title does, magically (and usually after hard work), seem just right, notice how much it helps you control and direct the piece of writing. The title—or the lead—becomes the focus for the piece of writing. It reveals its tone, limits, direction. Titles and leads can be the greatest help you will have in finding your way towards an effective piece of writing.

If, for example, the title is "Was Grandma alive?" I have to start with the scene of my tiptoeing into her room early in the morning and watching to see if the sheets rise and fall. If I start with "Married to a fiddle foot" I have to focus on the part of her life I know least about, and I can only handle it by writing about the mystery we all have in our backgrounds that can never be resolved.

I don't think any of these titles work, and that really doesn't worry me. I'll keep doodling titles until I find one that does. Usually I like to have the title first, but I'm not compulsive about it. If the title doesn't come I'll move ahead and try to write some leads.

Leads

Time a friend going through a newspaper or magazine to discover how long it takes a reader to decide to read an article. You will probably find you have three to five seconds to catch the reader.

In those few seconds the lead—the first line, the first sentence, the first paragraph, perhaps the first three paragraphs—has to capture and hold the reader.

The lead has to give the reader information that is specific and interesting; it has to be honest, for the story must be able to deliver on the promise of the lead. And it has to establish a voice, in just a few words.

As in the case of the title, a good lead is a marvelous help to the writer as well as the reader. It tells the writer what must be in the story and what must be left out. The lead provides the direction of the story. The lead establishes the pace and the tone.

Most writers have to have the lead right before they go on. There are writers who don't follow this rule. And every writer has times when he or she is stuck on the lead and has to get on with the story. But most of the time a writer who goes forward without having a lead finds that the story doesn't work. It goes off in tangents; it lacks direction; it is poorly organized; it doesn't have a consistent tone; it doesn't make a single dominant point; it doesn't serve the reader. It doesn't work. And trying to get a poor draft back on the road is like trying to back up a ramp to get on a busy superhighway. It's far better to know where you're going in the first place.

It doesn't take long to draft a lead. Usually they are about three lines long, and in the beginning the writing can be pretty sloppy. It will get polished later. The first thing to do is to discover, by using language, what the lead might be. Once you have that, the lead can be made stronger and surer.

I usually write at least fifty or sixty leads for an article, but that doesn't mean fifty or sixty hours of work. I can write a lead in three to five minutes, and so can my students. Each lead is, in a way, a draft of the story you may write. You get something down and you can see where that story is headed and how. Then you can decide if you want to follow it. Most of my lead writing is done in fragments of time, mostly in my daybook, sometimes on the typewriter, on sheets of paper I paste in my daybook afterward. As I write leads I'm doing two things at the same time: I'm writing new leads, new approaches to the story, and I'm also revising leads that I've written before. If I have sixty leads there may be fifteen different ways to approach the story and three or four variations on each of them.

Lead writing is fun, for you can see, surprising you on the page, all sorts of ways of starting what seemed like a very ordinary story, until you tried to write the lead.

My Grandmother Smith died in a letter when I was in combat—she thought I had gone to fight Napoleon—but thirty-eight years later I'm still trying to live up to her standards—and failing.

I like the phrase "died in a letter," which is left over from a poem. It got me started on this string of heads, but I may be trying to do too much here, I may be making the reader leap back and forth in time too much.

Grandma was tough. She'd broken the wrist of a robber with a cane, shoved her sewing scissors up the nose of an attacking bull, and scrubbed the tan away when I came home from camp.

Don't need the topic sentence. I show she's tough. Should read, "Grandma had broken. . . ." Would be better—more active— if I got rid of the past perfect tense—make it "broke."

My mother and her brothers loved Grandma the way they were supposed to love God: in fear.

This has a little surprise at the end. It's a bit quick, but it might work.

When Grandmother did housework she sang the hymn, "When the roll is called up yonder, I'll be there." There was never any doubt she would be there, but I wasn't so sure about myself.

Nice specific—and sets up a reflective tone for me.

I find myself sitting in the shadows, not yet turning on the lights, the way Grandmother used to sit "in the gloaming." And I find myself living with the very live people others think are dead, the way she used to.

I had a ceiling of maps, and I used to lie in bed staring at the places I would go—Arabia, the South Seas, Europe, China. At twelve I left home in my mind and became, in a sense, a boy of the streets. At seventeen I was gone, but I never escaped my grandmother's piercing eye, her stern back, her disapproving mouth.

When I was a boy my best friend was my grandmother, a tall, imperious woman who looked like Queen Mary of Great Britain. But when I tipped the living room chairs on their sides and pulled the rug over them she visited me in my cave, and when I put the fan in the front of the row of the dining room chairs she flew to Scotland with me. She was a shipmate, a fireman, a cowboy.

And when I was eight years old running upstairs to bed I found her on the dark stairway, hunched over on her side, grunting like a wounded animal.

She was used to seeing things that others could not see, her husband dead for twenty years and her daughter dead for nine, the bagpipers who came back to haunt the moors, the ancestors she had never met, and God who was as real as the gnarled mahogany hatstand in the hall.

Perhaps this would be a piece about me, not Grandmother. Should it be?

Like her "stern back." This may, through specifics, set up a nice perspective and tension—we can't leave home. (Title?)

"Grandma Never Died"

Would Queen Mary mean anything to present-day reader? No. Can't use that.

Notice how the second and third paragraphs of the lead can take me off in two directions—both possible.

A hundred times a day, it seemed, my mother and I, each on a side, would haul my grandmother up against the pillows at the top of the bed. She was paralyzed, and we never saw her move, but glacierlike she kept sliding toward the bottom of the bed. And Mother and I, laughing with Grandmother at her travels, would haul her up again.

I wanted to try some humor. It wasn't all that grim.

The bell would tinkle and we'd go to Grandma's room, where she'd ask, "Is lunch ready?" We'd just cleared the dishes after feeding her, but we'd learned to answer, "It won't be long."

Perhaps this creates, in a few words, what that world was like. Where's it going?

As you can see, each lead can start you in a different direction with a different tone. Notice how the piece of writing starts to take control of itself. When you choose a lead there are things you have to do and things you can no longer do.

Categories of Leads

It may be helpful to take a piece of paper and list the kinds of leads you have in your writer's toolbox. Most of us have many more ways of beginning a piece of writing than we realize. Some of the leads in my toolbox are:

▶ **News**   Tell the reader what the reader needs to know in the order the reader needs to know it. Check the five W's—who, what, when, where, why.

▶ **Anecdote**   This is a brief story that captures the essence of what you will be dealing with. It is the most popular magazine lead, but watch out—if it's a good story but doesn't aim the reader in the direction you want the reader to go, the whole piece may be lost.

▶ **Quotation**   A quote is a good device, for it gives additional authority and an extra voice to the piece. Like the anecdotal lead, however, it must be right on target.

▶ **Umbrella**   This is a lead that covers several equal, or almost equal, elements in the story. "Yesterday the governor took three actions to prevent forest fires . . ."

▶ **Descriptive**   The writer sets the scene for the story. Remember to use specifics.

▶ **Voice** Voice is an important element in every lead, but in some leads it is the most important element. It establishes the tone of communication between reader and writer. Read aloud and make sure that the voice is communicating information.

▶ **Announcement** This lead tells the reader what you are going to say. Most of the time you just want to say it. Get out of the way. Do not write an introduction.

▶ **Tension** This lead reveals the forces in the story in action. They are coming together on a collision course, or pulling against each other. The lead contains the forces, and makes the reader feel the tension between them.

▶ **Problem** The lead establishes the problem that will be solved, or not solved, in the piece.

▶ **Background** The writer first gives the reader the background of an event, argument, conflict, issue, or action.

▶ **Narrative** This lead establishes that the story will be told in narrative form. Be careful not to start too early. Start as near to the end as possible to involve the reader in the story.

▶ **Question** This sounds like it should work, but it rarely does. The writer usually knows the answer to the question and so it sounds patronizing, like the nurse who says, "Now we would like to take our medicine, wouldn't we?"

▶ **Point of View** The writer establishes the position from which the reader will be shown the subject.

▶ **Reader Identification** The inexperienced writer tries to do this by speaking directly to the reader in the second person, saying, "You . . ." That doesn't usually work. The reader identifies best with a "he" or a "she," best of all with a specific name.

▶ **Face** A character is revealed in action. The reader becomes interested in the person and then the issue.

▶ **Scene** The writer establishes a scene that is central to the meaning of the piece.

▶ **Dialogue** The reader hears one person speak and another react. It's not often you can use this lead, but when it's appropriate it is dramatic and provides a lot of energy.

▶ **Process** A process central to the story is shown in action, and the reader is carried forward into the story.

These are not all the ways to write leads. They are samples from my own toolbox. Make a list of the leads you like to write, and then look through periodicals and books to see other ways of writing leads. Steal them. And also pay attention to the leads you see in movies and on television. Those were all written too, and we can learn from each other.

Lead Writer's Checklist

Remember, in writing leads:

▶ *Be Quick*   The reader will decide to read on—or not to read on—in a matter of seconds.

▶ *Be Accurate*   The reader who spots a tiny error will refuse to believe anything you write.

▶ *Be Honest*   Don't hoke up a lead that will tease the reader, because a lead is a contract with the reader, a promise that must be kept.

▶ *Be Simple*   Cut back the underbrush. Use proper nouns, active verbs, and concrete details whenever possible.

▶ *Write with Information*   The effective lead gives the reader information, and that information makes the reader want to read on.

▶ *Read Aloud*   Voice is important in the lead. The reader should hear an individual writer speaking directly to the reader.

Ends

The end is a beginning.

John Irving says, "I don't know how far away the end is—only *what* it is. I know the last sentence, but I'm very much in the dark concerning how to get to it." "If I didn't know the ending of a story, I wouldn't begin," says Katherine Anne Porter. "I always write my last line, my last paragraph, my last page first." Eudora Welty agrees. "I think the end is implicit in the beginning. It must be. If that isn't there in the beginning, you don't know what you're working toward. You should have a sense of a story's shape and form and its destination, all of which is like a flower inside a seed."

Many good writers know where they want to end before they begin to write. It gives them a sense of destination. Sometimes they just have the ending in mind, but often they write the end first. They know, of course, that the ending may change after the piece is written, but it still helps during the writing to have an end in sight.

Only rarely in effective writing is the end a formal summary or conclusion in which the writer repeats in general or abstract terms what has already been said. The most effective endings are usually the same devices that make effective leads: specific detail, quotation, anecdote, scene, and all those other tools listed in the section on lead writing.

Look back at the leads I wrote about my grandmother. The first one would make a good ending as is. So would the third, fourth, and fifth, and possibly the sixth. But since I do not yet know how I'm going to begin the piece on my grandmother I will try to write some new endings, which, incidentally, might turn out to be leads.

When I remember Grandmother I remember the topknot on her hairdo, like a crown. I remember her singing at her work, and I remember her taking trips with me. But most of all I remember, and wish I did not, her disapproving mouth.

I'm catching up with her in years, and I know she must have had doubts, regrets, second thoughts. But none of us ever heard them.

Now I have my own children, grown, I can understand with a bit more compassion how these grown men, my uncles, were always children to her: Alec, head of his own family, was still the eldest son; Will was always working hard, trying to catch up; and Donald was still the favored baby, the beloved eccentric. And my mother, her hair already turning gray, had to be told just how to make the tea.

I knew for the first time that things were going to change when Grandma called and I found her sitting on the floor of the house on Vassell Street. She was angry at herself, and she was holding her arm, which had a huge swollen bruise above the wrist. She told me to call Dr. Bartlett. I was too young to go to school, but I did the job and became older. The most powerful person in the world had needed my help.

The last time I saw Grandmother was in August of 1944, when I was in a winter uniform and got illegal permission to go home for two hours. I was sailing the next day, a twentieth-century paratrooper going to Europe to fight Hitler.

I raced up the stairs and into Grandmother's bedroom, where I used to stand by the bed before I went out on the paper route to see if she was still breathing. She recognized me and called me by my name. She knew I was in uniform and was going off to war, but she thought I was the great-uncle for whom I was named and that I was a Highlander leaving to fight Napoleon at Waterloo.

She used to sing that old Scottish song that I think went, "I'll take the high road and you take the low road, and I'll be in Scotland afore ye." She did take the high road, and certainly at times I've taken the low road, and she did get there ahead of me, but I do think that when I take the final trip she'll be there waiting.

She won't hug me; we never did that sort of thing. She'll probably tell me to shave off the beard she never saw. Perhaps not. My Uncle Will, when he saw it, said, "You look just like Father." Perhaps she'll introduce me to the grandfather I never knew, Morison Smith, the man with the fiddle foot.

As I write endings, some of them echo the beginning and others make me see a new beginning. In each case the potential ending gives me a sense of the voice and the direction of the piece of writing. When I choose one and know where I'm going I may know how to get there.

Sequences

Another way to plan a piece of writing is simply to list the main points that will be made in the piece of writing. I call these points sequences, because I like to move them around until they're in a natural order so each point leads to the next one.

Most pieces of writing are built from three to five main points, and you can use your own code words to remind you of each point. If, for example, a scientist has given you a long quote about an environmental hazard, all you have to do is write "scientist" or "sci. qte." to remind you of that point and its documentation. If the chemical the scientist is talking about has polluted Upper Valley Lake, all you have to do is put down "Upper Valley Lake" or "describe lake" or "desc. UVL." Now you only have two points on your list, but already you can start thinking about whether you want to lead with the scientist's quote and then describe the stinking lake, or let the reader smell the lake and then explain it with the scientist's quote. It's better, however, not to stop at this point, but to put down the other main points: the cost of cleaning it up, the dangers to the people who drink the water that travels from the lake into the reservoir a hundred and fifty miles away, the effect on Valleyville of shutting down the industry that is polluting the lake. If those are your main points you can move them around until you have your piece of writing lined up in a natural, easy-to-read, and purposeful order.

▶ I accepted saint
I questioned
Now I accept Grandma as a person

▶ First memories of Grandma—murky
    Playing imaginary games
    Washing off tan
    Collapsed on stairs
    Paralyzed in bed
Last memories—going off to war

▶ Circle her—different points of view
    Her husband???
    Her sons
    Her daughter, my mother
    Other grandchildren—cousins
    My wife/my daughters
    Myself

▶ Born 11/8/55 Our Civil War
       Boer War/Spanish-American War
       WWI: 1917; she was 62 years old
                (I am 57—she was 57 in 1912)
       WW II: Died 1945 before her 90th birthday

▶ Islay
  London
  America
  England/Scotland
  America

▶ Hid her feelings about:
  Husband
  Sex
  Religious doubts
  Social background
  Struggle to survive

▶ I see in her what I need to see:
  Role model
  Connection with past
  Authority to rebel against
  Anti–role model—be a different kind of parent

▶ Tie piece together with tea

▶ Family:
  Sense of vocation—striving for success
  Scotch pride
  Belief in work
  Cynicism about how others get ahead
  God—we're the elect—the upper classes might have status in this
      world, but we would have status in the next
              Lead: (?) We lived in a rented flat, but we belonged to an
              aristocracy of the spirit. We might have to pay our nickel
              and ride the trolley car in this world, but we would have a
              Packard or a Pierce-Arrow—with a chauffeur—in the Great
              Beyond.

This kind of doodling allows me to look for a thread or order or spine that may hold the piece together. I look back and forth and see potential endings and titles and leads. I'm looking for a trail through the material I have, and I even allow myself to get off track for a moment or two and wonder if I should be writing about my father, or my mother, or even myself as a parent. That kind of daydreaming is important at this stage, and sometimes you'll want to follow the scent of a new order. But after staring out of the window for a while I realize I have to write about my grandmother; I'm committed, and I no longer have a choice.

Outlines

"Outline" is a nasty word for many students, and I was one of them, for it is often taught in such a rigid manner that it doesn't work. An outline is not a formal blueprint that has to be followed precisely; it is not a contract, and you can't be sued if you break it. An outline is a sketch, a guess, a scribbled map that may lead to a treasure.

Outlines are written by experienced writers with the knowledge that the writing will change the structure and the meaning of the writing. Writers may create outlines and then not refer to them during the writing, for what they learned by making the outline allows them to get on with the writing. Sometimes it is also helpful to make outlines in the middle of the writing to see where you've gone and where you might go, and at the end of the draft to see what you have discovered through the writing and how you have organized your material.

There are many ways to outline, but I will list a dozen here to show how different outlines can be. None of these is, *the* way to outline. Develop your own system of outlining. Outline only if it helps you, and then outline in a way that provides that help.

Outline 1

If you go back over what we have done in this chapter you will see that we have covered the elements in one form of outline—title, lead, sequence, and end. It is the form that I use the most, and it allows me to get all four elements on one page.

For me the title always comes first, and the lead is usually next, but sometimes the end is next. I usually do the end after the lead and then the sequence, just putting them down and then messing around with them until I get them in the right order.

Watching the Sheets Move

It was my chore when I got up at 4:30 in the morning to do the paper
route to stand by Grandma's bed, in the pale orange light of the night-
light, and watch to see if the sheets moved, if she was breathing and still alive.

▶ Establish Grandma as powerful figure
▶ Scene when she collapsed on stairs—turning point
▶ Caring for her; in control; her faith
▶ Last time I saw her

Grandma died in a letter (when I was overseas and surrounded by death) but . . . . . I still watch the sheets move (?).

I went back and worked on a title that seemed to have some action, some tension, and that gave me a central point to work on—something that has been influencing me all my life. The lead's okay for a draft (I used *x*'s when I heard myself write "light" twice, and then cut one out). The sequence is natural. The ending is not well written, but I have a sense of direction. I know where I may end.

Outline 2

The formal outline may be appropriate for a formal, very structured subject. It uses arabic and roman numerals and capital and small letters to break a subject down into categories and subcategories in a logical sequence.

The most formal outline requires a full and complete sentence for each entry, but most people just use fragments, as signals for what will be said.

Grandmother

I. Scotch
    A. Highlander
        1. Islay
    B. Father—Donald Bell—tenant farmer
        1. Social/economic distinctions
            a. Laborer (My father's family)
                i. bottom socially and economically
            b. Tenant
                i. In middle socially and economically.
                    a. Ran farm
                    b. Top person in residence
                    c. Lives to standards of middle-class behavior
            c. Landlord
                i. At top socially and economically
                    a. Owns land—this farm and many others
                    b. Absentee
                        1. English, not Scottish
                        2. Lives in London?

Too much for me at this stage. Could work on another writing task and does help me see a complex structure more clearly, but I couldn't follow it religiously on the kind of tonal piece I'll be writing.

Outline 3

A writer friend of mine, Donald H. Graves, uses this outline form. He lists everything that might be included in the piece of writing in the left-hand column; then he moves items to the columns marked Beginning, Middle, and End.

Some things don't get moved, of course, and others come to mind as the outline is being made and go right into the appropriate column.

?	Beginning	Middle	End
▶ Fiddle foot ▶ Helen—daughter, died flu epidemic ▶ See if she breathes ▶ Making tea ▶ Uncles ▶ Going overseas—last visit ▶ Scrubbing off tan ▶ Wood stove ▶ Sent London—putting on airs ▶ Great-uncle—Waterloo ▶ Paralyzed left side ▶ Forgets time ▶ Father tenant farmer ▶ Cane breaks robber's arm ▶ Back-scratcher ▶ Fragments of	▶ See if she breathes ▶ (Remember only fragments of a legend)	▶ Fiddle foot ▶ Helen—daughter, died flu epidemic ▶ Sent London—putting on airs ▶ Scrubbing off tan ▶ Found collapsed on stairs ▶ Cane breaks robber's arm	▶ Going overseas—last visit ▶ Great-uncle—Waterloo

Notice how some things in the left-hand column are not used. It's a brainstorming list, and it becomes an inventory of material that may be used. Also note that some things that are not on the list occurred to me while I was working on the right-hand columns. The items are ordered within the columns after the writer has finished. Then the writer is ready to write.

Outline 4

For this book I combined Donald Graves's outline with a space or box outline. Here is how I used it on my grandmother piece.

Usually when I use this outline for a book I go through and do all the collecting in the left-hand column, and then the ordering for each chapter in the right-hand columns.

What May Be Included

▶ As a young woman, must have been almost a girl, Grandma would be called out to help lay out the dead
▶ She was a Protestant saint
▶ Seeing if she breathed
▶ Collapsed on stairs
▶ Harsh religion:
    Glad Helen died
    Hated Rome
▶ Ran family
▶ Worked as servant (companion?) in London home of absentee landlord
▶ Husband had fiddle foot
▶ Father tenant, not laborer
▶ Sometimes mill owner's wife and sometimes had to bake bread to sell
▶ Had been a servant and had servants (they were Irish)
▶ (Our blacks were Irish)
▶ Great-uncle fought Napoleon
▶ Why such a fear of booze? (Joke: If they had to invent Scotch to keep the Scots from taking over the world.)

Title

Will the Sheets Move?

Lead

Boy starts each day standing by his grandmother's bed to see if she's died in the night.

Sequence

▶ Legend of grandmother
▶ How she runs family
▶ Collapsed on stairs
▶ Paralyzed—world limited
▶ How she still runs family

End

I'm catching up with her in age—she's been dead almost 40 years, but she's still running me.

Each outline gives me some new information and helps me see a slightly different pattern. I have a new title this time, and I came to a different ending. I was also interested in the parallel between how she ran the family before she was paralyzed and afterwards.

Outline 5

A way to use the outline to dramatize the importance of certain parts of the piece of writing to the reader is to make a box outline in which the space represents the importance of each part. The first paragraph, for example, is much more important to the reader than the pages that follow.

Watching the Sheets Move

> When I got up in the early hours of the dark New England morning to do my paper route I first did my most important chore. I walked down the long corridor and into the pale yellow light of Grandma's night-light and stood quietly by her bed, watching to see the sheets move. If they had not moved she would have left us during the night.

> Grandma family head

> I find Grandma collapsed on stairs. I'm the first one to understand what she's saying after the doctor leaves.

> Runs family from bed

> The last time I saw Grandma I was in uniform, ready to go to Europe as a paratrooper. She didn't know about jumping out of planes or much about Hitler. She thought I was her great-uncle, for whom I was named, and that I was going to fight Napoleon at Waterloo, wearing kilts.

This outline really forces me to face up to the importance of the opening and the ending—to the importance of what I'm going to say and how I'm going to say it. It also forces me to see the structure of the piece in stark, efficient terms.

In a fifteen-page essay, the first box may represent one paragraph, the second box eight pages, the middle box one page, the next-to-last box six pages, and the final box one paragraph. The boxes dramatize the impact of the text on the reader—an important thing to remember.

Outline 6

A fine way to outline, especially on a complicated subject, is to brainstorm the questions the reader will ask and then put them in the order the reader will ask them.

There will usually be five questions—sometimes three or four, sometimes six or seven, but most likely five. You don't want to use the questions in the text, but simply give the answers. The questions are in the reader's mind; the writer anticipates and answers them.

▶ What did it mean to you (+ the family) when she was found on the stairs?

▶ How did you feel?

▶ Why did you have to go in to see the sheets move? What did you see?
▶ "So what" question: What's so special about *your* grandmother? Everybody's got a couple.
▶ What's she mean to you now?
▶ How would she have been treated differently today?

Doing this, I have a better sense of the audience. I've got to reach readers who couldn't care less about my grandmother—or me, the little boy looking in to see if she's alive.

The last question is interesting, but doesn't belong. The outline brought it up, though. I may be able to weave it in or, more likely, write a separate piece about the care stroke victims receive today.

Outline 7

The writer can adapt outline forms from other disciplines. I often find it helpful to use a flow chart, similar to those used in systems engineering and in business organization study. These charts are designed to show how a factory works, how a material flows from a natural resource to a manufactured product, how power flows in a corporation. Using this device I can often spot a movement or force that can order my piece.

Proud Highlander's land owned by absentee Englishman	Highlander becomes proud of being tenant farmer not laborer	Daughter becomes servant in London to absentee landlord
Daughter mimics styles, manners, attitudes of landowners	Daughter marries older widow mill manager	They go to America where he can be mill owner
Wife looks down on Irish servant girls and my father's mother, a mill worker	Mill owner loses mill but their daughter has attitudes and manners of millowner	She marries man who has own business but fails
She (my mother) lives in tenements but spends as if she had money	I lived without money but have some of her attitudes about money	

Note how many ways this chart can flow—across, down, forward, backwards, or by row. Each reading reveals its own story. The flow chart can show where some of my attitudes about bargains and brand names come from. It could also take me, in a personal essay, back from the decision to buy a brand name camera all the way to Scotland and the Highlanders, who were occupied by a foreign country—England—and stripped of their lands.

Outline 8

A related outline form I find useful I've borrowed from computers. Computer users have developed a number of different forms of outlining that break complicated subjects down into their sequential parts. Most of these outlines flow from left to right.

			Soft-boiled eggs
		Scrubbing off tan	Wet the hairbrush for spanking
	As a child, big woman	Taking imaginary trips	Telling Scottish stories Teasing
How do I remember Grandma?	Caring for her when she was paralyzed	Bedpans for Victorian woman	Pain but never complain Real modesty, not false
		Her materialistic faith	Heaven would have a mill owner's house
	Remembering her today	As a parent being unlike her	Elect had direct payoff for being good Grandma shook hands, I hug
		Finding myself trying to get her approval	Try not to judge adult children Behaving like her in public Working more than need to work

There are many forms of flow charts designed to break down technical and complex subjects, but I find they help in every form of writing. Each outline is a quick sketch that gives me a new vision of the material. I may not use all the material, in fact I know I won't, but the process of making the outlines stimulates my memory and makes it possible for me to play around with many interesting combinations of information.

Outline 9

Outlines, called "skeletons" in Great Britain, can obviously take many forms. It helps to have an image of an outline in your head. The skeleton is a good image, and so is the tree, used for another purpose, described on page 29. This one I like to call the root outline. It can reveal the potential structure of a piece.

Grandma

Donald Bell		Morison		Edith
her father		her husband		her daughter
Scotland	Baptist	America	Failure	Me
Highlands		Scotland	Widow	
		England		
		America		
				My
				daughters

This root outline showed a way to write the piece about my grandmother, working from left to right—the Scottish Highlands; the severe Calvinist Baptists; the trips to America, back to Great Britain, and back to America; business failure; widowhood; and how all that has shaped my attitudes and those of my children.

Outline 10

In many effective pieces of writing, fiction as well as nonfiction, each chunk of writing—a paragraph, a page, a scene—answers a question and asks a new question. For example, will they get married? Yes, but will they be happy? Or, will the product sell? Yes, but will it make a profit?

It can be helpful to outline by using this question-and-answer method.

Q. *Even paralyzed in bed, Grandma acted as if she were a lady— someone the common people would be watching as a model. How come?*

A. She had been one of the common people who had studied how ladies acted, and had even become, at one time, a mill owner's wife.

Q. *What did this mean for her husband and her children?*

A. Her children were to be the children of a lady. They were to dress and behave properly, not to work with their hands, and to marry well.

Q. *And if they didn't?*

A. They were never to let the neighbors know. The part must be played, the play must go on; appearances are the reality.

Q. *What if the illusion is seen through?*

A. Grandma would become a common person again. The struggle to rise would have failed.

Each new form of outline seems to bring its own perceptions. It helps me see the familiar material in a different way. I'd realized, of course, something of why appearances were so important to Grandma, but never quite so clearly as when I wrote this above.

Outline 11

Many fine writers, such as John McPhee and John Gregory Dunne, use a card technique to outline. This is the most popular technique of movie script writers.

Each element in the writing is put on a card, sometimes using cards of different colors for different characters, or different kinds of material in nonfic-

I SLAY
   DESCRIBE SCENE
IN SCOTLAND
	FIDDLE FOOT
	   GRANDFATHER
	   ALWAYS MOVING

BULL
   JABS SCISSORS
UP NOSE
	SHOCK
	   PARALYZED, I
	   FIND HER

ROBBER BREAKS WRIST WITH CANE	BAPTIST
NORTH GRAFTON MILL OWNER'S HOUSE	LAMB / COAL HADDOCK / STOVE IN SCONES / KITCHEN

BREAD
      TO
FEED FAMILY
	WATERLOO
	   LAST TIME I
	   SAW GRANDMA

tion. Then the cards are pinned to a cork board and moved around so the writer can see the pattern of the entire piece—book, movie, or article.

Outline 12

A way to see how a piece of writing is shaping up is to make file folders for each topic within the piece of writing. This is helpful on a large project. You can renumber and move the file folders around, and you can put all your raw material right into a folder—clips, photocopied articles, notes, photographs. When a folder is full it may have to be divided. When it has nothing in it you may have to drop that topic, or do more research.

Try out these outline forms, and then try to make up others that fit the way your head works. There's no one way to outline, and no twelve ways to outline. But you should find some way of preseeing what you may write.

Yes, there are writers who say that they do not outline, but if you interview them, as I have, you find that most of them have outlined in their head, sometimes without being aware they were doing it. That happens to me sometimes.

I just know where the writing is going and how it is going there. It seems like a feeling, even though it's probably a very organized intellectual act.

What do you do if you feel that way? I write. I don't outline unless I feel the need to outline. But I do find that most of the time my drafts collapse unless I have outlined in my head or on paper.

Of course, when you outline you may realize that you need more information, or that you need a different focus, and you have to go back through one or both of the earlier stages of the writing process. That isn't failure. You haven't made a mistake. That's one of the big reasons to outline, so that you will see the information you need to have before you write the draft. You will see, by outlining, if you have the information to develop the focus.

Order from the Writing Task

In addition to the kinds of order we have been talking about, each writing task imposes its own demands—or order—on what we write.

None of us knows what we will be writing after we leave school. When I was in college I planned to write a few great poems. They would be short, no more than twelve lines long, and I would produce about three a year. I guess I expected to spend most of my time accepting great acclaim—casually, modestly. If I became bored with poetry I would produce an occasional fine novel.

When I graduated I got a job on a newspaper as a copy boy. I went out for coffee and sandwiches and watched others write. Since then I have published a few poems and several novels, but I've written thousands of newspaper stories, editorials, and all sorts of other kinds of prose—magazine articles, political speeches, juvenile and business nonfiction books, company reports, short stories, one Christmas carol, academic articles, eulogies, memos, fund-raising letters, state proclamations, applications for propane priority, and all sorts of other writing, some of it too embarrassing to mention.

Many of my students who expected to be writers never write, but many who did not expect to write have become writers. And many more became engineers, business executives, lawyers, research scientists, doctors, bureaucrats, and politicians and spend most of their time writing. Information is power, and information is best shared through the process of clarified thinking we call writing.

The person who can accept a new and unexpected writing task and perform it well will have a clear career advantage. Even more important, the person who is able to perform these writing tasks will have an opportunity to learn, think, and influence.

Just as important to me are the noncareer benefits, even though I have made writing a career. I have always kept some writing going that has no immediate professional or practical advantage, writing that I need to do for personal reasons, often for reasons I don't understand. Yet this writing and my family stand at the very center of my life. Beside my desk is a quotation from Graham Greene that may explain this: "Writing is a form of therapy; sometimes I wonder how all those who do not write, compose or paint can manage to escape the madness, the melancholia, the panic fear which is inherent in the human situation."

I hope that in the years ahead you will have the challenge and the satisfaction of performing many writing tasks, and I hope that some of them, at least, will be self-assigned.

When you face an unfamiliar writing task it may be helpful to look over the territory ahead to see just what the task involves. You may wish to consider the following checklist so that you will have some idea of what you have to do and how you may be able to do it.

Once you've completed your checklist you can start to use the writing process of collect, focus, order, draft, and clarify.

Eight Tips for Starting a New Writing Task

1. Purpose   The purpose may be most explicit—to persuade the government to support a research project, to convince the company to adopt a new marketing strategy. Or it may be appropriately unclear—"I wonder if I could write something that would help me understand why I didn't feel sad at the funeral." "Perhaps there's a story in the accident that happened Saturday night." Most writing tasks fall somewhere in between, and most of the time it helps to state the purpose of the writing, especially when we face a new writing task and are not used to the territory. As we become more experienced there may be times when the purpose is obvious and there may also be times when the purpose is unclear and will only come clear through the process of writing.

2. Audience   Some writing tasks have a single reader—the personnel officer who can give you a job, a parent who will send you cash, the teacher who will grade the paper—and other writing tasks have hundreds, thousands, or even millions of readers. It is helpful to know the size of your audience, and to remember that the larger the audience, the more specific you must be and the less you can assume the reader knows about the subject. There are almost infinite variations in audiences. There is the audience that knows the subject better than you and the audience for which you are the authority; there are audiences that fundamentally agree with you and those that are opposed to you or what you are saying. There are audiences that need to be attracted and entertained, that are not apparently interested in what you have to say. And there are times when you have no identifiable audience, or when the audience during the writing is simply yourself. Some writing tasks demand that you know the audience well and can anticipate and respond to the reader's questions and reactions. But in no case should you pander to the audience, by giving false information, withholding information, or distorting information to please the audience. Sometimes people mistakenly feel that an awareness of audience means you must tell the audience what you think they want to hear, in the way you think they want to hear it. That is not true; what you want to do is to know where the audience is so that you can speak honestly and clearly in terms they will understand.

3. *Sources* Effective writing is built on information, and it helps to identify those places where you can get the information you need, for the first stage in the writing process is usually collecting. Often when we face a new writing task it is not clear to us where we will be able to find the information we need to write well. In looking at the territory ahead we need to know where that information can be found. We should not forget, however, that our own experiences and observations are significant sources for most pieces of writing.

4. *Form* Some writing tasks require very specific forms. You can, for example, go to most stationery stores and get a form to fill in for a lease or a will. Many academic disciplines have professional societies that establish precise forms for writing in those disciplines. Be sure, however, that you get the form for the right branch of the discipline. Social psychologists, clinical psychologists, and experimental psychologists follow significantly different forms in their writing. It is often helpful to ask the person who has given you the writing task to suggest the names of writers who have performed that task well. Then you can study those writers to see what problems they faced and how they solved them. It is important, however, not to follow other writers or traditional forms slavishly. You should try to understand the reasons for a traditional form. Traditional argument, for example, anticipates the strongest argument of the opponent first, and tries to pull its teeth; scholarly publications provide footnotes and a bibliography, because its purpose is to serve other scholars who need to know where to get the information on which the publication is based. If you understand the reasons for the traditional forms, then you may be able to follow them easily when the traditions serve the reader well, and to abandon them when other approaches will serve the reader better.

5. *Tone* An effective piece of writing is written in a tone of voice that reinforces the purpose of the piece of writing, communicates its information, and pleases the writer. Each writer's voice is, of course, individual and distinct. But the experienced writer extends the range so the voice is appropriate for different writing tasks. The writer can maintain his or her own voice and yet be objective in a business report, evangelical in a lay sermon, angry with a complaint, chatty with a friend, passionate in an appeal to the zoning board. Adapting tone to purpose and audience is not a mystery. We do it all the time in speech, adjusting our voice at a family gathering, on the street corner, in class, in the locker room, in the dorm, at a formal dance, in church. Usually even the experienced writer has to try out different tones in a test paragraph or two, or thirty-seven, to find the voice appropriate to a new writing task.

6. *Problems* Some writing problems are a surprise, but most of them can be anticipated—and they should be. There's no sense wasting time writing an unsuccessful draft when a key problem could have been solved in advance. You may know that the reader you have in mind wants quotations cited, or is persuaded by statistics. If so, you'd better dig them out. You may know that the writing task is potentially dull, so you can decide, if you want to, to seek out anecdotes about people and quotations from people that will make the writing lively. It may be obvious that the story of a biochemical process or a state budget is complicated, and you may seek ways from the very beginning to simplify without oversimplifying. One of the nice things about problem hunting is that once you define the problem, solutions may become obvious.

7. Deadline If you know when the piece has to be delivered then you can pace yourself, establishing deadlines for each part of the writing process. If there is no deadline, then you're probably in real trouble, for most writing is done on deadline. What do you do? Set your own deadline, allowing double the time it ought to take you if you're sensible, triple if you're smart.

8. Length Know how long the piece of writing is expected to be, and face up to it. In some cases the length will be precise—500 words, or ten pages double-spaced; other times you'll be given a range of words or pages. If no length is given to you, make a guess. It will help you limit and focus your subject from the moment you start collecting information until you begin your draft. It always helps me to have a target. For example, I usually aim for thirteen pages, double-spaced, elite type, for a magazine article. If it runs a couple of pages under that or a couple of pages over, I don't worry; if I get down to nine pages or up to seventeen I begin to be aware that I'm running short or long. That may be fine, but I need to know that I may have a problem of saying too little or too much.

Tips for Special Writing Tasks

In the pages ahead I will pass on to you some tips from professionals who have experience with the different writing tasks you may be assigned or wish to attempt. Yes, these suggestions are brief and in some cases they may appear superficial, but they are designed to help a beginner face a new genre. If you spend a career writing book reviews or poems or scientific papers you will find complexities and challenges, year after year. Here you will find simplicities that are designed to help you get started.

A Book Review

There are two basic types of book review. One is the report to the teacher proving you have read the book; the other is the review written for the general public, to help people decide if they should read the book. The difference, of course, is that the teacher is familiar with the book and therefore should not have to be told what is in it, while the general public may need a summary of what the book covers.

Remember:
▶ Include either in a heading above the report or in the first paragraphs of the report the name of the book, the author, the publisher, where it was published, the number of pages, and the price. This rule can be adapted to the

needs of the reader when something of less than book length is being reviewed, for example a short story or a journal article.

▶ Summarize the contents of the book.

▶ Evaluate the book. Answer such questions as are appropriate: Is the author qualified to write on this subject? What does the book add to our knowledge? Is the work worth reading? Is the book well written? What are the book's strengths? What are its weaknesses?

▶ Document each point with examples, quotations, specific details from the text.

▶ If appropriate, place the book in the context of other books by the same writer; relate it to other books in the same genre or on the same subject.

A Letter Applying for a Job

When you write a job application you are selling yourself. You should remember that the person reading it will get the first impression of you from the letter. If the person's name is spelled wrong, the title inaccurate, the address in error, the letter will probably not be read; if the spelling is incorrect, the grammar eccentric, the mechanics erratic, the typing messy, the paper wrinkled or decorated with coffee stains, the letter will certainly not be taken seriously.

Remember:

▶ Role-play the reader. Provide the information you would want if you were doing the hiring.

▶ Be specific about what you have to offer and what experience you have. Vague, impassioned promises to do anything are not strong selling points.

▶ Avoid formal business jargon—"In response to your ad of the 16th, I am most willing to be of service to your corporation in the capacity of sales clerk"—and write your letter in simple, active, direct prose: "I can sell motorcycles. I have owned and repaired three motorcycles. I am able to get along with people from very different backgrounds. I have worked in a gas station, waited on tables at the Faculty Club, worked as a counselor at a summer camp for retarded children, and been an orderly in a nursing home."

▶ Let the person know where you can be reached and when you'll be there. Include telephone numbers as well as mailing addresses.

▶ Photocopy and include letters of recommendation, certification of skills, and other appropriate documentation.

▶ Don't be cute.

A Résumé

In a résumé as in a job application letter, neatness counts. The résumé shouldn't be printed on attention-getting paper in an eccentric typeface. It should be simple and professional.

It may be helpful to look at some of the job résumés available in your school's placement office or in books on the subject, but there is no one correct form to follow. You can design your own résumé by role-playing the person who will receive it. Deliver the information that person needs for that particular job.

Remember:

▶ Include your full name, address, and telephone number at the top of the page.

▶ Include personal information if it is appropriate to the job and if you feel comfortable including it. You should not include such information if it is inappropriate or if you feel it should not be considered.

▶ Organize the information the prospective employer needs into categories, such as education, skills, and job experience, and then put them in the order the person using the résumé will need them, with the most important information first. If your résumé is to be attached to a proposal for a grant for graduate study the education category may come first. If you're applying for a job to train baboons your skill certification or job experience may come first. Add categories such as awards, publications, exhibits, travel, languages spoken, and hobbies only if they are appropriate to the job. Including the fact that fishing or skiing is your hobby may tell an employer that you will live for the weekend, and somebody else will get hired. On the other hand, if you want to sell fishing gear or manage a ski lodge it may be appropriate.

▶ List the items under each category by date, with the most recent items first.

▶ Include enough information about each job or course or experience so that the person reading it will know its significance. Don't just say, "Summer 1984, ambulance attendant." Add this kind of information (if it is true): "Worked nights and weekends at Massachusetts General Hospital, a major trauma center. Discovered I work best under pressure and enjoy making tough decisions. Found that I did not want to become a doctor, but am interested in training as a stockbroker, because I think I would be making important decisions under pressure."

▶ Add a few photocopies of letters of recommendation or commendation, certificates of training, or examples of work, such as news stories, if appropriate.

A *News Story* or a *Press Release*

There are two differences between the press release and the news story. The first is minor: the date and time of release are noted above the story, in caps— "TO BE RELEASED AT 2:00 PM OCTOBER 11." The other difference is much more important. The news story is written in an objective style that is fair to everyone involved in the story. It gives everyone an equal opportunity to have his or her side of the story presented. The press release is written in an objective style, but its purpose is to present one point of view.

Remember:

▶ Print your name and a phone number where you can be reached, as well as your address, single-spaced, in the upper left-hand corner.

▶ Two spaces under your name write a slug that identifies the story, such as CHI O DANCE.

▶ In the top left-hand corner of each page after the first put your last name, the slug, and the page number: Murray—CHI O DANCE—2.

▶ Start halfway down on the first page so there is room for an editor to put in a headline above the story. Do not write a headline yourself; you do not know the size of the head, and therefore you do not know the word count.

▶ Type double-space, leave at least a fifteen-point margin on both sides, and use a deep ten-point indent for the beginning of each paragraph.

▶ Put the word "more" at the bottom of each page until the last one, where you put —30— or #.

▶ Write on one side of a piece of paper.

▶ Use a paper clip. Do not staple pages.

▶ Write in simple, direct sentences, using a minimum number of clauses.

▶ Write in short paragraphs. One-sentence paragraphs are acceptable, two-sentence paragraphs are normal, three-sentence paragraphs are exceptional. Paragraphs should average three to five lines of typewritten copy, because they will double when printed, and readers will not read paragraphs in newspapers that average fifteen or twenty lines of type. Keep it short.

▶ News stories are organized to answer the reader's question. The form often used is the inverted pyramid, in which the most important news is given to the reader first, the next most important second, and so on, trailing off at the end. This was the traditional news-writing form for decades. Today, many forms are used but all serve the reader by anticipating the reader's questions and answering them in the order they will naturally be asked.

▶ The first paragraph, the lead, is the most important part of the news story. It tells the reader the most important information in the story and lets the reader decide whether to read on. Check the materials on leads on pp. 91–96.

There are two basic forms of leads. One is the direct lead, in which the answers to the five W's are presented to the reader: who, what, where, when, why. The direct lead is the basic form used for the radio news program or the television brief.

The other principal form of lead is the delayed lead, in which the writer focuses on one aspect of the story, the one most significant for the reader, and then establishes the voice and direction of the article. It may be an anecdote, a quote, the beginning of a narrative, a case history, a process description, or a scene, but it always is information that the reader needs. This is followed by a paragraph that answers the W's not included in the lead.

A Research Paper

To understand how to write a research paper you have to understand that its purpose is to help other researchers. Your job is to collect information and order it into meaning. But the other researchers not only need the information you have collected and the order you have made of it; they also need the sources you have used so they can do their own research in the area. This means the reader needs footnotes that tell where the significant information comes from, or a bibliography that lists the important sources you have used, or both.

Remember:
▸ When you use a direct quote you put quotation marks around it and indicate in a footnote where it came from. When you paraphrase you put the information in your own words, but you indicate by a footnote where you got the information.

▸ To make your research paper flow it's usually helpful to put your notes aside and work from a simple outline. What you remember is usually what you should remember, and what you forget is usually what should be forgotten. You will have a chance after you have finished the draft check every quote and fact and to put in the footnotes.

▸ If you are doing a research paper for a specific discipline, such as sociology, English literature, or history, see if there is a specific form to be followed. If not, create your own form, one that serves the reader's needs. This will usually include an abstract that compresses the whole paper into a fat paragraph that the reader can scan to see if the paper will help him or her. The other elements in a research paper usually include a survey of the literature, a description of the research methods used, a description of the findings, and a conclusion that points out the significance of the findings.

A Poem

Writing poetry is the highest form of literary art, because more is said with less. Poetry distills life, and the writing of poetry is the toughest, most demanding form of writing. If you've never written poetry, a good way to start is by making a list poem, in which you use lists of specific, concrete details and manipulate them into a meaning.

Remember:
▸ Formal rhyme and meter are not often used in contemporary poetry. Those poets who did write in this way had a long apprenticeship which made this discipline natural. Unless you have had such an apprenticeship it's better not to begin by writing with rhyme in formal structures.

▸ Poetry depends on specific, concrete information. The raw material of good poetry is the revealing detail or image.

▸ The line is the basic unit of contemporary poetry. It is not a sentence, and it really isn't part of a sentence; it's a number of words that deliver information to the reader in an insightful way. The poet does not write in sentences or paragraphs; the poet arranges information into a series of lines that reveal significance.

▸ Good poetry is not gush. Do not write poetry with adjectives and adverbs, but with verbs and nouns.

▶ Effective poetry does not summarize and give the reader the poet's feelings, but reveals experience in such a way that the reader has his or her own feelings. The poet points out life, but allows the person looking in that direction to react individually.

▶ As in all good writing, but especially in poetry, do not take yourself, your subject, or your form too seriously. Poetry is play. Its truths are discovered through the play of language and vision. Have fun. Surprise yourself.

A Memo

When you write a memo you have a specific job to do and a specific audience to reach. In this kind of writing you should know your purpose and your audience before you start to write.

Remember:
▶ Date the memo in the upper right-hand corner and use the following format:

To: D. Horatio Graves, Corporate Vice-President for Marketing
From: Ian Morison, Comptroller
Subject: Unacceptable travel expenses

That format allows the reader to know who it is from and what its purpose is right away, and it allows both the sender and the receiver to file it accurately.

▶ The text should be clear and precise. No business, government, or academic jargon is necessary. Speak clearly and directly. Use lists, outlines, diagrams, and any other devices that will make the meaning clear.

▶ If you are going to give copies to other people either include their names at the top of the memo or list them at the bottom of the last page, preceded by the word "copies" and a colon. Sometimes people send "blind" copies to protect themselves or to play other office-politics games. That isn't good form. The person receiving the memo should know who else is seeing it.

▶ Try to stay on one page. You can attach supporting material if that's necessary.

A Biographical Sketch

It is a valuable skill to be able to make a person come alive on the page so that the reader can hear the person talk, see the subject move, observe the person acting and reacting. People like to read about people, and profiles are not only useful in themselves but are also one of the best ways of presenting a complex subject in a way the reader will care about and understand. The news magazines, with their cover stories, do this every week. They know, for example, that few readers will be interested in the World Bank, but that many readers may be interested in the powerful president of the World Bank or in the touching story of a particular farmer in a remote African village whose life was changed because of a World Bank loan.

Remember:

▶ Weave the essential details—the full name, the address, the age, the title, the accomplishments—of the subject into the story early on. Don't give them to the reader in an unpalatable lump; sneak this information into the prose.

▶ Let the reader see the subject.

▶ Let the reader hear the subject speak.

▶ Reveal the subject in action doing whatever it is he or she does.

▶ Put the person into context so the reader can see the environment in which he or she lives and works.

▶ Avoid summary statements about how wonderful or terrible the subject is. Give the reader the information, let the reader meet and get to know the subject. Then let the reader make up his or her mind.

▶ Concentrate on the few most significant or revealing incidents in the subject's life and make sure they add up to a single dominant impression.

An Argument

We often write to persuade, to convince someone else of our views. Arguments can appeal to the emotions or to the mind, or to both. Most written arguments are more effective if they appeal primarily to the mind. The points made and the voice used in appeals to the mind seem more objective and therefore more persuasive than those appealing to the emotions.

Remember:

▶ Argue with information—evidence and documentation—that is accurate and objective.

▶ Double-check every piece of evidence you use. The reader who catches you in one error of fact will mistrust the entire argument.

▶ Be sure you write in a consistent voice appropriate to the subject you are discussing and the reader you are attempting to persuade. Many readers will be persuaded, to some degree, by the authority in the writer's voice as well as the force of the evidence.

▶ Identify your opponent's strongest arguments and dispose of them first. Conclude with your own strongest arguments.

An Opinion

When we are asked—or invite ourselves—to give an opinion we usually roar instead of persuade. We let the "I" carry the day, when the work should be done with information.

Remember:

▶ Be brief. The shorter your statement, the larger your audience.

▶ Make your case with information.

▶ Make your opinion clear, but don't lecture. Converse. Speak as you would to a person of intelligence who has a right to his or her opinion, but who may be persuaded by rational talk.

Literary Analysis

The purpose of literary criticism is not, as many students seem to think, just to prove you've read the book. The purpose is to share an understanding of the book, an evaluation of it, an appreciation of where it fits within a literary tradition. The focus is not on the story as such, but on those matters of meaning and style which you find significant.

Remember:
▶ Make one principal point. Everything in the text should support and develop that point.
▶ Use documentation from the text, from other texts, and from other critics to make your understanding of the text clear.
▶ Don't run all over the landscape trying to cover *every* point and use *every* critical tool. Concentrate on one critical approach.
▶ Make sure your reader knows enough about the work you are examining to understand what you're saying, even if the reader has not read it.
▶ Make sure the reader understands what critical approach you are using and what your principal point is.

An Essay Exam

Most students plunge into an essay exam and splash wildly without thought or purpose. The essay exam is an ideal task on which to use the writing process. Whatever the time limits—two hours, one hour, twenty minutes, even ten—take some time to *collect, order,* and *focus* before you *draft,* and allow some time to *clarify.* This may mean only a minute or two, but it can make the difference between an effective exam answer and a failing one.

Remember:
▶ Read the question twice. Many students fail essay exams because they answer the question they thought was going to be asked, not the one that actually was asked.
▶ Make your answer explicit, and document it with appropriate evidence.
▶ Write clearly and forcefully with specific information.
▶ Read over your question and make corrections neatly and legibly.

A Speech

A speech involves a personal relationship that writing does not; there are considerations of dress (the less sure I am of what I am going to say, the brighter the tie I wear), gestures and body language, enunciation, pace, and inflection.

When speaking, it is a good idea to work from notes and not to read a text, because it takes great art to read a text and make it sound spontaneous and personal.

Speak slowly, for nervousness makes you accelerate your speech. Keep your hands and feet under control so they don't dance about, distracting from what you have to say. Speak loudly, as if you had the confidence you don't. Make eye contact with individual members of the audience.

A speech or talk is usually written, however, before it is spoken, and there are some things you should keep in mind as you construct a speech.

Remember:

▶ The beginning of a speech does not have the impact of a lead in a written text. The speaker has to respond to the introduction and make human contact with the audience. This does not mean that the speaker has to start with a joke: if you're not good at jokes, don't start with one. But at the beginning of a speech you have a chance to demonstrate that you are a human being interested in some of the same concerns as the audience. That should not take long—two or three paragraphs is adequate.

▶ Make sure the audience knows, right after the introduction, what you're talking about.

▶ Establish your knowledge of the subject in a graceful, humorous way, especially if the introduction has failed to do so.

▶ Make each point in your talk clear, repeat it if necessary, and then provide documentation.

▶ Vary the documentation to keep the audience interested and to support each point in an appropriate way. Use anecdotes, quotations, statistics, analogies, and personal experiences, as appropriate.

▶ End on a specific note. Use an anecdote, an example, or a piece of specific documentation so that the audience is left with a solid piece of information in its memory.

A Business Letter

Don't fool around with tricks of language or traditional formalities. You're writing a purposeful letter to a busy person for a clear reason. Write in taut, concrete terms, making it clear what you want to say and what response you hope to achieve.

Remember:

▶ Put the date in the upper right-hand corner.

▶ Put the full name, title, and address of the person you are addressing above the salutation. Be accurate.

▶ Address the person by title and name and avoid sexist salutations such as "Dear Sir" or "Gentlemen."

▶ Make the body of the letter clear and precise, using lists and diagrams if that will help make your case.

▶ Put your name at the bottom right-hand corner of the letter, following a simple "Sincerely"; type your name and sign above it.

▶ Put your address at the top right or bottom left of the letter, if you don't have a printed letterhead. Include your phone number if you want the addressee to respond by telephone.

A Personal Letter

Make it personal. Speak in any way that is appropriate to what you have to say and to the person to whom you are saying it. It may be a letter of sympathy or congratulations, a thank-you note, a chatty keeping-in-touch, a letter home, travel notes during a trip. In every case you should sound natural, the way you would speak if you were with the person to whom you are writing.

A Personal Essay

This form of writing is able to recreate those rare moments in our lives when conversation becomes both witty and insightful. The craft of personal essay writing is so well hidden by its art that the person who starts to write a personal essay often thinks there is no craft at all, and just wanders off. The personal essay always has focus and meaning. Read the master, E. B. White, and analyze one of his essays to see traces of his invisible craft.

Remember:
▶ The personal essay has the quality of conversation. It depends greatly on voice, on language that is so carefully crafted it seems natural. Read aloud and jiggle the language until it flows spontaneously.
▶ Allow humor on the page, or anger, or nostalgia, or any other emotion when it is appropriate. But keep it under control. Give the reader the information so the reader will laugh or cry or itch to act. Don't keep telling your readers what to feel; let them have room to feel—and think—for themselves.
▶ Have a single main point and make sure that no matter how casually the prose may appear to flow, everything in the essay develops or documents that main point.

A Laboratory Report

The laboratory report has a specific purpose: to inform other researchers what you have done so that they can build on your findings. It may be a laboratory in sociology or psychology, engineering or education, physics or chemistry, zoology or botany, but the purpose is the same—to advance our knowledge of our world in a disciplined manner that can be tested and proved, or disproved. Check with your instructor or lab supervisor, or with the published guidelines for laboratory reports in your discipline, and follow the format that is required. If there is no set format, create a pattern that would serve you well if you were a person who wanted to make use of the experimental results your report is presenting.

Remember:
▶ Put the work you are doing, briefly, in a context. Relate it to other experiments or hypotheses and theories.
▶ Make sure the reader understands the reason for the experiment—what you hope to discover.

▶ Make sure the reader understands the method you chose and the reasons you chose it.

▶ Make the results clear and specific.

▶ Identify the significance of each result, the implications of the results, and the questions that need to be answered by further research.

Narrative

Story satisfies a fundamental human need. The cave drawings at Lascaux in France document the observations of man 17,000 years ago. We know that long before written history man was telling stories to bring order to the disorder of the world. Observe any child and you will recognize the need to tell stories and to listen to stories. In a sense every piece of writing, even nonfiction, has an imbedded narrative. The reader reads to find out what comes next.

Remember:

▶ Start as near the end as possible. The biggest mistake every writer makes is to write what Donald Graves calls the "breakfast-to-bed" story, in which everything the child did during the day is given equal space and importance—peanut butter on toast ranks with the capturing of the whale. The experienced writer of narrative distorts time, and gives space to those parts of the narrative that must be developed fully.

▶ Pay attention to cause and effect. Each action in a narrative is motivated, in the sense that it comes from somewhere, even if that somewhere is irrational craziness. The narrative moves forward on a chain of action and reaction.

▶ The narrative takes place in an environment, and that setting should be described in details that are woven through the text.

▶ Characters are the most memorable element in narrative most of the time. The people in narrative should be revealed in action, and they should interact with each other.

▶ The narrator should be at the right place to see what is happening. The narrator may be a participant—the "I"—or an observer. The writer needs to know where the narrator is—where the camera is—and then should work toward getting out of the way so the reader is not aware of the writer, but only of the story that is being revealed.

▶ Narrative should have significance. It should have a single principal meaning. This meaning should not be told to the reader but revealed to the reader through the story.

Fiction

Writing a short story or a novel is the art of making up an untrue story to reveal a Truth. It is a lie that becomes true when it is told. Fiction allows us to go within the minds and souls of our characters and reveal what they do, think, and feel—and why. Next to poetry it is the highest form of literary art, and great fun to write.

Remember:

▶ Fiction most often starts with character, and is most often remembered because of character. "I never started from ideas but always from character," said Ivan Turgenev. Neil Simon agrees: "Dialogue surprises me. Dialogue comes last. I think of characters first." Get one person walking on your page, then have that person bump into another person. Out of their action and reaction comes drama. The characters should be seen and heard, revealed.

▶ Build your fiction with scenes, where the action is onstage and the characters are reacting to each other. Most beginning fiction writers make the mistake of presenting a lone character mumbling about an action that has taken place before, offstage. Write the central scenes and let the story build on them.

▶ Place. Have the story take place in the world by using background details that support and illuminate the principal actions.

▶ Plot implies a formula, but most stories that work grow out of the actions and reactions of the characters within the story. The writer watches and listens as the characters act out their own story, and records what they do.

A Play, TV Script, or Movie

Writing fiction that is to be observed rather than read is a demanding discipline. Most of the time this is showing rather than telling, in its most sophisticated form.

Remember:

▶ Dialogue is usually the way in which the significant action that moves the drama forward takes place. It is helpful to remember that dialogue is not talk but action: it is what people do to each other and that sets off further reaction.

▶ Dialogue approximates speech. It is casual, colloquial; most of all it is built on the knowledge that the characters speaking to each other have in common. The inexperienced writer tries to drag exposition in with dialogue— "When I spent that weekend with you last summer at Aunt Naomi's cabin, it was apparent that you cared for waterskiing more than you cared for me"— that real people would never say to each other. They both know about that weekend:

"All you were interested in was waterskiing."
"Until your bikini busted."

Note that each time a person speaks you start a new paragraph.

▶ Write scenes in which something happens between characters. A question is answered—will they go off on another weekend?—and a question is asked—will it be another disaster?

▶ As much as possible the writer should not try to tell the actor how to perform. The dialogue itself should force the actor to be angry, impatient, cute, nasty, scheming.

Travel

Most people who write an account of their travels merely catalogue what they have done, and the reader is subjected to an unedited slide show. Effective travel writing gives the reader the experience of taking the trip.

Remember:
▶ Distort time as you do in narrative. Give more time to describing what happened when the grizzly got into the car with Uncle Joe than what happened when you stopped for a cup of coffee at Ivanhoe Falls and were shortchanged thirty-seven cents.
▶ Take adequate time and space to develop those anecdotes and scenes that deserve development.
▶ Include your observations and reactions, but emphasize the details that caused those thoughts and feelings.
▶ Make sure that everything you say about the trip adds up to a single overall meaning. The trip must have a purpose for the reader beyond the fact that you went to visit Ninnie and Nannie at Oak Corners and returned.

Humor

Good luck. Humor can't be taught by a teacher or commanded by an editor. It can only be encouraged. It has to *be* natural as well as appear natural.

Remember:
▶ Humor comes more from the point of view of the writer than from contrived situations or artificial gag lines. We enjoy and need humorists, because they see the ordinary in our world in an extraordinary and insightful way.
▶ Humor has meaning that reveals the world. It is always serious at base, and idealistic. It shows us what is, compared to what ought to be.
▶ Underplay. Most humor, even zany humor, has discipline. Everything is under control even when it seems spontaneous.
▶ Give the reader room to look in the direction you're pointing, and to laugh. Don't say so much that the reader has no space in which to observe and laugh. The humorist's job is to initiate another way of looking at the world.

A Case History

The purpose of a case history is to document the changes in a person that occur because of medical treatment, institutionalization, psychiatric conditions, teaching methods, and so forth. It is also one of those forms of writing designed to serve someone in a specific discipline. Follow a professional pattern required by the discipline, or role-play the person using the case history and satisfy that person's needs.

Remember:
▶ Describe the subject with the specific details appropriate to the use to which the case history is being put. The details should be accurate and precise.
▶ Make sure the reader knows the purpose of the case study—the treatment or condition that is being examined.

▶ Describe the subject during the course of the study in chronological detail, being specific about changes that occurred during the course of the study.

▶ Evaluate the study and put its significance in context.

▶ Make appropriate recommendations for further treatment or research.

A Description

One of the most important services writing can perform is to describe. It can record a physical process or a thought process, capture an event, reveal a person, place, theory, or idea. Writing description has a side benefit for the author, for the more you describe the more you see.

Remember:

▶ Effective description has a dominant impression that is similar to a focal point in a photograph or a painting. Inexperienced describers simply catalogue, or move from right to left, or top to bottom, or near to far. The effective description is created from details that all lead toward or away from a dominant impression.

▶ Precise, concrete pieces of information are the raw material of effective descriptions. The reader's hunger for descriptive details is almost insatiable.

▶ Whenever possible make the description active, not static. Show a person in action, put the reader in movement through the scene. Describe something happening as a way of revealing a person, place, or event. Descriptions of thinking should also be active. The reader should be taken along on a trip within the mind as problems are defined and solved, theories proved or disproved, ideas developed and challenged.

Minutes or a Secretary's Report

Performing such tasks can be a pain, but can also make you much more aware of what is going on. And making a record of significant information can put you in a position of considerable power.

Remember:

▶ Keep taking notes during the entire meeting. Identify who said what, and record the actual votes and decisions made.

▶ Write up the minutes as soon after the meeting as possible, while your memory is fresh.

▶ Use a form that seems natural and serves the needs of the group. But make sure that at the top it is clear what group is meeting, when they met, who was present, and who was absent. Then sign your name at the bottom.

A Proposal

The ability to write can put a person in a position of power in any institution. One example is the writing of proposals asking for money, a new position, a change in policy, or other forms of support.

Remember:
▶ Make clear immediately what you want. Many proposals I have read while working as an administrator and on review panels and committees lost out because it was not clear exactly what the people making the proposals wanted.

▶ Avoid jargon or other forms of private language that will be unclear to those reviewing the proposals who are not in your area—and perhaps to some who are. Speak in clear, simple prose.

▶ Don't make obviously inflated promises. Just say what you want to do and why.

▶ If money is involved don't duck the issue. Say how much you need and for what.

A Term Paper

A term paper—or a master's thesis, or a doctoral dissertation—is a difficult form and a rather unique one, because you're writing for a small audience, usually just one person, that knows the subject better than you do. And it is also difficult because of the myths that have gathered around this kind of writing. Try to avoid the legends and the myths and just tell what you know about the subject as clearly as possible.

Remember:
▶ Discover the specific traditional devices involving footnoting, organization, bibliography, and style that you are required to follow, and follow them.

▶ Put your notes aside and write a draft as fast as possible. What you remember will most likely be what you should remember; and what you forget is probably what should be forgotten.

▶ Write early so that the writing will tell you what you know and what you need to know—then you'll have time to fill the holes that will appear in the draft.

▶ Use a test reader to help you get distance on the subject. Term papers should be the result of such intense research involvement that it is difficult to get perspective and to know if what you are saying is clear to a reader.

▶ Develop an opinion. A term paper is not just a vacuum-cleaner bag full of what you have researched. It should have a point of view; it should be a demonstration of thought based on research.

Questions about Ordering

What if I'm working on a lead and I think it might make an ending?

Make a note in the margin beside it, "end?" Or make a note in your "end" file. This often happens, and you shouldn't let the idea get away. Good leads often make good endings, and the other way around.

What if the leads won't come?

Switch around and try titles or outlines. Try any of the other ordering strategies. You can outline first and then go back and write titles or leads. Endings can come before beginnings. Go with what works.

I do all this stuff in my head—why do I have to write it down?

You don't. If you do it in your head and your writing is well organized, don't do it. There are people who never write down outlines, and others who only do it when they face a new and difficult writing task—writing about a complex, unfamiliar story; trying to appeal to a new audience; writing in a different form than they are used to. If your writing works well follow the process that is succeeding. If you're having problems writing well, then try some of the techniques proposed in the text.

How can I do all this planning when I've got to write the paper tonight?

Planning helps you write more efficiently and more quickly. If you have an hour, take five or ten minutes to collect the information with which you'll be writing. Take a few more minutes to make sure you have the focus, and then a few minutes to put the information in order. If you take ten minutes for each of those tasks you'll only have invested half an hour. You'll have twenty minutes to write and ten minutes to check over what you've written. The planning will make your draft quicker, often longer, and better.

Do you have to follow the outline?

Of course not. It isn't a legal contract; it's merely a sketch or a plan. It is a tool to help you. Writing isn't completed thought written down; writing is thinking. The draft should change under your hand. It will teach you about the subject. When you're writing best you are often writing what you did not expect to write. Remember John Fowles's counsel: "Follow the accident, fear the fixed plan—that is the rule."

Ordering Activities

1. Look through half a dozen magazines and write down the article titles that make you want to read. Do the same thing with book titles in a library or bookstore. Work alone or in a group to decide what the qualities of a good title are.
2. Share your idea for a piece of writing with another person in the class or with a small group; then write titles for each other. Write new titles for textbooks or pieces of literature you are reading.
3. See how many titles you can write for the piece you're working on. Do at least twenty. Do them quickly, in small chunks of time.
4. Find ten leads, for articles, stories in magazines or newspapers, or chapters in books, that make you want to read. Share them with others and decide what elements they have in common.

5. Collect by yourself or with others fifty to a hundred good leads and list the different techniques used by these successful lead writers.
6. Write ten new leads, taking no more than five minutes a lead, for something you've just read.
7. Write at least twenty-five leads for the piece of writing you're working on.
8. Look back at pieces of writing you've read recently or that you consider good and list the techniques the writers used.
9. Share the idea you're working on with others and draft endings for each other.
10. Take a piece of writing you've read and see how many different ways you can end it.
11. Draft as many endings as you can—at least twenty-five—for the piece of writing you're working on.
12. Take a piece of writing you like and write down the three to five principal points that are made in it.
13. Share your subject with someone else and write down, for each other, the main points that will be made and the order in which they'll have to be made.
14. Sketch out ten different sequences that might be used to get you from one of your leads to one of your endings. (What if the sequence reveals you need a new lead, a new ending, or both? Good. That's one of the reasons to play with sequence.)
15. Design your own outline form and share it with others who are sharing theirs with you.
16. Outline your piece at least five different ways.

5

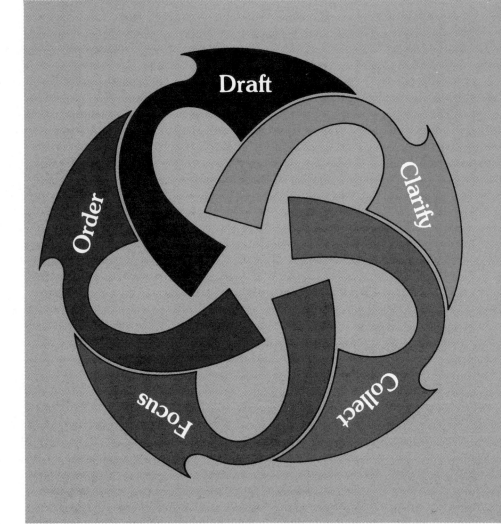

Draft

There are some kinds of writing that you have to do very fast, like riding a bicycle on a tightrope.

William Faulkner

I try to write without consulting my material; this avoids interruption and prevents me from overloading my text with quotations. In this way, I establish a comfortable distance from the mass and pressure of data. It helps the narrative flow; it is a guard against irrelevancy.

Leon Edel

The language leads, and we continue to follow where it leads.

Wright Morris

It never gets easier to write. All writers are masters of avoidance. If there are no interruptions they create them. They make phone calls, travel far on unnecessary errands, cut wood in July, buy a snow shovel in August. When it is time to write, writers read, attack the correspondence and the filing, sharpen pencils, buy new pens, change the typewriter ribbon, shop for a word processor, make coffee, make tea, rearrange the furniture in the office. When writers get together they often, shamefaced, share new ways to avoid writing.

But some of that avoidance is good. E. B. White reminds us, "Delay is natural to a writer. He is like a surfer—he bides his time, waits for the perfect wave on which to ride in. Delay is instinctive with him." This waiting is purposeful, for most writers discover that starting a draft prematurely causes a total collapse three, five, or seven pages along, and it's harder to pick up the pieces and repair a train wreck of a draft than to start one along the right track.

Writers, of course, being writers, are never sure whether they are allowing their subject to ripen properly or are just being lazy. This waiting is often the worst part of writing. It is filled with guilt and doubt, yet it is essential.

A Checklist for Writing Readiness

Experienced writers usually find that there are six elements that produce the essential ripeness. They don't come in any particular order, and sometimes not all of them are present before an effective draft begins. But it may be helpful to go over this checklist. If you have these elements in hand you are usually ready to write.

▶ *Information*   Frank Lloyd Wright declared, "God is in the details." And an abundance of accurate, specific details is what the writer needs at the moment of creating a first draft. Experienced writers have learned the impossibility of building an effective piece of work without information and prefer to have an inventory of detail far greater than they will ever be able to use.

▶ *Concept*   Writers are great guessers. Anton Chekhov explained, "An artist observes, selects, guesses, and combines." Most writers will not begin a draft until they have some idea of what their writing may mean. Sometimes it is as firm as a thesis, but many times it is just a hint, a shape seen in the fog, an educated guess. It may be something that can't be placed in words; that's all right, the final piece of writing will *be* the meaning. But the writer will not proceed with a draft until a potential meaning can be guessed from the material.

▶ *Problem*   Again and again as we study creative people, we discover that they see problems that others do not see, and they delight in solving them. Diane Wakoski says, "I think that poetry is an act of problem solving, which means that if there are no problems to solve there is no poetry to be written." Usually the writer has a problem of meaning, a problem of form, a problem of audience, a problem of language to be solved through the writing. Sometimes there is more than one problem, but this doesn't keep the writer from writing. In fact, most writers write a draft as a way of solving the problem or problems they perceive.

    ▶ **Form**   Writers, as we saw in the last chapter, may have a rough sketch of the form their writing will take, or a detailed blueprint. But few writers proceed into a draft without a sense of where they are going. Ernest J. Gaines says, "A novel is like getting on a train for Louisiana. All you know at the moment is that you're getting on the train, and you're going to Louisiana. But you don't know who you're going to sit behind, or in front of, or beside; you don't know what the weather is going to be when you pass through certain areas of the country; you don't know what's going to happen south; you don't know all these things, but you know you're going to Louisiana."

    ▶ **Need**   Effective writing is usually the result of the writer's need. Sometimes the writer has an internal need; something has to be gotten rid of by writing. As Jean Rhys said, "I wrote because it relieved me." The writer has an itch that has to be scratched, or the urge to persuade, educate, entertain, or explain. Or the writer may have, instead, an external need—an assignment, a need to make money, a need to get promoted and get tenure, a need for fame or attention, a need to answer a question from a reader. It doesn't make much difference if the need is internal or external, but few writers will begin a draft until they convince themselves, one way or another, that the draft is needed.

    ▶ **Voice**   Few writers will plunge into a draft until they have a sense— in the ear—of how the draft may sound. Each piece of writing must have its own consistent and appropriate voice. There is further discussion of the importance of voice later in this chapter. The writer may have the voice worked out in detail, or may just have a fragment or two of voice on the page. But few writers know how to proceed into a draft until they have a sense of how the draft will speak to the reader.

    If the writer is working on those elements, and if there is time before the deadline, then the hesitation before starting the draft may be appropriate. However, if the writer has some sense of each of these elements, then it's time to get writing.

Twenty-Six Ways to Start Writing

A promise: If you write until your hair's white, your eyes make the print blur, and your hands tremble on the typewriter keys, it will still be hard to start writing.

    Writing reveals us to ourselves and eventually to others, and we do not want to be exposed on the page. The writing is never as good as we hoped, so it is natural that we resist this exposure. We have to find ways to get over this understandable psychological hurdle, this normal stage fright before the blank page.

Writing is also a commitment. Once we have put down one line, sometimes just one word, we have made a choice, and the direction of our writing, its limits, its pace, its dimensions, its voice, its meaning are all constrained. Everything is not possible, and we face the realities of making meaning with language.

The process approach described in this book is itself an attempt to get us writing in a normal way. We collect material, focus it, and order it. At least 60 percent of our time and effort is spent in planning and preparation for writing so that we will be ready, often eager, to make a run at the blank page. If we aren't ready to write it may mean that we need to go back to collect, focus, or order.

Experienced writers, however, still find it hard to get started writing. Here are some of the tricks they use:

1. *Make Believe You Are Writing a Letter to a Friend* Put "Dear _____" at the top of the page and start writing. Tom Wolfe did this on one of his first New Journalism pieces. He wrote the editor a letter saying why he couldn't write the piece he'd been assigned. The letter flowed along in such a wonderful, easy fashion that the editor took the salutation off and ran it. It established a new style for contemporary journalism.

2. *Switch Your Writing Tools* If you normally type, write by hand. If you write by hand, type. Switch from pen to pencil or pencil to pen. Switch from unlined paper to lined paper, or vice versa. Try larger paper or smaller, colored paper or white paper. Use a bound notebook or a spiral notebook, a legal pad or a clipboard. Tools are a writer's toys, and effective, easy writing is the product of play.

3. *Talk about the Piece of Writing with Another Writer, and Pay Close Attention to What You Say* You may be telling yourself how to write the piece. You may even want to make notes as you talk on the telephone or in person. Pay attention to words or combinations of words that may become a voice and spark a piece of writing.

4. *Write Down the Reasons You Are Not Writing* Often when you see the problem you will be able to avoid it. You may realize that your standards are too high, or that you're thinking excessively of how one person will respond to your piece, or that you're trying to include too much. Once you have defined the problem you may be able to dispose of it.

5. *Describe the Process You Went Through When a Piece of Writing Went Well* You may be able to read such an account in your journal. We need to reinforce the writing procedures that produce good writing. A description of what worked before may tell us that we need to delay at this moment, or it may reveal a trick that got us going another time. We should keep a careful record of our work habits and the tricks of our trade, so that we have a positive resource to fall back on.

6. Interview Other Writers to Find Out How They Get Started   Try your classmates' tricks and see if they work for you.

7. Make Writing a Habit   For years I started every day by putting a pocket timer on for fifteen minutes and writing before I had a cup of coffee. Now the timer's not necessary. When writing, any kind of writing, is a normal activity it's much easier to start on a particular writing project. You are used to spoiling clean paper the same way joggers are used to wearing out running shoes.

8. Switch the Time of Day   I tried to write this chapter just before noontime. Nothing. Well, not nothing, just the first paragraph and a feeling of total hopelessness. Now it is early morning the next day and the writing is perking. Sometimes writing at night when you are tired lowers your critical sense in a positive way, and other times you can jump out of bed in the morning and get a start on the writing before your internal critic catches up with you.

9. Call the Draft an Experiment or an Exercise   All my courses are experimental, so I don't have to worry too much about failing as a teacher—failure is normal during experiments—and I'm ready to try new ways to teach. Good writing is always an experiment. Make a run at it. See if it will work. The poet Mekeel McBride is always writing "exercises" in her journals. Since they are just exercises and not poems she doesn't have to get uptight about them, but of course if an exercise turns into a poem she'll accept it.

10. Dictate a Draft   Use a tape recorder, and then transcribe it from that. You may want to transcribe it carefully, or just catch the gist of what you had to say. No matter how experienced we are as writers we are a million times more experienced as speakers, and it's often easier to get started writing by talking than by simply writing.

11. Quit   Come back later and try again. You can't force writing. You have to keep making runs at it. Come back ten minutes later, or later that day, or the next day. Keep trying until the writing flows so fast you have to run along behind it trying to keep up.

12. Read   Some writers read over what they've written, and they may even edit it or recopy it as a way of sliding into the day's writing. I can't do that; I despair too much, and when I read my own writing I feel I have to start over again; it's worthless, hopeless. If you don't feel that way, however, it may be a good device to go over the previous day's work and then push on to the new writing, the way an experienced house painter will paint back into the last brush stroke and then draw the new paint forward.

13. Write Directly to a Reader   The too-critical reader can keep us from writing, but we can also get writing by imagining an especially appreciative reader, or a reader who needs the information we have to convey. If we can feel that reader's hunger for what we have to say it will draw us into the text. Sometimes as I have been writing this book, I must confess, I've imagined the enjoyment I expect Don Graves, Chip Scanlan, or Nedah Abbott to feel at an unexpected turn of phrase, a new insight, or a different approach. I read their faces as I write the way I read and speak to friendly faces in an audience.

14. Take a Walk, Lift Weights, Jog, Run, Dance, Swim Many writers have found that the best way to get started writing is by getting the blood coursing through the body and the brain. As they get their physical body tuned up their brain starts to get into high gear. Exercise is also the kind of dumb, private activity that allows the mind to free itself of stress and interruption and rehearse what may be written when the exercise is done.

15. Change the Place Where You Write I write in my office at home, but I also write on a lap desk in the living room or on the porch. I like to take the car and drive down by Great Bay, where I can look up from my lap desk and watch a heron stalk fish or a seagull soar—the way I would like to write, without effort. Some writers cover their windows and write to a wall. I like to write to a different scene. Right now, for example, I'm looking at the green ocean of Indiana farmland and a marvelously angry gray sky as I drive west and write by dictation. In the 1920s writers thought the cafés of Paris were the best places to write. I don't think I could work on those silly little tables, but my ideal writing place would be in a booth in a busy lunchroom where nobody knows me. Yesterday morning I started writing in a Denny's in a city in Michigan; it was a fine place to write. When my writing doesn't go well I move around. I imagine that the muse is looking for me, and if it can't find me at home I'll go out somewhere where I may be more visible.

16. Draw a Picture, in Your Mind or on Paper Take a photograph. Cut a picture from a magazine and put it on your bulletin board. When small children start writing they usually first draw a picture. They do on paper what experienced writers usually do in their mind—they visualize the subject. Last summer I started my writing sessions by making a sketch of a rubber tree that stands on our porch. I wasn't writing about the rubber tree, but the activity of drawing seemed to help me get started and stimulated the flow of writing.

17. Free Write Write as hard and as fast and free as you can. See if language will lead you towards a meaning. As I have said before, free writing isn't very free, for the text starts to develop its own form and direction. But the act of writing freely is one of the techniques that can unleash your mind.

18. Stop in the Middle of a Sentence This is a good trick when the writing is going well and you are interrupted or come to the end of the day's writing during a long project. Many well-known writers have done this, and I've found that it really helps me at times. If I can pick up the draft and finish an ordinary sentence, then I am immediately back into the writing. If I've stopped at the end of a sentence or a paragraph it's much harder to get going. And if I've stopped at the end of a chapter it may take days or weeks to get the next chapter started.

19. Write the Easy Parts First   If you're stuck on a section or a beginning, skip over it and write the parts of the draft that you are ready to write. Once you've got those easy, strong pieces of writing done then you'll be able to build a complete draft by connecting those parts. A variation on this is to write the end first, as I've suggested in other parts of the text, or to plunge in and grab the beast wherever you can get hold of it. Once you have a working text you can extend it backwards or forwards as it requires.

20. Be Silly   You're not writing anyway, so you might as well make a fool of yourself. I've numbered the day's quota of pages and then filled them in. One of my writer neighbors loves cigars, but he won't let himself have a cigar until he finishes his daily quota. Reward yourself with a cup of coffee or a dish of ice cream, or a handful of nuts. It is no accident that some writers are fat; they keep rewarding themselves with food. Do whatever you have to do to keep yourself writing. Jessamyn West writes in bed the first thing in the morning. If the doorbell rings she can't answer it; she isn't up and dressed. Use timers, count pages, count words (you may not be able to say the writing went well, but you'll be able to say "I did 512 words," or "I completed two pages"), play music, write standing up (Thomas Wolfe wrote on the top of an icebox, Ernest Hemingway put his typewriter on a bureau), start the day writing in the bathtub as Nabokov did. Nothing is silly if it gets you started writing.

21. Start the Writing Day by Reading Writing that Inspires You   This is dangerous for me, because I may get so interested in the reading I'll never write, or I'll pick up the voice of another writer. I can't, for example, read William Faulkner when I'm writing fiction: a poor New Hampshire imitation of that famous Mississippian is not a good way to go. The other day, however, when I couldn't get started writing I read a short story by Mary Gordon, one of my favorite authors. Reading a really good writer should make you pack up your pen and quit the field, but most of us find reading other writers inspiring. I put down Mary Gordon's short story and was inspired to write.

22. Read What Other Writers Have Written about Writing   I may not write as well as they do, but we work at the same trade, and it helps me to sit around and chat with them. You may want to start a "commonplace book," an eighteenth-century form of self-education in which people made their personal collections of wise or witty sayings. I've collected what writers have said about writing in my own commonplace book, which has now grown to twenty-four three-inch-thick notebooks. Some of my favorite quotes from that collection appear before each chapter in this book as well as in the text. I find it comforting to hear that the best writers have many of the same problems I do and browse through these quotes as a way of starting writing.

23. Break Down the Writing Task into Reasonable Goals   A few years ago I watched on TV as the first woman to climb a spectacular rock face in California made it to the top. It had taken her days, and as soon as she got over the edge a TV reporter stuck a microphone in her face and asked her what she'd thought of as she kept working her way up the cliff. She said she kept reminding herself that you eat an elephant one bite at a time. You also write a long piece of writing one page, or one paragraph, at a time. John Steinbeck said, "When I face the desolate impossibility of writing 500 pages a sick sense of failure falls on me and I know I can never do it. Then I gradually write one page and then another. One day's work is all I can permit myself to contemplate." If you contemplate a book you'll never write it, but if you write just a page a day you'll have a 365-page draft at the end of a year. If you're stuck, you may be trying to eat an elephant at one gulp. It may be wiser to tell yourself that you'll just get the first page, or perhaps just the lead, done that day. That may seem possible, and you'll start writing.

24. Put Someone Else's Name on It   I've been hired as a ghostwriter to create a text for politicians or industrialists. I've had little trouble writing when someone else's name is on the work. Most of the time when I can't write I'm excessively self-conscious. Sometimes I've put a pseudonym on a piece of work and the writing has taken off.

25. Delegate the Writing to Your Subconscious   Often I will tell my subconscious what I'm working on, and then I'll do something that doesn't take intense concentration and allows my subconscious mind to work. I walk around bookstores or a library, watch a dull baseball game or movie on TV, take a nap, go for a walk or a drive. Some people putter around the house or work in the garden. Whatever you do, you're allowing your mind to work on the problem. Every once in a while a thought, an approach, a lead, a phrase, a line, or a structure will float up to the conscious mind. If it looks workable then go to your writing desk; if it doesn't shove it back down underwater and continue whatever you're doing until something new surfaces.

26. Listen   Alice Walker says, "If you're silent for a long time, people just arrive in your mind." As Americans we are afraid of silence, and I'm guilty too. I tend to turn on the car radio if I'm moving the car twenty feet from the end of the driveway into the garage. One of the best ways to get started writing is to do nothing. Waste time. Stare out the window. Try to let your mind go blank. This isn't easy, as those who have tried meditation know. But many times our minds, distracted by trivia, are too busy to write. Good writing comes out of silence, as Charles Simic says. "In the end, I'm always at the beginning. Silence—an endless mythical condition. I think of explorers setting out over an unknown ocean. . . ." We have to cultivate a quietness, resist the panic that the writing won't come, and allow ourselves to sink back into the emptiness. If we don't fight the silence, but accept it, then usually, without being aware of it, the writing will start to come.

These are some ways to get writing. You will come up with others if you make a list of techniques from other parts of your life that may apply here. A theater major may have all sorts of exercises and theater games that can spark writing. A scientist will be able to apply techniques of setting up experiments to setting up the experiment of writing. Art majors know how to attack a white canvas, and ski team members know how to shove off at the top of a steep slope. Keep a record of methods of starting writing that work for you. The more experienced you become, the harder it may be to start writing, but you will also have developed more ways of starting words down a page.

Writing the Draft

When starting to write it is wise to remember that all writing is an experiment in meaning—and that most experiments fail. You have to try to write to discover what you have to say, and then read it afterward to see whether it is working or not. One of my friends, Chip Scanlan, one of the best writers on the Providence (Rhode Island) *Journal-Bulletin,* keeps reminding himself, "You have to write badly to write well."

Lower Your Standards

Some writers suffer that terrible paralysis of the pen called writer's block. Its principal cause is inappropriate standards. The writer wants to write better than the writer can at that moment. The writer is producing for someone else who has a critical eye, or for the writer's own too-critical eye. William Stafford offers the best antidote for writer's block: "I believe that the so-called 'writing block' is a product of some kind of disproportion between your standards and your performance. . . . One should lower his standards until there is no felt threshold to go over in writing. It's *easy* to write. You just shouldn't have standards that inhibit you from writing."

Lowering your standards may sound like poor advice, but it isn't. The standards can be raised after you have produced the draft. For the moment you have to follow de Maupassant's advice and "get black on white." There will be another draft if you need it; there will be a chance to read, edit, and revise.

This means, of course, that you have to set early deadlines, deadlines ahead of your deadlines, so that you can pace yourself and have time for rereading, reconsideration, and rewriting. And it helps to write early. By drafting what you hope you will be able to say you will discover what you need to know, as well as what you know.

Write Fast

When drafting, write fast. The faster the better. Language should carry you forward towards meaning. At times it will almost feel as if you are out of control. William Faulkner described this feeling when he said, "A writer writing is like a man building a chicken coop in a high wind. He grabs onto any board he can and nails it down fast."

When the writing is going well it is almost automatic writing for me. I dictate, or scribble, or hack away at the typewriter with two wildly dancing fingers. I'm not aware, consciously, of what I've just said or what I'm going to say. In fact, I'm not really aware of what I am saying. I'm just moving forward as fast as I can. I am not thinking about writing, I am writing.

Not everybody writes this way, and not everybody should write this way. There are writers who carve their copy out of stone, making each word, line, paragraph, and page right before they move on. But they're in the minority. Most of us have to write fast, have to write badly to write well.

Write Without Notes

It's a good idea to put your notes aside before you start to write the draft. You've done the collecting and the focusing and the ordering. The important thing now is what's in your head, not what's on the paper. Too often writers become bound by their notes, and they write a draft that is really a transcription of their notes. It is usually dull prose that is clogged with excessive, indiscriminate information.

Sometimes you may have to take a quick glance at your notes. I'm writing this while driving a car west on Route 80, dictating to my wife, who is typing on a lap desk. Once in a while I peek at my scribbled notes, I admit, but I'm going down the highway at sixty-two miles an hour, and I certainly can't read my notes and survive.

There are tricks which help you to write fast. When I worked on *Time* Magazine and came to a statistic or a quote that wasn't handy I put in the capital letters "TK" to indicate that that information was to come. I had left blanks for the Stafford and Faulkner quotes in this chapter, for example. I don't have a good memory; I remember enough to know I want to use the quotes, but I certainly can't quote them accurately, so I leave a blank I'll fill in when I get back to the office.

Write with Information

Effective writing is built from concrete, accurate information. Too many beginning writers think that writing is made with words and literary flourishes that are detached from meaning. Good writing is not a collection of colorful balloons that bob aimlessly against the ceiling. Good writing—poetry as much as non-fiction—delivers information to the reader.

During the writing of the draft the writer should be conscious of the information that is being delivered to the reader, and the writer should try to make that information as abundant and specific as possible. Words, after all, are symbols for information. Words that have no information behind them are as valuable as checks drawn on an account with no money in it.

Readers hunger for information, and the writer should satisfy this hunger by constructing a piece of writing with solid chunks of information.

Show, Don't Tell

The advice "Show, don't tell" is often given in fiction writing, but it is just about as important in nonfiction writing. The skillful writer usually does not tell the reader about the subject, but instead reveals the subject to the reader.

It isn't easy for a writer to learn how to get out of the way. Most beginning writers call attention to themselves rather than the subject. The reader should see the subject and then have the room to make up his or her own mind about it. The most quoted, remembered, and probably influential parts of the Bible are the parables, little stories that tell by showing.

George Orwell said, "Good writing is like a windowpane." The effective writer knows how to get out of the way and let the reader see the subject. When I wrote editorials I often played a secret game. I imagined I was a defense attorney and my client was charged with murder. In my summation to the jury I wanted to be able to say, "I'm not going to tell you how to vote. I'm just going to remind you of the evidence." My editorial was the evidence, as unadorned as possible. I just wanted to reveal the information so that readers would absorb that information and think for themselves—what I wanted them to think.

Some examples of telling and showing are:

Telling: My grandmother was a very brave little girl.
Showing: One day when my grandmother was a little girl she and her friends cut across a pasture on the way home from school. When a bull charged them she turned, got her friends behind her, pulled out her long sewing scissors from her school bag, and stuck them up the nostrils of the bull. He didn't bother them any more.

I don't need an announcing or topic sentence to tell the reader that I'm going to show she was a brave girl, and I don't need a concluding sentence to tell the reader she was a brave girl. What I need to do is to get out of the way. The reader will absorb the evidence, feel sympathy for the bull, and know that my grandmother was a brave little girl.

Select and Develop

The inexperienced writer tries to jam all the information that has been collected into the story. That is not the way good prose is created. When I was at *Time* an editor there used to say, "You can tell a good story by the amount of good stuff that is thrown away."

When a student is asked to write a short paper the student, naturally, tries to compress. And the result is what I call the garbage compactor story. All the information is jammed together into a tiny, unreadable little block.

Brevity is achieved not by compression so much as by selection. The writer has to select the information the reader needs, and then develop it properly. Each anecdote, definition, argument, description—whatever needs to be said— has to be set up and developed adequately so that the reader can experience that part of the story at an appropriate pace, a pace that will allow the reader to absorb the information.

Answer the Reader's Questions

There's a myth that popular writers write down to the reader, that the reader is a slob with a fifth-grade education who picks his teeth with a beer can. Not so. The reader is an intelligent person who may not know the subject, but is no dope.

The reader will ask good, intelligent questions of any piece of writing, and the experienced writer will answer those questions, not by writing down but by writing across to the reader, using a tone of voice the writer would use to an equal.

Sometimes it helps me to imagine a reader sitting across from my desk, sprawled in an armchair, a skeptical, surly doubting Thomas. I make a statement, and my reader snarls, "Who says?" And I stick in an attribution. I say something else, and the reader asks, "How come?" I stop and tell the reader how come. I write another paragraph and the reader says, "What's that mean?" I tell the reader what it means. The reader snarls, "Who cares?" And I make sure the reader knows the importance of what I'm saying.

Other times I imagine a specific person, an individual who is not at all impressed by me or what I know about the subject. And by writing to that person I make my draft clear.

Sometimes we have to write for several very different readers. In that case, I pick one of them and write for that person. In the revision process I will read and revise for each of the other readers. But I must focus on a single reader at a time.

Good writing almost always seems to be a conversation between an individual writer and an individual reader. The writer has to anticipate where the reader is in that conversation and deliver the information the reader needs when the reader needs it.

Sometimes the reader asks so many nasty questions I can no longer write. I get mad at this surly, overly critical baboon who makes me feel dumb and inadequate. When that happens I send him out of the room. I'll deal with him later, after the draft is done, during the last stage of the writing process, when I have to invite him in anyway. He isn't polite about leaving. Sometimes he even makes obscene gestures, and he wears that all-knowing sneer that says, "I'll get you later." Fair enough. I will have to deal with him later, but when I do there will be a text we can read together. If I don't get him out of the room there will be no text at all.

Vary Documentation

Most of us write with the evidence we feel most comfortable using. One writer will always make the point with a quotation from an authority; another will salt the page with statistics; a third will back up each assertion with an anecdote;

still another writer will walk on stage and use an "I" to speak directly to the audience. We have to watch out that we don't always choose the form of evidence with which we are comfortable, instead of using the form of documentation that will most effectively persuade the reader.

Write with Your Ear

Even the most experienced writer speaks a thousand times more than he or she writes. When drafting we should consciously use this oral sense and listen to what we are saying as we say it.

When I visit a newspaper's city room as a consultant on writing, I look around and then I guess who the best writers are. More often than not, the editors think I've made good picks. What did I look for? I looked to see which writers' lips were moving as they wrote. Most writers read aloud when they're writing. Sometimes they speak right out, but usually they have taught themselves to speak under their breath. Their lips, however, betray them.

Conscious reading aloud is especially helpful on the most difficult passages, as the speaking voice tells the writing voice how to make the prose flow.

Writing is not speaking written down, as anyone who has been tape-recorded knows. Effective writing, however, creates the illusion of speech. The flow and music and pace and rhythm and individuality and intimacy and experience of speech has to be created with the written word. And that brings us to the question of voice, the single most important element in writing.

Voice—The Vital Difference

Voice separates writing that is not read from writing that is read. Voice gives a text concern, energy, humor, individuality, music, rhythm, pace, flow, surprise, believability. Voice includes the elements in writing that make it possible for printed marks on a page to become a single human being—a writer—speaking privately to another single human being—a reader.

Voice is language in use, language seeking and achieving meaning and communication. Sometimes people call voice "tone," but that, it seems to me, only relates to one kind of language use. Often we talk about style. But I don't like the term "style," for it has the connotation of something that is external from the writing, that can be bought off the rack and put on.

Voice is the writer revealed. Voice is the character of the writer, and the point of view of the writer towards the subject, the caring of the writer, the honesty of the writer. "The most difficult task for a writer is to get the right 'voice' for his material," says John Fowles. "By voice I mean the overall impression one has of the creator behind what he creates." And Blaise Pascal adds, "When we encounter a natural style we are always surprised and delighted, for we thought to see an author and found a man."

Each of us has his or her own voice. We can tell the step of each member of the family on the stairs in the dark, and we can tell who is speaking without understanding the words or seeing the speaker. Only weeks into a writing course you will know who has written each paper without seeing the name on the paper. Our voice tells the reader how we think, how we feel, how we live, who we are.

We must teach ourselves to recognize our own voice. We want to write in a way that is natural for us, that grows out of the way we think, the way we see, the way we care. But to make that voice effective we must develop it, extending our natural voice through the experience of writing on different subjects for different audiences, of using our voice as we perform many writing tasks.

The Spoken Voice

The question of voice is complicated, but reasonably easy to understand, for we all practice the process of extending and refining our inner voice. This is the voice with which we speak to ourselves, the voice of reverie, the voice we use when we are talking silently to ourselves. One of the most shocking things about visiting a mental hospital is to hear inner voices out loud, uninhibited, streaming forth, confused, searching for meaning. All of us have this voice, or rather these voices, for we talk differently to ourselves when we are angry, when we're trying to solve a problem, when we are preparing an argument, when we are happy, when we are musing.

When we speak aloud it still is *our* voice, it still sounds like us as we select and practice those inflections and pauses and rhythms that are natural to us. But when we speak we have an audience, and our spoken voice is adjusted to that audience. We speak differently—though some of the elements of our voice may be the same—when we go to meet a possible employer than when we chat with an old friend. Our voice will often reveal our tension, our happiness, our anger, our sadness, our anxiety. We use our voice to reinforce our arguments, to make others laugh, to reach out with sympathy, to persuade, to sell, to share.

The Written Voice

Our written voice is still more removed from our inner voice, for it must exist without gesture, expression, body movements, spoken inflection—all the things we normally do to reinforce our speech. We say something that sounds angry, but smile; our friend knows we are teasing. In print the smile will not be there, unless we learn the high skill of placing it there. We write more carefully than we speak to others or to ourselves.

The written voice will be heard by people we will never see. It may even be heard after we are dead. To be effective, it must create the illusion of personal speech. There must be a human being standing behind the page. But we have to achieve that when we know that the reader may be much more critical than any audience to which we will ever speak.

This takes craft and experience. What we attempt to do is to sound natural, to develop a voice for the text which sounds like a human being. I hope that if you met me and heard my speaking voice it would be similar to my written voice in this book. My written voice is natural, in the sense that it is me, but it is not natural in the sense of being spontaneous, unpracticed, accidental. All writers have, through writing, polished their written voice so that it can be adapted to many texts and many tasks—to many readers. It is natural-seeming, I hope. I've spent a lot of time, as you can understand having read this far in the book, on that question of seeming.

The Personal Voice

I will describe my grandmother, using my voice in different ways. First I will write the descriptions, and then comment on what I did to demonstrate how a single voice on a single subject may be varied by the writer.

This is an exercise that you may want to try yourself. Make sure that you limit it. The first time I tried it I wrote off in all directions. I had to back up and pick a very limited area. I couldn't, in other words, just describe my grandmother. To reveal the range of my voice to myself, I had to describe my grandmother on an afternoon when I came home from school and went in to report to her as she lay paralyzed on her bed. Limit your subject and try it yourself. After all, you have many variations on your own voice that you use at home, at school, on the street corner. Demonstrate these variations and discover some others.

I stood at the door of Grandma's room and watched the good right side of her face smiling and nodding, regally. She was visiting Morison in the big house in Heaven, where she was the mill owner's wife again. I waited. She would return to the double-decker behind the Amoco station.

I don't like the tag-along adverb "regally," but it let me see and hear her. Sounds glib, staccato to me. Too much like a superficial journalist.

I watched Grandma from the door of her bedroom. She smiled. She nodded. She spoke in that superior way. Did she really think that Jesus had the big house in North Grafton waiting for her up in Heaven, that when she died she would always be the mill owner's wife?

The short, staccato sentences set up my anger and the sarcastic question. This sarcasm—"superior way"—turns nasty. I sound like a snotty kid.

I remember waiting at the door of Grandma's bedroom on Chester

The first sentence is too abrupt and then I rush on nervously like

Street. I'm angry now—but I was never angry then—that I believed the myth she had made up about herself, that she was a Protestant saint, that no one else could be as good as she was, the myth that castrated her sons, kept my mother a little girl, and made my father ashamed of what he was. She made them all believe they could never measure up to her.

Standing in the doorway of her bedroom I could feel the force from this wonderful woman who had three times crossed the Atlantic, survived the death of a stepdaughter, a husband, and a daughter, survived failure, sent two sons to war, recovered from one stroke, and now, paralyzed on one side, still ran the family.

Others standing in the doorway of Grandma's bedroom might feel pity or embarrassment; I never did. She was too tough to pity, had too much presence to tolerate embarrassment. She was herself.

Grandma never complained. I would stand in the doorway of her bedroom hoping to catch a moan or a complaint so I could help her. But not that tough turkey. She might be paralyzed and she might hurt, but she would never let pain know he had touched her.

I brought my doubts home after church, and would stand with them in the door of Grandma's bedroom.

Grandma's skin hadn't seen sun in ten years and was as pale as the white sheets, the white coverlet, the white pillows, her white hair.

an inexperienced door-to-door salesperson. The awkwardness of the sentences demonstrate my questioning and searching. The litany starts to lead me toward answers. Clumsy writing. Not final draft, but language that is leading me toward meaning.

"Wonderful woman"—cheap alliteration. Soupy. Sounds like a greeting card. I did, however, discover the word "force" by writing it. That's enough to justify this draft paragraph.

Come off it—"never"??? Not true, but there's something to work with here in the phrase "too tough to pity." I hear respect for her in my voice here.

Starts a bit dishonestly, like a realtor pitching a handyman's dream. But the respect and admiration come through in "tough turkey" and the tone of the sentence following.

Nice surprise for me when the doubts are as real as people standing beside me.

A kind of nice spooky feeling here. White is usually spooky. The voice tells me that I feared her too. Falls all apart with the "you." Sounds

You looked for her, trying to find her, and then you felt her dark eyes examining you.

The patient is paralyzed on the left side and confined to bed. The family seems to have kept her clean, although there are bed-sores on her buttocks. The patient is, except for time disorientation, rational.

When I talked to Grandma she would leave in the middle of a sentence, floating up to visit with Morison in the big house in Heaven. She would nod and smile regally, once more the mill own-er's wife. I learned to wait. She would return to the tenement be-hind the Amoco station.

I stood where I could watch Grandma in her bureau mirror without her knowing I was watch-ing her. I never caught her face changing, never found a lack of resolution or faith, never glimpsed the despair I found on my moth-er's face when she didn't think I was watching.

I watched from the hall when one of the uncles came, Alec, Will, or Donald—each different, each the same before the old lady in the bed. Each would hail her, each would be jovial and male hearty, and each grown man would be-come a little boy, home from school reporting to Mother.

Other children knew the Alps or the Rockies, but I was as familiar

like a sickening nurse: "You do want to take your shot, don't you?"

A distant, professional voice. A visiting nurse or social worker? Could it be appropriate, or is it just ho hum?

This builds on the earlier para-graph. I'd still cut "regally" and show her being regal. I like the actions of leaving, floating, waiting, returning. This voice is knowledgeable and accepting— uncritical. More active than be-fore. Maybe it works, maybe I could take the reader with me. Sounds as if a sympathetic grandson could say this to an-other family member in a hos-pital waiting room.

"Nevers" are awful and my voice is unsure, but it is leading me towards a nice piece about the kind of spying kids do, watching the grownups with whom they live, catching the grownups un-awares. (That might be a sepa-rate piece.)

False jovial, false hearty is im-plied in the voice without saying it right out. I like that. Does my voice capture their false-cheery, apprehensive voices?

Pompous. Sounds like a college president at commencement.

with the mountains and valleys of Grandmother's white covers, knew the ever-changing contours of her feet, her knees, her belly under the covers, as almost hourly she slid down the bed. The mountains are moving but you can never see them move, and I never caught a glimpse of Grandma moving in her hourly slide towards the foot of the bed.

That cranky old woman in the bed was our Hitler. There was no democracy in this family. Mother, Father, uncles, and I, all children.

Her windows would be wide open in the summer, and when the lace curtains hung unmoving she would take a great bamboo fan in her right hand and slowly fan herself. I would go in, take the fan from her and wave it wildly until her hair would blow in my breeze and she would laugh.

I'm filled with a sad happiness when I see in my memory's eye how the dappled shadows of the broad-leafed maple lay across her white coverlet, blurred by the lace curtains. I can feel that gentle light in the room, soft on my skin today.

Grandma had crossed the ocean three times, moved from farmer's cottage to London mansion to mill owner's house to worker's tenement, back and forth, and now was prisoned for life in this small bed.

Grandma was evil with goodness. Her strength made her children weak, her certainty made them doubt, her virtue was always be-

Doesn't work, but there is workable material here, and wonder in the voice that could be developed the way you bring up an enlargement in the darkroom.

From "cranky"—a loaded word, but honest-sounding—the voice leads me to one of the ways I felt about Grandma. And perhaps a true vision of the family.

This, for me, is almost pure voice. Nostalgic. I am there again as the tone starts slowly and accelerates. Sounds like a kid, a bit fresh but okay.

Unctuous, the sappy mortician, all practiced sympathy. This is almost all tonal: "dappled, shadows, blurred, gentle, soft." The voice puts me there at a special time, in a special mood. I feel I could work on this so the reader would feel that too.

Too remote. Sounds like a term paper. But still an interesting try. It's shorthand and would have to be translated for the reader. But I feel potential in the word "prisoned."

A bit slick—the professional player-with-words. That phrase in the first sentence does, however, set me off. I probably

yond their reach. I think she knew this and gloried in it.

wouldn't lead with it so baldly in the final version; I'd set it up so the reader discovered it. But there is a strong, critical tone that tells me one way I could write about her.

Looking back, I realize Grandmother was not so much a prisoner of disease as she was a prisoner of being a Scot, a Scottish Baptist who proudly out-Calvinized the Presbyterians, and a woman who had responsibility without power. She tried for eighty-eight years to be what she had been taught to be: a lady of propriety, a Christian worthy of being elect, a member of the middle class, a stern, righteous, hard-working, responsible person who would never reveal fear, emotion, or doubt.

And here my voice tells me to be understanding—and how to be understanding. I am not so much thinking this as listening to my voice tell me to think about it.

When I look at the "me" generation I think of Grandma. She was of the "them" generation. She lived according to what "they" said. And "they" were the Scottish people, especially Highlanders; Christians, especially Baptists; and the family.

Now I'm playing with voice—the voice of my time with the voice of her time. Fun. Might be an op ed essay in this.

To understand what I was doing in the paragraphs above you must realize that there was no planning, no calculating, no conscious thinking before the writing of each paragraph. The best analogy, I suppose, is jazz improvisation.

I brought my own voice or style, as the jazz musician does, to the session. And I also brought, of course, all my experience. But at the time of writing I tried to put it aside and let the voice lead me. I respect voice and try to follow it, for I know it is the great central intangible in writing. Without voice there is no writing.

The Academic Voice

The voice I used in the previous examples is a personal voice appropriate to the subject. There are, of course, other voices, voices that are more professional. There are the voices used by the corporation and the government agency, the voice of the military and the voice of the church, the voice of the lawyer and the voice of the doctor, and there is also the voice that you will use most in school, the academic voice.

There are several elements of the academic or professional voice that you should consider in adapting your own voice to these more professional purposes. They are:

▶ *Appeal to Reason*   In academic discourse the writer appeals to the intellect. The arguments are objective, arguments that would appeal to the mind, and the tone is rational. It is the voice of an intellectual speaking to an intellectual. It is easy to call this tone stuffy, and sometimes it is, but it doesn't have to be, and in fact should not be. In academic writing writer and reader are speaking of matters of the mind, and the tone used would be different if the writer were writing poetry, a short story, a humorous essay, or a letter to an old friend.

▶ *Distance*   Since the matters being discussed in professional writing are not personal, the writer stays at a greater distance from the reader. The style is not familiar, it is objective and detached. That does not mean that the writer is not committed to the subject (criticize a scholar's writing and you'll see how involved academics are), but it does mean that the posture the writer assumes is more that of the professor giving a paper than a friend having a private conversation.

▶ *Evidence*   All writing, as I have often said, should be built from accurate, specific information. Academic writing, like some other forms of writing, gives special importance to clear documentation. The reader of academic writing not only wants to know the conclusions that the writer drew from the evidence but also wants to know the evidence itself. The reader wants to be able to draw his or her own conclusions, which may or may not coincide with those of the writer.

▶ *Attribution*   In personal writing much of the attribution comes from common experience. The writer is able to make the reader recall observations or feelings from the reader's life that makes the reader believe the text. In academic writing the reader needs to know where the evidence came from. The reader may be reading the piece to follow his or her own research trail. The reader needs to know where the fact can be found, how it can be put in context. Each significant fact in academic writing should have attribution, either woven into the text or attached to the text by footnotes or a bibliography.

▶ *The Review of the Literature*   Sometimes the section that reviews the literature in academic writing seems only to be a peacock display of plumage—"Look, colleague, I read all this stuff"—but it has an important purpose. Most academic writing is written in response to previous academic writing. Our scholarly knowledge is built in increments of small additional bits added to previous knowledge. The review of the literature tells the reader the ancestry of this particular work, and therefore puts the work within a tradition.

▶ *Conclusions*   The writer of academic prose should not just report what has been done, but should come to conclusions about its significance. Opinion, yes, personal opinion, is at the heart of academic writing, but it is opinion based on evidence, an opinion argued in a rational manner, an opinion based on thinking, with the process of thought revealed to the reader.

The academic voice can and should be vigorous, lively, and opinionated. It shouldn't be stuffy, dull, boring, and uncommitted. But its liveliness comes from information and the interpretation of that information. It is lively thought written down.

Whatever voice I write in—and I write academic prose as well as personal prose, sometimes write corporate prose, and often write institutional prose—it brings together everything I know about writing: word choice, sentence structure, mechanics, rhetoric, form, style, pace, rhythm. But it also brings together everything I've lived and felt and thought. It is that element in writing that combines both the intellectual and emotional, the brain and the heart.

I hope that you will experiment with voice and have the fun I have had in playing writing. Improvise. Don't think then write; just write, letting voice bring everything that you know and feel together, so that you have the satisfaction and the joy of listening to your writing play a meaning you have never heard before.

The Draft Demonstrated

Now I will write a draft of the piece about my grandmother, trying to demonstrate all the points made in this chapter—and more. But I will try not to think too consciously of these points (or even of grammatical rules), or I will write woodenly, as if I were trying to dribble a basketball with a rule book in my left hand.

And I am terrified, as I would be at the end of the diving board high above a pool that seems smaller and smaller. I don't know what I will say, or if any reader will find it worth saying. I know that I have an itch I want to scratch: I want to know my grandmother better, and I want to share what I discover with my children and, perhaps, with others. I will be writing a discovery draft with all the notes I've collected and all the focusing and ordering behind me. I will have my memory of the first outline on page 100 in my mind, but I will have nothing in front of me except the blank page.

Waiting for the Sheets to Move

When I woke in the black, New England mornings to do my paper route I had a chore to perform first. I had to go and stand in the pale orange of her night-light and watch to see if the sheets rose and fell.

This tall authority of my childhood, who was more powerful than God, and was loved with fear by all the uncles and her daughter, my mother, was so frail now she hardly had to move the sheets to breathe. I tried not to look at the black hole of her mouth—her teeth grinned in a glass on the night table—and studied the top sheet. It did not move. This was the night Grandma had died. Just as I was ready to go and wake my parents the sheet suddenly fluttered and fell.

(Death had always seemed to live in our dark houses, not in the shadows but sitting right there, his legs crossed, wearing his terrible smile, just seated in the living room chair, waiting. The sermons talked of a real life hereafter. There were houses in Heaven and a universal broiler down below. Grandma lived with Morison, who had gone before, and she was glad that Helen, her daughter, had died in the flu epidemic, because she went with a man who drank beer. Every night I got down on my knees in my dark bedroom and prayed, ". . . if I should die before I wake . . .")

My first memories of Grandma must have been when I was seated or crawling on the floor. A great column of skirts that rose to the vast swellings, and above them her face looking down, disapproving, and her hair gathered into a topknot like a crown. Queen Mary, whose picture was in the living room with King George, wore her hair the same way.

I knew the legends of Grandma from my mother, from the uncles, and from herself. She would tell me, to teach me I should never disobey, that she had disobeyed when she was a schoolgirl on Islay, an island in the Hebrides off Scotland. She had led her friends through the shortcut across the forbidden pasture. She had looked for the bull, but hadn't seen it, and taken the chance, as if she had known better than her parents. And then the bull charged.

She put her friends behind her, pulled out her huge sewing scissors from her schoolbag, and rammed them up the nostrils of the bull.

She reminded me to obey my parents, but I started looking for shortcuts hoping for bulls.

In the front hall there was a great, tall porcelain jar, and in it a bouquet of umbrellas and canes. Every day it reminded me of the story about what happened to the robber. It was after Grandmother had moved to this country and when the grandfather I never knew still had the mill. The payroll was in the safe at the house, and Grandfather was away on business, when Grandma heard a sound downstairs. She found the robber in the kitchen, and he pointed a big six-gun at her. She told him to wait, and anyone who knew Grandmother knew he waited. She went to the front hall and selected a heavy cane from the same porcelain jar, went to the kitchen, broke the robber's wrist with one stroke, then called my Uncle Alec, her oldest son, and told him to get the constable.

I never really began to understand why the uncles and my mother loved my grandmother so, or were so dependent on her. It was something even beyond the natural extreme of Scottish duty and obligation. But while researching this paper I found that Grandma's husband, Morison Smith, who looked so successful in the brown photograph, his face so sure above his beard, had died a failure. Mother and Grandma had protected his image. He had, indeed, been an owner of a mill, and that was held up to me. I did belong in the middle class. But he had lost the mill and lost many jobs, and Grandma had had to cook bread in the kitchen to keep the family going. The farm girl from Islay, who had been the servant girl in London, and who had married the older widower as he was leaving for America, had been a mill owner's wife. We lived in a working-class flat, but we were down on our luck in the Great Depression, but we were middle class.

I despised her pretensions, her concern with the neighbors—the shades drawn just so. She changed her clothes every afternoon. We never ate in the kitchen until she was paralyzed and didn't know. Her Sunday dinners were ceremonies, and all the family came back for every holiday. She always sat at the head of the table.

It was a strange household. Grandma was in charge, and the four of us lived in her house, all children somehow. My mother, who did not cook, for it was Grandma's kitchen and Grandma's special wood stove; my father, who wore his salesman's smile to work or church; my spinster uncle, the accountant, who worked late on account books on the oak desk in the corner of the bedroom; and myself.

They all feared Grandma. In fact, our home seemed glued together by fear, fear of God whose lightning-fast rod was held by Grandma, fear of the neighbors, but especially the Irish Catholics, fear of Drink—the curse of Scotland, fear of Roosevelt, fear of smoking, fear of sex, fear of failure, fear of what the others might think, fear of being found to have dirty underwear when they take you to the hospital after the accident, fear of being hit by lightning, fear of irregularity and perpetual constipation, fear of food that would poison you, fear of the flu that had killed Helen, fear of rust that could cause the blood poisoning that left Uncle Alec with the bent finger, fear of the bruise that would become the lump that would become cancer, fear of what you might say and what you might not say. And above all the other fears for the rest of them was the fear of Grandma.

But she did not entirely terrify me. When I said "darn" I had my mouth scrubbed out with laundry soap, and when I got tanned in the summer she took the same brown soap and the scrubbing brush she used on the linoleum in the kitchen to scrub the tan away. She believed that "to spare the rod was to harm the child." And I was not harmed;

the rod was not spared. I was spanked with a shaving strap, with the back of a hairbrush soaked to make it hurt the more, and with my father's hand. My grandmother could press her hand together at the hinges of my jaw and force soft-boiled egg down my throat. But I also knew her in a way that her own children did not seem to know her.

When I was young my mother was away most days with her friends, shopping in Boston, and I was alone with Grandma. I heard her singing hymns as she did the housework, heard her talking, casually, with Morison or with God. I could get her to tell me stories of Scotland, and I could make her laugh.

She was the only one I knew who knew my friends who lived in the walls were real. She did not talk at them, smiling knowingly and winking over my head; she visited with them, and they could play with us. She always remembered the imaginary cake in the invisible pan, and when I painted and repainted the back steps with water, she always knew to step over the wood where the paint had not yet dried.

When I tipped the woven cane living room chairs over and covered them with a blanket, she would visit me in the igloo, the cave, the tent. When I lined up the dining room chairs she would sit in the bow and paddle the war canoe, or when I put the fan in front she would fly with me to Paris, as Lindbergh had just done. And at the end of the day, when all the chores were done and it was too early to light the lamps and start supper and too dark to read, she would let me sit with her in the gloaming, when she seemed most alone.

Then one Saturday night when I was rushing up to bed, leaping two steps at a time, I found her collapsed on the stairs, curled up like the dead dog I found curled up under the bush. Her dress moved, but she only grunted, she could not seem to speak.

Late that night, after they had told me time and time again to go to bed and I had paid no attention, long after Dr. Bartlett had gone, we all stood around her bed, where she lay propped halfway up on pillows. I was closest to her on her right side, and when she grew agitated, trying to speak with a terrible animal sound and flailing wildly with her one good arm, I think it was I who brought her a pad of paper, and I think it was I who was able to translate the meaning that lay between the scrawled note and the face that was so terribly pulled down on one side. I think it was I who laughed, and I think I remember Grandmother nodding, "She's telling you when to put the leg of lamb in the oven for Sunday dinner."

Grandma was still in charge, and Grandma might have suffered a stroke—a shock she would have called it—but she would survive, and she would tell us what to do.

And she did just that. She lived until she was eighty-nine, another eleven years, and she never got out of bed except when we carried her in a special canvas sling to the couch in the living room for a few special holiday dinners.

She grew thin, and her auburn hair that had been gray turned pure white. Her left arm, which had always been so busy making bread or grape jelly or kidney soup lay curled and useless outside of the covers, unless we put it in. The skin on that hand grew soft; it was almost transparent, and it had the shiny pale colors I only saw on the inside of seashells.

In the mornings when I went out on the paper route and when I returned and when I came home from school or in from playing, I always checked to see if the sheets still moved. I gave my Victorian grandmother the urinal or the bedpan when it was needed, and I cleaned her afterwards, and I helped lift her up in the bed, and I helped change the bed and put salve to her bedsores, and helped her eat.

Her physical world shrank to her bedroom and to her bed. It seemed to be as far as she could reach with the bamboo back-scratcher that is still on my desk. With it she could pull up the dark green Black Watch shawl she had brought from Scotland. She lost her sense of time and would ask for lunch just after we cleared the dishes away, and she talked more often with Morison and with God. But still she was in charge.

I always checked in with her first after school or work or church. She told my spinster uncle when to marry. And each week there were visits from each of the uncles. My father always stayed at a distance. His father and mother had both worked in a mill and never owned or lost one. And my mother, in her forties and her fifties, still took instruction on how to make tea, and never felt she did it right.

I went away summers to get tans Grandma could no longer scrub off. More and more my life was lived in my room, where I had a ceiling of maps—Arabia, Antarctica, Africa, China and Japan—or where I worked after school on weekends, or on street corners or in gas stations, hanging out. I thought I was escaping this tight Scottish family that lived so in fear.

I hung out with the Irish. I smoked two packs of cigarettes a day. I learned to let a cigarette hang from the corner of my mouth, and learned to squint my eyes against the smoke. I took that first drink, and then I took more. I ate strange Mediterranean food—spaghetti and ravioli. I ate pepper and salads. I flunked out of high school to show them there was a Scot who could betray the heritage, and I went off to college to play football and never returned home.

The last time I saw Grandmother I was in the army, a paratrooper going overseas to fight Hitler. It was a hot, muggy August in Boston, and I was in my itchy woolen winter uniform on a bus going from camp to a Red Sox game. I'd won the chance by luck.

When I saw that the bus was going to pass ten blocks from my home I told the lieutenant that my grandmother was dying. I didn't mention that I had been watching for the sheets to move since I was a child. He told me he would slow down the bus, but if I weren't at this corner when they passed by on their way back to camp I would be a deserter, because we were going overseas, and I would face a general court-martial. I nodded, swung off the bus, and even in my woolens ran the ten blocks home.

My mother shook my hand. We were Scots, and we did not show emotion. We went to stand by my grandmother's bed. She was delighted to see me. She smiled her crooked smile and held my hand with her good hand. She knew what I was doing. I was going off to war, but as we talked I realized I was not this Donald going off to World War II, or Donald her son for whom I was named and was in the Navy in the First World War, or Donald, her brother, or Donald, her father, but Donald, her great-uncle who had sat around the fire when she was a girl in the 1860s, and had shown her the bent leg that had taken a ball when he fought with the Black Watch at Waterloo. And with that great bringing together that the elderly can do, spanning centuries in a sentence, she was talking to that uncle long before she was born, and I became him when he was a boy going off to fight Napoleon.

Grandma died in a letter that I received when I was living in the rubble of a German city. But I think I knew by then that although I would only for a few weeks return home, I would never leave home, and I would never live without the sense of death nearby. Now I have, like Grandma, buried my father, my mother, and a daughter. And when I wake early or come home late it is first with a sense of dread. I am still waiting in the shadows to see if the sheets will move.

The draft is done. I feel a sense of relief and apprehension. I had the usual problem, as I wrote the draft, of maintaining faith in it. I kept wanting to quit. It wasn't coming out the way I wanted. It was terrible. It was awful. It was, at best, people fertilizer.

But that isn't all. At times I really thought it was great. I was surprised where it was taking me. Everything seemed to weave together, and I came up with little phrases like "spinster uncle" that surprised and excited me. They seemed especially clever. And as soon as I felt that way I began to doubt them. I was too clever. It was too tricky, too cute. I had to force myself to suspend both despair and elation and plunge on.

Note that the third paragraph in the piece is in parentheses. I heard that paragraph and liked what I heard, but I was afraid that it would take me off on a tangent. I put it in parentheses and got back on track in the fourth paragraph.

I have no idea if this draft works or not. That isn't important. That will be decided when I perform the skills introduced in the next chapter. What is important is that I have a draft. I have made the most important step in the writing process and created a complete text, what Peter Drucker calls a "zero draft" and what Calvin Trillin calls "the vomit all."

My draft was written in two hours, but I was able to write it this fast because of all the collecting, planning, rehearsing I had done. I had a sketch in my head, I had the hint of a voice, I had a potential beginning, a turning point, an end.

Questions about Drafting

What if the writing doesn't come? What if there's absolutely nothing in my head when I start to write?

I always feel that way—and many times it's true, there's nothing but space between my ears.

I don't try to force the writing. I back up, stop, do something else, and try again, perhaps in ten minutes, perhaps the next morning. I'm a morning writer, and I find that if the writing doesn't come one time it will come the next.

But what if it doesn't?

Then I haven't planned well enough. I go back and wallow about in the information, mess around with focusing activities, or do some ordering. I use the techniques listed on pages 100–110. If the writing isn't ready to come then I haven't prepared it well.

But won't I get writer's block?

Few students have writer's block. Some writers do, but not enough that they're filling the back wards of institutions. Writer's block is a convenient thing to say to someone who wouldn't understand planning activities or the necessary rehearsal that precedes writing. It's also a convenient term to use when you haven't got yourself into the chair and waited for writing. John McPhee used to tie himself into the chair the first thing in the morning with his bathrobe cord. Getting into the chair and waiting for writing is the hardest thing to do.

Stick some mottoes or quotations from writers above your writing desk. A few of mine:

> "I have to write every day because, the way I work, the writing generates the writing."
>> *E. L. Doctorow*

> "Two simple rules. (A) You don't have to write. (B) You can't do anything else. The rest comes of itself."
>> *Raymond Chandler*

> "If you keep working, inspiration comes."
>> *Alexander Calder*

Most cases of writer's block are the direct result of inappropriate standards. The writer is trying to write better than is possible for this writer to write at this particular time. Just write; worry about how well it works after you have finished the draft.

My writing changes. I mean, I have all these outlines and stuff, and then it takes off and goes on its own.

Good. Writing is thinking, not just reporting what you've thought. Writing is a dynamic, forward-moving force, and when the writing is going well most writers feel they are following the writing. E. M. Forster advised, "Think before you speak, is criticism's motto; speak before you think, is creation's."

But what if it's really out of control, I mean, doesn't make any sense at all?

You have two choices: go back and start over again, or edit with a firm hand and get it under control.

My piece doesn't so much get out of control as run off in a dozen directions, like when I take my beagle for a walk and she follows her nose, chases cats, investigates garbage pails, chases shadows, keeps circling around. She isn't out of control—we get home—but she walks ten miles more than I do.

I used to write like a beagle myself. Then the late Hannah Lees suggested I write each paragraph on a separate page. For years I did just that, using half pieces of paper—8″ × 5″. When I got the piece done I spread all the paragraphs on a large table or on the floor and rearranged them into an efficient pattern. Some of the trails I had followed belonged in the piece; others didn't, and they had to go.

But sometimes I have to write right on deadline.

So do I, and for years I was a newspaper rewrite person spending five nights a week writing fifteen to fifty stories a night, on deadline. When you write under that pressure you have to follow the patterns of writing laid down in long-term memory. The experience of writing when you had time—the lessons you learned—is on call when you have to write in a hurry.

Drafting Activities

1. Try a different tool. If you usually write by hand, write directly on the typewriter, or dictate into a tape recorder, and then copy down what you've said. Different ways of writing can help capture a working draft.
2. Write a discovery draft, writing as fast as you can to find out what you're going to say.
3. Tell the story to someone else to hear what you say when you have an audience; read the person's reactions by paying attention to body language, interest, and so forth. Don't do this if you think you'll lose the piece. Some writers find this very helpful, but others find that if they have told the piece to someone they won't write it.
4. Write one paragraph each describing a place, defining an idea, introducing a person, presenting an argument, revealing a process; then write a second paragraph for each one in which you show instead of tell.
5. List the questions the reader will ask about your piece of writing and put them in the order the reader will ask them.
6. Read aloud something you've written before and make notes about what reading aloud reveals to you. One significant thing it may reveal is that it's hard to make notes—you hear the flow of the piece of writing and want

to be carried on by that flow; in other words, reading aloud is the best way of testing to see if a piece of writing flows.

7. Take a significant piece of information from the writing you're working on and list all of the ways it can be documented—quotation, statistic, description, anecdote, and so on.

8. Write a draft.

9. Go back and use one of the techniques of collecting, focusing, or ordering to see if it will help you get a draft flowing.

10. Imagine a person you feel comfortable with and write the draft to that person, speaking as you would in a conversation. You may even want to start the draft as a letter to that person.

11. Imagine that you are a ghostwriter writing the piece for someone else. Put your "client's" name at the top to see how the piece would go if you were writing it in that voice. Make believe you're James Baldwin, Joan Didion, George Orwell. Try on another style as a way of seeing how that style works and as a way of getting into a text that you can make your own.

12. Write the draft backward, writing the end first, the next to the end next, until you've worked your way back to the beginning.

13. Write the section that is easiest for you to write, then the next easiest, and so forth until you get all of the parts written and can fit it together into a working draft.

14. Give yourself a quota of time (an hour, an hour and a half, two hours) or of pages (one page, or three, or five), and then write to fill the time or the number of pages. Don't worry for the moment about the whole piece and its final quality; just deal with the chunk of writing time or the number of pages you have assigned yourself.

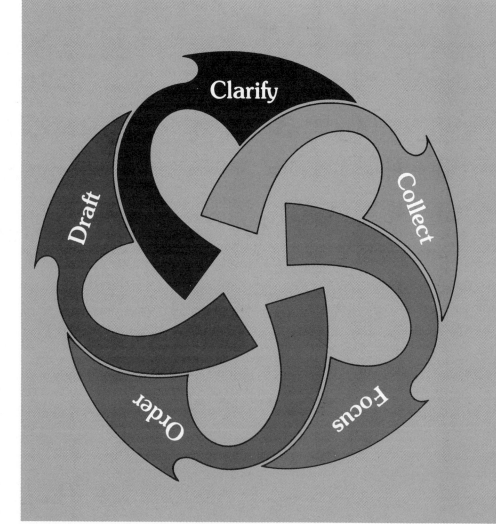

Clarify

I work with language. I love the flowers of afterthought.

Bernard Malamud

What makes me happy is rewriting. In the first draft you get your ideas and your theme clear, if you are using some kind of metaphor you get that established, and certainly you have to know where you're coming out. But the next time through it's like cleaning house, getting rid of all the junk, getting things in the right order, tightening things up. I like the process of making writing neat.

Ellen Goodman

When I see a paragraph shrinking under my eyes like a strip of bacon in a skillet, I know I'm on the right track.

Peter De Vries

Now that you have a draft you are ready to make it clear, first to yourself and then to other readers.

It is important to remember that you are your own first reader. You have to read your own copy to make sure that it is clear to you, that you are saying what you want to say.

Then you have to read as a devil's advocate. When a person is proposed for sainthood in the Catholic Church, a high church official is appointed to be the devil's advocate. That person attempts to find out everything bad about the prospective saint. You have to be a devil's advocate in regard to your own copy, role-playing the most critical reader.

Four Ways to Clarify

The first choice is to *discard* the whole text or part of it. You may be able to do this without even reading the draft, but that is dangerous, for most writers feel an unjustified despair when they face their own copy. There are times, however, when you know that the writing doesn't work. It hasn't gone anywhere

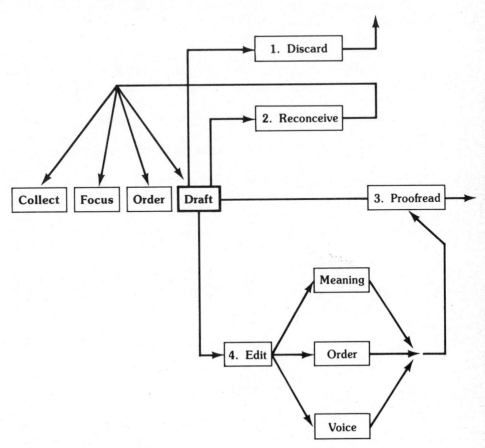

you want it to go or that you want to go following it. Sometimes the decision to discard comes after reading a draft. The important thing is not to feel that you have failed. Isaac Bashevis Singer has said that "the wastepaper basket is a writer's best friend. My wastepaper basket is on a steady diet." All writing is experimental, and you should expect that some drafts—experiments in meaning—simply will not work.

The next choice is to *reconceive*. This decision, like the one to discard, can be made without reading the draft, but it is usually made after at least a quick reading. In this case the experiment in meaning has revealed that you need to go back and recollect, refocus, or reorder.

I have pointed out all the way along that writing is recursive, that you have to keep circling back through the writing process. Again, this isn't failure, just a normal part of the writing process—the writer's search for meaning.

The third choice is to *proof* the text. When you have a deadline and the text you have is the text you're going to have, or when you have done all the reconceiving and revising that you are willing to do, then you have to go through the copy to eliminate the superficial problems that will prevent the reader from having an uninterrupted opportunity to experience the text.

The fourth choice is to *edit*. This is the one we use most frequently. Few texts are produced that need only to be proofed; most texts have to be edited in order for the writer to be able to discover the meaning and to be able to share that meaning with the reader.

I have worked for the past few years with editors on some of the best newspapers in the country, and I have found these editors make the same mistake most teachers do. It is the same mistake that every one of us, as writers, will make unless we have trained ourselves to be effective editors. The mistake is to plunge in and start editing language first, working from the written line back to form and then to meaning. It is the backward way of editing, and it simply doesn't work.

You choose one word and reject another word in relation to meaning. If the meaning isn't clear the choice will be arbitrary and often wrong. There are no rules for word choice unrelated to meaning. And when you choose to write a short sentence or a short paragraph it is usually for emphasis, and unless you know what you want to emphasize you won't know whether to make the sentence or the paragraph short.

When most drafts are edited the meaning isn't yet clear—that's the primary purpose of editing. A careful line-by-line editing before the meaning is clear is a waste of time.

The Three Readings

Effective editing is usually the result of three separate and distinct readings, each with its own pace, strategies, and techniques.

The highly skillful editor or writer may be able to perform all three readings simultaneously, moving from the large global questions of meaning to structural questions of order, and to line-by-line questions of voice. But those interrelated skills are best developed by separating the readings—reading first for meaning, next for order, and third for voice.

And of course in each case the writer has to keep an eye cocked for the audience, standing back and making sure that what is being said and resaid on the page is clear to the reader.

This seems a slow process, but the first reading is usually a very fast reading—a quick flyover of the territory to make sure that there is a single dominant meaning and an abundant inventory of information to support that meaning.

The second reading is a bit slower, but not much. The piece is still read in chunks to see if the sections support the main point and appear when the reader needs them.

The third reading is a slow, careful, line-by-line editing of the text to make sure that it is ready for a final proofreading. Here the reader cuts, adds, and reorders, paragraph by paragraph, sentence by sentence, word by word.

The process of the three readings sounds tedious and boring, but it shouldn't be. In each case there should be the excitement of discovery, of finding a meaning that you did not expect to find and having the chance to make it come clear. Writing gives us the satisfaction of craft, the feeling we have when we lean our weight into the corner and make our bicycle swing gracefully where we want it to go. Writing is similar to stroking a tennis ball, baking bread, building a sturdy shelf, sewing a dress, planting a garden. It is a process of making, and it is fun to make something well, to handcraft a piece of prose that will carry meaning and feeling to another person.

Editing Principles

There are some principles to keep in mind during each of the three readings:

▶ *Build on Strength*   The focus should be on the positive as much as the negative. Of course, the editing writer solves problems and corrects mistakes. But most of all, the writer builds on strengths. It is important to be able to identify what works well in the text so it can be extended throughout the text. For example, if the voice is strong and appropriate in one part of the text, that voice can be taken and applied to the rest of the text.

▶ *Give the Reader a Full Serving of Information*   Most beginning writers underdevelop; they serve a meal on which you see mostly plate. The reader needs a full serving of specific information to satisfy the reader's natural hunger.

▶ *Cut What Can Be Cut*   Everything in the text must relate to the single dominant meaning of the text. If it doesn't, it has to go.

▶ *Simplicity Is Best*   This doesn't mean simply writing headlines or sentences without clauses; it does mean that the writing should be as simple as the task allows. The pro in any sport makes it look easy. Don't showboat and call attention to yourself; don't write to impress; write to communicate.

▶ *Listen to the Writing*   Read aloud, for your ear is a better editor than your eye, and if you listen to how the piece reads it will tell you when it needs a definition woven in, some description, more evidence, a change of pace. A writer who listens well to the evolving text will find out that the text is teaching the writer how it should be written.

At this stage of the writing process the reader cannot be sent out of the room. The writer still must write for himself or herself, making sure the text is understood. But there is always a double reading: will the reader understand this, will the reader think, will the reader feel, will the reader keep reading?

The writer will find it helpful at times to role-play the reader, to become the person who picks up the text, who is busy, skeptical, intelligent but unknowledgeable, quite willing to go to something else. Writing without a reader is an incomplete act, and the writer must make every honest effort to achieve a reader.

A Checklist for the First Reading

Reading for Meaning

Read the text fast, the way the reader will. If you have to make notes in the margin, make big notes, quickly—a C for something that may have to be cut, an arrow suggesting a movement of material, a double-headed arrow for expansion. But try not to get too close to the text. I do the first reading without a pen or a pencil, in an easy chair, away from my desk, so that I am almost free of worrying about the details of language; so I can see if the piece has a meaning worth developing.

▶ What does the piece of writing mean?
▶ Is the meaning built on undocumented assumptions?
▶ Does the reader need more information?
▶ Does the form contain the meaning and carry it to the reader?
▶ Is it too long?
▶ Is it too short?
▶ Does it go off on tangents that can be cut out?
▶ Are there other pieces of writing within the text—other subjects—that could be cut out and developed later?
▶ Is there convincing evidence for each point?
▶ Are the reader's key questions answered?
▶ Does the writing place the reader at the most effective distance from the subject?
▶ Does the piece answer the reader's question: Why should I read this?
▶ Does the the piece of writing have an imbedded narrative or thread that runs through the entire text and keeps the reader reading?

▶ Does the piece of writing deliver on the promise made in the title and the lead?

▶ Is there scaffolding that was important when the piece was being written but gets in the reader's way now and has to be taken down?

Doing three readings sounds like a triple assignment, but it actually is a time-saver. Trying to read for content, form, and language simultaneously causes the writer to do an unnecessary amount of scurrying back and forth. There is enormous waste of motion and a great deal of doing over. It is a time-saver to read three times, because the first two readings are relatively quick, and the time and care it takes for the third reading can not be spent efficiently until the questions brought up in the first reading are answered.

In the following pages I will read my draft for meaning and show my concerns with that text in the margin. Write your own comments in the margin. Mark it up. Second-guess me, third-guess me. Come on in, the water's fine.

Waiting for the Sheets to Move

When I woke in the black New England mornings to do my paper route I had a chore to perform first. I had to go and stand in the pale orange of her night-light and watch to see if the sheets rose and fell.

> What do I think I am saying in this piece? That you can never run away from home? If that's true I've got to tie this—and other experiences—to now. Do I do that?

This tall authority of my childhood, who was more powerful than God, and was loved with fear by all the uncles and her daughter, my mother, was so frail now she hardly had to move the sheets to breathe. I tried not to look at the black hole of her mouth—her teeth grinned in a glass on the night table—and studied the top sheet. It did not move. This was the night Grandma had died. Just as I was ready to go and wake my parents the sheet suddenly fluttered and fell.

(Death had always seemed to live in our dark houses, not in the shadows but sitting right there, his legs crossed, wearing his terrible smile, just seated in the living room chair, waiting. The sermons talked of a real life hereafter. There were houses in Heaven and a universal broiler down below. Grandma lived with Morison, who had gone before, and she was glad that Helen, her daughter, had died in the flu epidemic, because she went with a man who drank beer. Every night I got down on my knees in my dark bedroom and prayed, ". . . if I should die before I wake . . .")

> Is this the tie to the past? Isn't it too much—and off the track?

> Do I want to be this personal? No. But if I want to explore how we are tied to our background I must.

My first memories of Grandma must have been when I was seated or crawling on the floor. A great column of skirts that rose to vast swellings, and above them her face looking down, disapproving, and her hair gathered into a topknot like a crown. Queen Mary, whose picture was in the living room with King George, wore her hair the same way.

> It's hard to read fast, the way the reader will read. My pen wants to attack the bad writing. Put it away—decide if there's a piece worth attacking first.

I knew the legends of Grandma from my mother, from the uncles, and from Grandma herself. She would tell me, to teach me I should never disobey, that she had disobeyed when she was a schoolgirl on Islay, an island in the Hebrides off Scotland. She had led her friends through the shortcut across the forbidden pasture. She had looked for the bull, but hadn't seen it, and taken the chance, as if she had known better than her parents. And then the bull charged.

> I'd forgotten the moral lesson in the story until now. Did she really think I'd buy the moral, or was she just proud of goring the bull?

She put her friends behind her, pulled out her huge sewing scissors from her schoolbag, and rammed them up the nostrils of the bull.

She reminded me to obey my parents, but I started looking for shortcuts, hoping for bulls.

In the front hall there was a great, tall porcelain jar, and in it a bouquet of umbrellas and canes. Every day it reminded me of the story about what happened to the robber. It was

> If I'm going to use such anecdotes they

after Grandmother had moved to this country, and when the grandfather I never knew still had the mill. The payroll was in the safe at the house, and Grandfather was away on business, when Grandma heard a sound downstairs. She found the robber in the kitchen, and he pointed a big six-gun at her. She told him to wait, and anyone who knew Grandmother knew he waited. She went to the front hall and selected a heavy cane from the same porcelain jar, went to the kitchen, broke the robber's wrist with one stroke, then called my Uncle Alec, her oldest son, and told him to get the constable.

<blockquote>are going to have to be developed at this length—or more.</blockquote>

I never really began to understand why the uncles and my mother loved my grandmother so, or were so dependent on her. It was something even beyond the natural extreme of Scottish duty and obligation. But while researching this paper I found that Grandma's husband, Morison Smith, who looked so successful in the brown photograph, his face so sure above his beard, had died a failure. Mother and Grandma had protected his image. He had, indeed, been an owner of a mill, and that was held up to me. I did belong in the middle class. But he had lost the mill and lost many jobs, and Grandma had had to cook bread in the kitchen to keep the family going. The farm girl from Islay, who had been the servant girl in London, and who had married the older widower as he was leaving for America had been a mill owner's wife. We lived in a working-class flat, but we were down on our luck in the Great Depression, but we were middle class.

<blockquote>Like this phrase. Like it too much? Will the reader get it?

I want to find out more about him. Maybe not this piece.

I wonder if I'm moving too swiftly through all of this. Will the "sociology" of it be understood? Will the reader understand how important it was to get into the middle class and stay there?</blockquote>

I despised her pretensions, her concern with the neighbors—the shades drawn just so. She changed her clothes every afternoon. We never ate in the kitchen until she was paralyzed and didn't know. Her Sunday dinners were ceremonies, and all the family came back for every holiday. She always sat at the head of the table.

<blockquote>Yes, I'm going to have to work back and forth from how I felt then and feel now. Is piece not you can't run away but you can begin to understand—have compassion? Can the essay reveal the dawning compassion?</blockquote>

It was a strange household. Grandma was in charge, and the four of us lived in her house, all children somehow. My mother, who did not cook, for it was Grandma's kitchen and Grandma's special wood stove; my father, who wore his salesman's smile to work or church; my spinster uncle, the accountant, who worked late on account books on the oak desk in the corner of the bedroom; and myself.

They all feared Grandma. In fact, our home seemed glued together by fear, fear of God whose lightning-fast rod was held by Grandma, fear of the neighbors, but especially the Irish Catholics, fear of Drink—the curse of Scotland, fear of Roosevelt, fear of smoking, fear of sex, fear of failure, fear of what the others might think, fear of being found to have dirty underwear when they take you to the hospital after the accident, fear of being hit by lightning, fear of irregularity and perpetual

<blockquote>This is helpful insight: the FEAR. Is that the piece?</blockquote>

constipation, fear of food that would poison you, fear of the flu that had killed Helen, fear of rust that could cause the blood poisoning that left Uncle Alec with the bent finger, fear of the bruise that would become the lump that would become cancer, fear of what you might say and what you might not say. And above all the other fears for the rest of them was the fear of Grandma.

But she did not entirely terrify me. When I said "darn" I had my mouth scrubbed out with laundry soap, and when I got tanned in the summer she took the same brown soap and the scrubbing brush she used on the linoleum in the kitchen to scrub the tan away. She believed that "to spare the rod was to harm the child." And I was not harmed; the rod was not spared. I was spanked with a shaving strap, with the back of a hairbrush soaked to make it hurt the more, and with my father's hand. My grandmother could press her hand together at the hinges of my jaw and force soft-boiled egg down my throat. But I also knew her in a way that her own children did not seem to know her.

When I was young my mother was away most days with her friends, shopping in Boston, and I was alone with Grandma. I heard her singing hymns as she did the housework, heard her talking, casually, with Morison or with God. I could get her to tell me stories of Scotland, and I could make her laugh.

She was the only one I knew who knew my friends who lived in the walls were real. She did not talk at them, smiling knowingly and winking over my head; she visited with them, and they could play with us. She always remembered the imaginary cake in the invisible pan, and when I painted and repainted the back steps with water, she always knew to step over the wood where the paint had not yet dried.

When I tipped the woven cane living room chairs over and covered them with a blanket, she would visit me in the igloo, the cave, the tent. When I lined up the dining room chairs she would sit in the bow and paddle the war canoe, or when I put the fan in front she would fly with me to Paris, as Lindbergh had just done. And at the end of the day, when all the chores were done and it was too early to light the lamps and start supper and too dark to read, she would let me sit with her in the gloaming, when she seemed most alone.

Then one Saturday night when I was rushing up to bed, leaping two steps at a time, I found her collapsed on the stairs, curled up like the dead dog I had found curled up under the bush. Her dress moved, but she only grunted, she could not seem to speak.

Late that night, after they had told me time and time again to go to bed and I had paid no attention, long after Dr. Bartlett

Is this moving too fast for reader to absorb, or is it supplying energy by its speed? Don't worry about that until the next reading. See if you've got a piece to write.

If I open this door, I've got to show the cruelty. And I've got to try to understand that all these years later. Perhaps that's the way to deal with it here. It can't be understood— or forgiven. Is that the piece? You can escape and be different? I don't treat my children this way. How do my children see it? Have I been as bad in my own way?

This wasn't consciously done, but after some criticism of her (I set her up as a somewhat harsh forbidding figure) I show the "secret" grandmother I knew. And then show her on the stairs. I think the piece is working in here— but of course it'll need more working.

had gone, we all stood around her bed, where she lay propped halfway up on pillows. I was closest to her on her right side, and when she grew agitated, trying to speak with a terrible animal sound and flailing wildly with her one good arm, I think it was I who brought her a pad of paper, and I think it was I who was able to translate the meaning that lay between the scrawled note and the face that was so terribly pulled down on one side. I think it was I who laughed, and I think I remember Grandmother nodding, "She's telling you when to put the leg of lamb in the oven for Sunday dinner."

Grandma was still in charge, and Grandma might have suffered a stroke—a shock she would have called it—but she would survive, and she would tell us what to do.

And she did just that. She lived until she was eighty-nine, another eleven years, and she never got out of bed except when we carried her in a special canvas sling to the couch in the living room for a few special holiday dinners.

She grew thin, and her auburn hair that had been gray turned pure white. Her left arm, which had always been so busy making bread or grape jelly or kidney soup lay curled and useless outside of the covers, unless we put it in. The skin on that hand grew soft; it was almost transparent, and it had the shiny pale colors I only saw on the inside of seashells.

In the mornings when I went out on the paper route and when I returned and when I came home from school or in from playing, I always checked to see if the sheets still moved. I gave my Victorian grandmother the urinal or the bedpan when it was needed, and I cleaned her afterwards, and I helped lift her up in the bed, and I helped change the bed and put salve to her bedsores, and helped her eat.

Her physical world shrank to her bedroom and to her bed. It seemed to be as far as she could reach with the bamboo back-scratcher that is still on my desk. With it she could pull up the dark green Black Watch shawl she had brought from Scotland. She lost her sense of time and would ask for lunch just after we cleared the dishes away, and she talked more often with Morison and with God. But still she was in charge.

I always checked in with her first after school or work or church. She told my spinster uncle when to marry. And each week there were visits from each of the uncles. My father always stayed at a distance. His father and mother had both worked in a mill and never owned or lost one. And my mother, in her forties and her fifties, still took instruction on how to make tea, and never felt she did it right.

I went away summers to get tans Grandma could no longer scrub off. More and more my life was lived in my room, where I had a ceiling of maps—Arabia, Antarctica, Africa, China and

Set up as turning point? Is it? If so I must tie it to the meaning of the piece.

These "I's" may begin to provide tie in to present. I get distance, grow up?

I like this. I think I've begun to capture that hand. Set up? Show how busy it used to be? Not now. Do that later.

This writing is bad. It's hard to keep my hands off it. One minute I think it's great and the next minute I think it stinks. Probably neither is right—at best, it's a piece that needs working on. Normal amount of work.

Are these paragraphs too quick? Hold back that question for the next reading. Am I staying on target?

Is this the meaning? Trying to escape—will think I can——but I won't.

Japan—or where I worked after school on weekends, or on street corners or in gas stations, hanging out. I thought I was escaping this tight Scottish family that lived so in fear.

I hung out with the Irish. I smoked two packs of cigarettes a day. I learned to let a cigarette hang from the corner of my mouth, and learned to squint my eyes against the smoke. I took that first drink, and then I took more. I ate strange Mediterranean food—spaghetti and ravioli. I ate pepper and salads. I flunked out of high school to show them there was a Scot who could betray the heritage, and I went off to college to play football and never returned home.

The last time I saw Grandmother I was in the army, a paratrooper going overseas to fight Hitler. It was a hot, muggy August in Boston, and I was in my itchy woolen winter uniform on a bus going from camp to a Red Sox game. I'd won the chance by luck.

When I saw that the bus was going to pass ten blocks from my home I told the lieutenant that my grandmother was dying. I didn't mention that I had been watching for the sheets to move since I was a child. He told me he would slow down the bus, but if I wasn't at this corner when they passed by on their way back to camp I would be a deserter, because we were going overseas, and I would face a general court-martial. I nodded, swung off the bus, and even in my woolens ran the ten blocks home.

My mother shook my hand. We were Scots, and we did not show emotion. We went to stand by my grandmother's bed. She was delighted to see me. She smiled her crooked smile and held my hand with her good hand. She knew what I was doing. I was going off to war, but as we talked I realized I was not this Donald going off to World War II, or Donald her son for whom I was named and was in the Navy in the First World War, or Donald, her brother, or Donald, her father, but Donald, her great-uncle who had sat around the fire when she was a girl in the 1860s, and had shown her the bent leg that had taken a ball when he fought with the Black Watch at Waterloo. And with that great bringing together that the elderly can do, spanning centuries in a sentence, she was talking to that uncle long before she was born, and I became him when he was a boy going off to fight Napoleon.

Grandma died in a letter that I received when I was living in the rubble of a German city. But I think I knew by then that although I would only for a few weeks return home, I would never leave home, and I would never live without the sense of death nearby. Now I have, like Grandma, buried my father, my mother, and a daughter. And when I wake early or come

---

Margin notes:

How explicit should I be? How much implied?

Last page and this, I've gotten the itch. There is a piece here. I want to get my hands on it, to cut, develop, shape, form. My hands want to grab hold of it. Work it.

I can feel the closure, coming to the end of the race.

Too much. Too slow. End must come fast. Be tight. A fist.

This seems awful. Clumsy. Rhetorical. But it is where I want to end. I want to go back and work towards it—more carefully.

home late it is first with a sense of dread. I am still waiting in
the shadows to see if the sheets will move.

It is so hard to accept the necessary bad writing. It's hard to read without
plunging in with my pen and making the writing right. But how can I do that
until I know what the piece may mean? I have to stand back—the artist from
the canvas, the carpenter from the bookshelves—to see it whole.

The first reading is a constant battle with despair. I feel I write so badly.
It's so far from what I had hoped it would be. It's sloppy, a mess, worthless.
And at the same time I am so proud of its potential, eager to get on with making
it work.

Okay. I think the piece is, you can't escape. I feared and loved my grandmother, hated (too strong a word) and liked her. She represented the family I
fled but didn't flee. (How set up end to say that?) Density will come in details
of this particular family—and from the fact that everyone has this ambivalence:
fear of and attraction to the powerful people in their lives, a desire to be part
of a tradition (family, race, heritage) and to escape it.

A Checklist for the Second Reading

Reading for Order

Continue to read at a pretty good pace. Do not stop for the problems of language. Now you're dealing with chunks, to make sure that each section of the
writing is developed well and is in the right order.

- ▶ Is the title on target and will it catch the reader?
- ▶ Does the lead catch the reader in three seconds or less?
- ▶ Does the lead establish the voice for the draft?
- ▶ Is the lead honest?
- ▶ Does the draft show as well as tell?
- ▶ Does the writer get out of the way and let the text speak directly to the
  reader?
- ▶ Is each section an answer to a reader's question?
- ▶ Are the questions in the order the reader will ask them?
- ▶ Is the documentation varied, and is each piece of documentation ap-
  propriate to the point being made?
- ▶ Does the pace keep the reader moving, but allow enough time to
  absorb each point?
- ▶ Does the end echo the lead and give the reader a sense of completion?
- ▶ Does the piece stay within the limits of the genre or form that is being
  used?

In the following pages I will read my draft again, and deal with these issues
in this second reading.

Waiting for the Sheets to Move

What's the title got to do with the meaning? Should it be "Still Waiting For . . ."?

When I woke in the black, New England mornings to do my paper route I had a chore to perform first. I had to go and stand in the pale orange of her night-light and watch to see if the sheets rose and fell.

I really like this lead. I've wanted to tell this ever since my wife was startled to hear it. It probably has colored my life. Set up differently . . . when a daughter is home and I wake early to write I walk to the door and watch—???

This tall authority of my childhood, who was more powerful than God, and was loved with fear by all the uncles and her daughter, my mother, was so frail now she hardly had to move the sheets to breathe. I tried not to look at the black hole of her mouth—her teeth grinned in a glass on the night table—and studied the top sheet. It did not move. This was the night Grandma had died. Just as I was ready to go and wake my parents the sheet suddenly fluttered and fell.

Should I go back a bit further and lead with "My real life was on the streets (or in my head?) when I was twelve and I left home when I was seventeen"? Or should I focus on my grandmother—"She died in a letter when I was overseas" . . . ???

(Death had always seemed to live in our dark houses, not in the shadows but sitting right there, his legs crossed, wearing his terrible smile, just seated in the living room chair, waiting. The sermons talked of a real life hereafter. There were houses in Heaven and a universal broiler down below. Grandma lived with Morison, who had gone before, and she was glad that Helen, her daughter, had died in the flu epidemic, because she went with a man who drank beer. Every night I got down on my knees in my dark bedroom and prayed, ". . . if I should die before I wake . . .")

Cut this. Too much. Garbage.

My first memories of Grandma must have been when I was seated or crawling on the floor. A great column of skirts that rose to the vast swellings, and above them her face looking down, disapproving, and her hair gathered into a topknot like a crown. Queen Mary, whose picture was in the living room with King George, wore her hair the same way.

Not too sure about this, but I may be able to edit it into shape. The reader has got to see her early in the piece.

I knew the legends of Grandma from my mother, from the uncles, and from herself. She would tell me, to teach me I should never disobey, that she had disobeyed when she was a schoolgirl on Islay, an island in the Hebrides off Scotland. She had led her friends through the shortcut across the forbidden pasture. She had looked for the bull, but hadn't seen it, and taken the chance, as if she had known better than her parents. And then the bull charged.

This anecdote will stay. It reveals her and is in the right place in the piece. Needs sharpening, though.

She put her friends behind her, pulled out her huge sewing scissors from her schoolbag, and rammed them up the nostrils of the bull.

I like this phrase. A nice, tiny surprise that makes a point.

She reminded me to obey my parents, but I started looking for shortcuts, hoping for bulls.

Put in anecdote about how she was called to lay out the dead?

In the front hall there was a great, tall porcelain jar, and in it a bouquet of umbrellas and canes. Every day it reminded me of the story about what happened to the robber. It was after Grandmother had moved to this country and when the grandfather I never knew still had the mill. The payroll was in the safe at the house, and Grandfather was away on business, when Grandma heard a sound downstairs. She found the robber in the kitchen, and he pointed a big six-gun at her. She told him to wait, and anyone who knew Grandmother knew he waited. She went to the front hall and selected a heavy cane from the same porcelain jar, went to the kitchen, broke the robber's wrist with one stroke, then called my Uncle Alec, her oldest son, and told him to get the constable.

Poor transition. Where am I? Where's the hall? The next editing will smooth over these seams. Is information in right order? I think so.

This anecdote will stay here. Should it be shaped better?

I never really began to understand why the uncles and my mother loved my grandmother so, or were so dependent on her. It was something even beyond the natural extreme of Scottish duty and obligation. But while researching this paper I found that Grandma's husband, Morison Smith, who looked so successful in the brown photograph, his face so sure above his beard, had died a failure. Mother and Grandma had protected his image. He had, indeed, been an owner of a mill, and that was held up to me. I did belong in the middle class. But he had lost the mill and lost many jobs, and Grandma had had to cook bread in the kitchen to keep the family going. The farm girl from Islay, who had been the servant girl in London, and who had married the older widower as he was leaving for America, had been a mill owner's wife. We lived in a working-class flat, but we were down on our luck in the Great Depression, but we were middle class.

Clumsy transition.

Good stuff in here, but all jumbled up. How does it relate to meaning of the piece? Explain some of Grandma's toughness?

Must untangle all this if I am to use it. Start with his portrait, end with baking bread?

Tie any of that grandfather stuff to me? Ambition, unrealistic dreams, fiddle foot vs. tenure?

I despised her pretensions, her concern with the neighbors—the shades drawn just so. She changed her clothes every afternoon. We never ate in the kitchen until she was paralyzed and didn't know. Her Sunday dinners were ceremonies, and all the family came back for every holiday. She always sat at the head of the table.

It was a strange household. Grandma was in charge, and the four of us lived in her house, all children somehow. My mother, who did not cook, for it was Grandma's kitchen and Grandma's special wood stove; my father, who wore his salesman's smile to work or church; my spinster uncle, the accountant, who worked late on account books on the oak desk in the corner of the bedroom; and myself.

Editorial pen will go to work here.

They all feared Grandma. In fact, our home seemed glued together by fear, fear of God whose lightning-fast rod was held by Grandma, fear of the neighbors, but especially the Irish Catholics, fear of Drink—the curse of Scotland, fear of Roosevelt, fear of smoking, fear of sex, fear of failure, fear of what

I'm carried along by this and like it, but what's it do for meaning?

the others might think, fear of being found to have dirty underwear when they take you to the hospital after the accident,
fear of being hit by lightning, fear of irregularity and perpetual
constipation, fear of food that would poison you, fear of the flu
that had killed Helen, fear of rust that could cause the blood
poisoning that left Uncle Alec with the bent finger, fear of the
bruise that would become the lump that would become cancer, fear of what you might say and what you might not say.
And above all the other fears for the rest of them was the fear
of Grandma.

I may have to outline
what I've written to
see order, the propor-
tion and dimension
and pace.

But she did not entirely terrify me. When I said "darn" I
had my mouth scrubbed out with laundry soap, and when I
got tanned in the summer she took the same brown soap and
the scrubbing brush she used on the linoleum in the kitchen
to scrub the tan away. She believed that "to spare the rod was
to harm the child." And I was not harmed; the rod was not
spared. I was spanked with a shaving strap, with the back of a
hairbrush soaked to make it hurt the more, and with my father's
hand. My grandmother could press her hand together at the
hinges of my jaw and force soft-boiled egg down my throat.
But I also knew her in a way that her own children did not
seem to know her.

The genre seems right.
It is a familiar essay—
not an argument, a
short story, a poem. It
really isn't a profile or
character sketch. It's
not just about my
grandmother, but
about not escaping.

Has to be less or
more. Cut it or de-
velop it.

When I was young my mother was away most days with
her friends, shopping in Boston, and I was alone with Grandma.
I heard her singing hymns as she did the housework, heard her
talking, casually, with Morison or with God. I could get her to
tell me stories of Scotland, and I could make her laugh.

I think this transition
probably works.

She was the only one I knew who knew my friends who
lived in the walls were real. She did not talk at them, smiling
knowingly and winking over my head; she visited with them,
and they could play with us. She always remembered the imaginary cake in the invisible pan, and when I painted and repainted the back steps with water, she always knew to step
over the wood where the paint had not yet dried.

I think these para-
graphs work.

When I tipped the woven cane living room chairs over
and covered them with a blanket, she would visit me in the
igloo, the cave, the tent. When I lined up the dining room
chairs she would sit in the bow and paddle the war canoe, or
when I put the fan in front she would fly with me to Paris, as
Lindbergh had just done. And at the end of the day, when all
the chores were done and it was too early to light the lamps
and start supper and too dark to read, she would let me sit
with her in the gloaming, when she seemed most alone.

This worries me. I'm
not seeing chunks to
cut or reorder or in-
serts to be made. Am I
too close to it, or did
my planning really
work? No need to
change just to change.
Leaving alone is as
much an act of craft
as cutting. Try to re-
member that.

Then one Saturday night when I was rushing up to bed,
leaping two steps at a time, I found her collapsed on the stairs,
curled up like the dead dog I found curled up under the bush.
Her dress moved, but she only grunted, she could not seem to
speak.

Late that night after they had told me time and time again
to go to bed and I had paid no attention, long after Dr. Bartlett
had gone, we all stood around her bed, where she lay propped
halfway up on pillows. I was closest to her on her right side,
and when she grew agitated, trying to speak with a terrible
animal sound and flailing wildly with her one good arm, I think
it was I who brought her a pad of paper, and I think it was I
who was able to translate the meaning that lay between the
scrawled note and the face that was so terribly pulled down
on one side. I think it was I who laughed, and I think I remember Grandmother nodding, "She's telling you when to put the
leg of lamb in the oven for Sunday dinner."

Grandma was still in charge, and Grandma might have
suffered a stroke—a shock she would have called it—but she
would survive, and she would tell us what to do.

And she did just that. She lived until she was eighty-nine,
another eleven years, and she never got out of bed except
when we carried her in a special canvas sling to the couch in
the living room for a few special holiday dinners.

She grew thin, and her auburn hair that had been gray
turned pure white. Her left arm, which had always been so
busy making bread or grape jelly or kidney soup lay curled
and useless outside of the covers, unless we put it in. The skin
on that hand grew soft; it was almost transparent, and it had
the shiny pale colors I only saw on the inside of seashells.

In the mornings when I went out on the paper route and
when I returned and when I came home from school or in
from playing, I always checked to see if the sheets still moved.
I gave my Victorian grandmother the urinal or the bedpan
when it was needed, and I cleaned her afterwards, and I helped
lift her up in the bed, and I helped change the bed and put
salve to her bedsores, and helped her eat.

Her physical world shrank to her bedroom and to her
bed. It seemed to be as far as she could reach with the bamboo
back-scratcher that is still on my desk. With it she could pull
up the dark green Black Watch shawl she had brought from
Scotland. She lost her sense of time and would ask for lunch
just after we cleared the dishes away, and she talked more often
with Morison and with God. But still she was in charge.

I always checked in with her first after school or work
or church. She told my spinster uncle when to marry. And
each week there were visits from each of the uncles. My father
always stayed at a distance. His father and mother had both
worked in a mill and never owned or lost one. And my mother,
in her forties and her fifties, still took instruction on how to
make tea, and never felt she did it right.

I went away summers to get tans Gandma could no longer
scrub off. More and more my life was lived in my room, where

Boy, does this need editing. But at least I got a draft to work on. It does seem in the right place, but its importance has to be woven in. I'm growing up, I'm escaping her power, I'll have power over her—but of course I won't.

Can some of this be cut?

Or will the proportions and emphasis change if I show other ways she influenced us?

Values:
S S. Pierce
dress for church
not buy on sales
brand names
toughness
honesty
moralist—
   good
   and snotty

Make my feelings about this clearer? (Discover my feelings by revising.)

Is this what I mean to say—the emphasis on her being in charge? What's that got to do with my leaving home? Perhaps a lot, if she's still in charge.

I liked "spinster uncle," thought it clever. That made me suspicious. I asked my wife about it. She didn't like it. I'll reconsider it. But I still think it's clever.

Now I am back on course.

I had a ceiling of maps—Arabia, Antarctica, Africa, China and Japan—or where I worked after school on weekends, or on street corners or in gas stations, hanging out. I thought I was escaping this tight Scottish family that lived so in fear.

I hung out with the Irish. I smoked two packs of cigarettes a day. I learned to let a cigarette hang from the corner of my mouth, and learned to squint my eyes against the smoke. I took that first drink, and then I took more. I ate strange Mediterranean food—spaghetti and ravioli. I ate pepper and salads. I flunked out of high school to show them there was a Scot who could betray the heritage, and I went off to college to play football and never returned home.

This trails off and needs to be explained at the end. Maybe go on with a paragraph of later life?

The last time I saw Grandmother I was in the army, a paratrooper going overseas to fight Hitler. It was a hot, muggy August in Boston, and I was in my itching woolen winter uniform on a bus going from camp to a Red Sox game. I'd won the chance by luck.

This is too slow. Too many unnecessary details. Get to the point.

When I saw that the bus was going to pass ten blocks from my home I told the lieutenant that my grandmother was dying. I didn't mention that I had been watching for the sheets to move since I was a child. He told me he would slow down the bus, but if I wasn't at this corner when they passed by on their way back to camp I would be a deserter, because we were going overseas, and I would face a general court-martial. I nodded, swung off the bus, and even in my woolens ran the ten blocks home.

What is the point? I love this anecdote and wrote towards it, but does it make my point?

My mother shook my hand. We were Scots, and we did not show emotion. We went to stand by my grandmother's bed. She was delighted to see me. She smiled her crooked smile and held my hand with her good hand. She knew what I was doing. I was going off to war, but as we talked I realized I was not this Donald going off to World War II, or Donald her son for whom I was named and was in the Navy in the First World War, or Donald, her brother, or Donald, her father, but Donald, her great-uncle who had sat around the fire when she was a girl in the 1860s, and had shown her the bent leg that had taken a ball when he fought with the Black Watch at Waterloo. And with that great bringing together that the elderly can do, spanning centuries in a sentence, she was talking to that uncle long before she was born, and I became him when he was a boy going off to fight Napoleon.

This does run on. If I keep it, 75 percent should be cut.

Grandma died in a letter that I received when I was living in the rubble of a German city. But I think I knew by then that although I would only for a few weeks return home, I would never leave home, and I would never live without the sense of death nearby. Now I have, like Grandma, buried my father, my mother, and a daughter. And when I wake early or come

This seemed rhetorical when I wrote it. Perhaps the note I'm ending on is right, but I need to write more with information and let that information

home late it is first with a sense of dread. I am still waiting in speak for me, by im-
plication.
the shadows to see if the sheets will move.

I don't need to reoutline. The structure seems to stand up. The proportions are a bit off, but I don't need to build a new piece of writing. Just plane and set, cut and fit—I hope.

Maybe after I edit I'll need to back up and recast the piece. The only way I'll find out is to get in there and edit.

A Checklist for the Third Reading

Reading for Language

Now get out your sharpest pencil or favorite pen and be ruthless. You're a surgeon—cut, add, and reorder. Work in short chunks of time. I find that after fifteen minutes I begin to get kind to my prose. I can take a five-minute break and become an unfriendly stranger again. Read aloud, read every line, and solve the problems caused by every change. Each time you touch the text there is a chain reaction. You put in a new word and find you are repeating a word when you don't want to, or that this word casts a shadow on a word ahead. Now you are deeply into your craft, and you have the challenge of making an effective text line by line.

- ▶ Can the piece be read aloud? Will the reader have the illusion of the writer speaking to the reader?
- ▶ Are important pieces of specific information at the ends and beginnings of key sentences, paragraphs, sections, and the entire piece itself?
- ▶ Is the piece built on the subject-verb-object sentence?
- ▶ Have unnecessary clauses been cut?
- ▶ Are there sentences that announce what you are going to say, or sum up what you have already said, and therefore can be cut?
- ▶ Does the reader leave each sentence with more information than when the reader entered it?
- ▶ Is the sentence length varied, with shorter sentences usually used for clarification or emphasis?
- ▶ Is each word the right word?
- ▶ Is each word the simplest word?
- ▶ Is the piece written with strong verbs?
- ▶ Have unnecessary adverbs been eliminated?
- ▶ Has the verb "to be" been cut whenever possible?
- ▶ Have "ings" been eliminated whenever possible?
- ▶ Have the verbs been made active when they can be made active?
- ▶ Is the simplest tense used?
- ▶ Are the tenses consistent?
- ▶ Are the nouns strong and as specific as possible?
- ▶ Have adjectives been eliminated whenever possible?

▶ Is the writing as specific as possible?

▶ Is there sexist or racist language that should be cut or changed?

▶ Is every unnecessary word cut—especially thats, woulds, quites, verys?

▶ Have the parts of the sentences been reordered so they read naturally and smoothly?

▶ Has private language—jargon—been translated into public language?

▶ Have clichés—worn-out language—been replaced with meaningful language?

▶ Have the rules that clarify meaning been followed—and the rules that confuse meaning broken?

▶ Have people been put into the text whenever possible?

▶ Has the writing made the reader see whenever possible?

▶ Are all the elements of the writing woven into the text so they seem to occur naturally?

▶ Does each paragraph make one point?

▶ Does each paragraph develop that point and carry a full load of meaning to the reader?

▶ Do the paragraphs vary in length, with the shorter paragraphs used for clarification or emphasis?

▶ Are the paragraphs in the order the reader needs them so transitional phrases are unnecessary?

▶ Have unnecessary introductory and concluding paragraphs been cut?

▶ Is there an explicit or implied authority for the information in each paragraph?

▶ Does the reader need more information?

▶ Is each piece of information accurate, in fact and in context?

▶ Does the text flow easily and strongly from beginning to end?

▶ Is the piece of writing fair to the subject and to the reader?

▶ Are the repetitions purposeful?

▶ Does the reader receive a definition or other clarification at the precise moment in the text when it's needed?

▶ Does it sound like you?

Editing Marks

Here are some common marks editors make that you will find helpful in polishing a draft:

paragraph	¶ My grandmother grew small but still ruled with fear.
capital	my grandmother grew small but still ruled with fear.
close	My grand mother grew small but still ruled with fear.
separate	My grandmother grew/small but still ruled with fear.
transpose	My grandmother grew small, but still ruled with fear.

insert punctuation	My grandmother grew small͜but still ruled with fear.
take out	My grandmother ⁄grew small but still ruled with fear.
cut	My grandmother ~~grew small but~~ still ruled with fear.
restore	My grandmother ~~grew small but~~ still ruled with fear.
lower case	My ¢randmother grew small but still ruled with fear.
period	My grandmother grew small but still ruled with fear⊙
move to other place in text	My grandmother grew small but still ruled with fear.
insert	(stayed in bed and) My grandmother⁄grew small but still ruled with fear.
Insert A ＞	Large inserts should be marked in the left margin with an arrow and should follow on the next page, marked (Insert A).

Whatever marks you make, they should be clear and logical. Use common sense and imagine what you would need to be shown if you were the teacher or the editor.

In the next pages you will see what I have done on the third reading, and how the text reads after it has been edited and proofed.

I Still Waiting for the Sheets to Move

Made more active, immediate.

Problem—how to work in my age? Necessary?

~~When~~ I woke in the black, New England mornings to do (my paper route,) ~~I had a~~ *a family that came before* chore, ~~to perform first. I had to go and~~ *and stood* stand in the pale orange of ~~her~~ *my grandmother's* night light *to* ~~and~~ watch ~~to see~~ if the sheets rose and

fell.

Forgot to introduce "her."

In each line there are a hundred possibilities considered and reconsidered. I considered and reconsidered "authority of my childhood" a dozen times.

This tall authority of my childhood ? *a personal,* ~~friend of~~ *who was more powerful than* God, ~~and~~ *acquaintance of* ~~was loved with~~ fear *ed* by all the uncles and her daughter, my mother, was so frail ~~now~~ *now   her* *breathing barely* ~~she hardly had to~~ move/ the sheets ~~to~~ *d* ~~breathe.~~ I tried not to look at the black

hole of her mouth—her teeth grinned in

a glass on the night table—and studied the

top sheet. It did not move. This was the

night Grandma ~~had~~ died. Just ~~as I was ready~~ *before I decided*

to ~~go and~~ wake my parents, the sheet sud-

denly fluttered and fell.

This is the fun of editing—I have a piece of writing now that I can work on. It's meaning may come clear to me.

It was important to write this, and important to cut it.

(Death had always seemed to live in

our dark houses, not in the shadows but

sitting right there, his legs crossed, wear-

ing his terrible smile, just seated in the

living room chair, waiting. The sermons

talked of a real life hereafter. There were

Too much.

houses in Heaven and a universal broiler down below. Grandma lived with Morison, who had gone before, and she was glad that Helen, her daughter, had died in the flu epidemic, because she went with a man who drank beer. Every night I got down on my knees in my dark bedroom and prayed " … if I should die before I wake …"

(margin note: I thought "swelling" was clever when I wrote it. That should have told me. It wasn't—a distraction.)

~~My~~ *I* first ~~memories~~ *remember* of Grandma ~~must are~~ ? ~~have been when I was seated or crawling~~ ~~on the floor.~~ A great column of skirts ~~that~~ ~~rose to the vast swellings, and above them~~

her face looking down, disapproving, ~~and~~ *(Changed punctuation for emphasis.)* her hair *was* gathered ~~into~~ *or* a topknot like ~~a~~ *the*

(margin note: I hope these details establish the atmosphere of British lower middle class respectability.)

crown, *on* Queen Mary, *'s head* whose picture was *the Bible, and the gilt-framed steel* in the living room with King George, ~~wore~~ *engraving crated from Scotland and always hung in the front room.* ~~her hair the same way.~~

¶ ~~I knew the legends of~~ Grandma ~~from~~ *taught me her own legends. How* ~~my mother, from the uncles, and from~~ ~~herself. She would tell me, to teach me~~ I *(margin note: I hope there's a little surprise in this.)* should never disobey, ~~that~~ *as* she had disobeyed when she was a schoolgirl on Is

(margin note: How hard it is to fight that weed, the verb "to be.")

lay, an island in the Hebrides off Scotland. *led her friends through* She had ~~taken~~ the short cut across the forbidden pasture. ~~She had~~ *Grandma had* looked for the bull, but hadn't seen ~~it~~ *him,* and *had* taken the *he was not there,* chance, as if she had known better than *(margin note: The order must deliver the information in an efficient (graceful) order that emphasizes what is important.)*

her parents. ~~And then~~ the bull ~~had~~ charged.

She ~~put~~ *shoved* her friends behind her, pulled

~~out~~ her huge sewing scissors from her

school bag, and rammed them up the nos-

trils of the bull.

¶ *At the end of the story,* ~~She~~ reminded me to obey my par-

always ents, but I started looking for shortcuts, *of course*

hoping for bulls.

¶ *When I was a child, still living in a single-family house,* (In the front hall) there was a great,

~~tall~~ porcelain jar and, in it, a bouquet of

umbrellas and canes. ~~Every day~~ it re-

minded me of ~~the story about~~ what hap-

pened to the robber. It was after Grand-

mother ~~had moved to this country~~ *sailed to America from Scotland for the first time,* and

when the grandfather I never knew still

owned ~~had~~ the mill. The payroll was in the safe

at the house, and Grandfather was away

someone on business, when Grandma heard ~~a sound~~

¶ downstairs. She found the robber in the

kitchen, and he pointed a ~~big~~ six-gun at

said, " right there" her. She ~~told him to~~ wait, ~~and~~ anyone who

mother knew ~~Grandma~~ knew he waited. She went

to the front hall, ~~and~~ selected a heavy cane

returned from the same porcelain jar, ~~went~~ to the

kitchen, broke the robber's wrist with one

Grandmother stroke, then, called my Uncle Alec, her old-

fetch est son, and told him to ~~get~~ the constable.

Marginal annotations:

- I liked this last line, but does it draw one off the track?
- Oops, abrupt transition.
- Every day just not true.
- I had to take a break here; editing like this is so intense I have to walk away from it for a few minutes, then return.
- Am I weaving in too much family history or does it add texture?
- All six-guns pointed at you are big.
- Do I know this was what she said? I know it was in the legend I was told.
- Cutting "and" speeds it up.

I never really began to understand

why the uncles'/and my mother ~~loved my~~
~~grandmother so, or~~ were so ~~dependent one~~ *tied to Grandmother for direction*
and approval. She certainly gave them direction, but precious little approval.
~~her.~~ ~~It was something even beyond the~~
Scots felt duty, *obligation, and guilt were better motivators than*
~~natural~~ *extreme* ~~of Scottish duty and ob-~~
praise and earthly rewards
~~ligation. But~~ while researching this paper

I found that Grandma's husband, Morison

se
Smith, who ~~looked so successful~~ in the
on the wall *looked* *of itself*
brown photograph, ~~his~~ *face* so sure ~~above~~

~~his beard,~~ had died a failure. Mother and
never let on about that. I was told.
Grandma ~~had protected his image,~~ He had
he
~~indeed,~~ been an ~~owner of~~ a mill, and ~~that~~
as a standard of achievement and proof
-ed
was held up to me. I ~~did~~ belong/in the
Grandfather, it turns out,
middle class. But ~~he had~~ lost the mill and
other positions. *baked*
lost many ~~jobs, and~~ Grandma ~~had had to~~

~~cook~~ bread ~~in the kitchen~~ to keep the fam-

ily going. The farm girl from Islay, ~~who~~
a *on the command of the absentee landlord,*
had been ~~the~~ servant girl in London, ~~and~~ *but*
she escaped that life a decade later by marrying a
~~who had married the older~~ widower as he
left ~~to operate~~ *manage a linen mill. Eventually he*
~~was leaving~~ for America ~~had been~~ a mill, *started his own mill, and she had servants of her own as*

owner's wife.

But he had a "fiddle foot." He was

always looking for a better position, a
made
quicker way to become rich. Once he ~~sold~~

chocolates ~~and he had~~ Grandma cook them
he
on her kitchen stove and sold them door-

to-door, dreaming he was a Cadbury. Their

of Grandma's bedroom,

The inflated diction of "positions" will, I hope, imply the family's pretensions.

children saw it was Mother who kept them

together. *was their Father failed in America, in England,*
in Scotland, and then back in America again, where he died, his
youngest son still in high school.

neighborhood and I could not understand how important
We lived in a working-class flat, but
it was that we believed ~~we were down~~ on our luck in the Great

Depression, but we were middle class *when I was young.*

¶I despised her pretensions, ~~her con-~~

she was obsessed *what* *thought.* *had to be*
cern with the neighbors—the shades drawn

and
just so, she changed her clothes every

afternoon. We never ate in the kitchen

until she was paralyzed and didn't know.

Her Sunday dinners were ceremonies, and

; all the family came back for every holiday.

She ~~always~~ sat at the head of the table.

¶ *My mother, my father,* ~~and my~~
~~It was a strange household. Grandma~~
uncle, and I all
~~was in charge, and the four of us lived~~ in

Grandmother's *always.*
~~her~~ house, all children ~~somehow~~. My

mother, ~~who~~ did not cook, for it was

Grandma's kitchen and Grandma's special

wood stove; my father, who wore his
always kept his distance from my grandmother, as if he were still
salesman's smile to work or church, my *my mother's suitor;*
ate his meals quickly, then
spinster uncle, the accountant, ~~who worked~~
returned to his
~~late on,~~ account books on the oak desk in
his *I took to living the streets.*
the corner of ~~the~~ bedroom; and, ~~myself.~~
too much to leave.
They ~~all~~ feared Grandma, ~~In fact~~ our

home seemed glued together by fear: fear

of God whose lightning fast rod was held

by Grandma; fear of the neighbors, ~~but~~

This didn't flow at all and it certainly wasn't clear to the reader. I won't be sure of the changes until the piece is typed.

Show it, don't tell it.

Too cute?

I must put in a transition here.

I hope this litany works. I'll read it again to be sure.

especially *those who were* ~~the~~ Irish Catholics *or*; fear of Drink,

the curse of Scotland; fear of Roosevelt;

fear of smoking; fear of sex; fear of failure;

~~fear of what the others might think~~, fear

of ~~being found to have~~ *having* dirty underwear

when they take you to the hospital after

the accident; fear of being hit by lightning;

fear of irregularity and perpetual consti-

pation; fear of food that ~~would~~ *might* poison ~~you~~;

fear of the flu that had killed Helen *Aunt in 1917*; fear

of rust that could cause the blood poison-

ing that left Uncle Alec with ~~the~~ *a* bent fin-

ger; fear of the bruise that would become

the lump that would become cancer; fear

of what you might say and *fear of* what you might

not say~~,~~*;* And ~~above all~~ the ~~other~~ *greatest* fear~~s for~~ *or of all was*

~~the rest of them was the~~ fear of Grandma.

and I didn't know why

But she did not entirely terrify me.

When I said "darn" ~~I had~~ *she* (my mouth)

scrubbed out with laundry soap *or*, and when

~~I got~~ tanned in the summer she took the

~~same~~ brown soap and *the* scrubbing brush she

used on the linoleum in the kitchen to

scrub the tan away. She believed that "to

spare the rod was to harm the child." ~~And~~

I was not harmed; ~~the~~ *her* rod was not spared.

I was spanked with a chaving strap, with

Side notes (left margin):

I hope these specifics recreate the climate in which we and Grand-mother lived. And sets up how we felt when she collapses on the stairs.

I am exploring—dis-covering how I feel about her—and my childhood.

Side notes (right margin):

I worry that young readers will not under-stand what I'm talking about. I'll have to have test readers.

I must make Grandma into what she was— something less than a monster.

the back of a hairbrush soaked to make it

hurt the more, and with my father's hand, *on my grandmother's command.*

It was true, but it might not be believed. And it isn't necessary for what I want to say.

~~My grandmother could press her hand to-~~   I hate to cut this; I'm still mad about it, but

~~gether at the hinges of my jaw and force~~   it doesn't fit here.

~~soft-boiled egg down my throat.~~ But I also

knew her in a way that her own children

did not seem to know her.

When I was young my mother, ~~was~~ *not allowed to cook or clean in Grandma's house, spent her* ~~away most~~ days with ~~her~~ friends, shopping *as if my father owned a mill instead of selling ladies' hosiery.* in Boston, ~~and~~ I was alone with Grandma,

I ~~heard her~~ *sang* singing hymns, as she did the *with her* *and kept quiet when I* housework, ~~heard her talking, casually, with~~

~~Morison~~ or with God. ~~I could get her to~~

~~tell me stories of Scotland, and I could~~   Too general. Cut it.

~~make her laugh.~~ ¶ *Grandmother,* ~~She~~ was the only one ~~I knew~~ who

knew my friends who lived in the walls, ~~were real.~~ She did not talk at them, smiling

knowingly and winking over my head; she

visited with them, ~~and they could play with~~

~~us.~~ She always remembered the imaginary

cake in the invisible pan, and when I

painted and repainted the back steps with

water, she always knew to step over the   It's just as important to leave works as to

wood where the paint had not yet dried.   change what doesn't, so I leave this alone. it seems to recreate the

When I tipped the woven cane liv-   quality and mood of those times.

ing room chairs (over) and covered them

with a blanket, she would visit me in the

igloo, the cave, the tent. When I lined up

the dining room chairs she would sit in

the bow and paddle the war canoe, ~~or~~ when *[and]*

I put the fan in front she would fly with

me to Paris, as Lindbergh had just done.

~~And~~ *[or]* at the end of the day, when all ~~the~~ *[her]*

chores were done and it was too early to

light the lamps and start supper ~~and~~ too *[yet]*

dark to read, she would let me sit with

her in the gloaming, *[sharing her quiet]* ~~time~~ *[so]* ~~when she seemed most~~

~~alone.~~

Then one/night *[Saturday]* ~~when~~ I ~~was~~ rush~~ing~~ *[ed]*

up to bed, leaping two steps at a time, ~~Ie~~ *[and]*

[Grandmother] found ~~her~~ collapsed on the stairs, ~~curled~~

~~up like the dead dog I found curled up~~

~~under the bush.~~ Her dress moved, *[at last,]* but she

only grunted, ~~she~~ *[and]* could not seem to ~~speak.~~ *[make sounds]*

[with her mouth, now strangely lopsided, and I can still hear myself scream for help.]

Late that night, after they had told

me time and time again to go to bed and

I had paid no attention, long after Dr. Bart-

lett had gone, we all stood around her

bed, where she lay propped halfway up

on pillows. I was closest to her on her

right side, and when she grew agitated,

trying to speak with a terrible animal sound

and flailing wildly with her one good arm,

I ~~think it was I who~~ brought her a pad of

paper, and I ~~think it was I who was able~~

Margin notes:

Her dress moving was written because I "saw" it as I wrote. I kept it during editing because it echoes the title and lead.

Using the name—which, of course, the reader doesn't know—seems to give the piece more authority than "the doctor." And it was what I would have thought then.

The dog draws the reader away from Grandmother.

~~to~~ translat~~e~~/the meaning that lay between

the scrawled note and the face that was

so terribly pulled down on one side. ~~I think~~

it was I who laughed, and I ~~think I~~ re-
when I said,

member Grandmother nodding, "She's

telling you when to put the leg of lamb in

the oven for Sunday dinner."

Now I leave in the "it was" I cut out above. Why? It sounds right here and didn't sound right there.

~~Grandma was still in charge, and~~

¶Grandma might have suffered a stroke—a

shock she would ~~have~~ called it—but she

would survive, and she would tell us what

to do.

~~And she did just that.~~ She lived until
eighty-nine

she was ~~89~~, another eleven years, and she

never got out of bed except when we car-

ried her in a special canvas sling to the
awkward

couch in the living room for a few ~~special~~

holiday dinners_) that never went right without Grandma in the kitchen._

She grew thin, and her auburn hair

that had been gray turned pure white. Her

left arm, which had always been so busy
the thick   _I loved,_

making bread or grape jelly or kidney soup

lay curled and useless outside of the cov-

ers, unless we put it in. The skin on that

hand grew soft; it was almost transparent,

and it had the shiny pale colors I ~~only~~ saw

on the inside of seashells.

I am re-seeing what I once saw. A writer's life is at least twice-lived.

Refers back to lead.

In the ~~early~~ mornings when I went out on ~~my~~ ~~the~~ paper route, ~~and~~ when I returned, *for breakfast,* ~~and~~ when I came when I came home from school, ~~or~~ in from *when I came* ~~playing,~~ *street hockey,* I always checked to see if the sheets still moved. I gave my Victorian grandmother ~~the urinal or~~ the bedpan when it was needed, ~~and~~ I ~~cleaned~~ *wiped* her afterwards, ~~and~~ I helped lift her up in the bed, ~~and~~ I ~~helped change the bed and~~ put salve ~~to~~ *on* her bedsores, and ~~helped her eat.~~ *I fed her who had once fed me.*

Her physical world shrank to, ~~her bedroom and to her bed. It seemed to be~~ as far as she could reach with ~~the~~ *her* bamboo back-scratcher ~~that~~ *That backscratcher* is still on my desk. ~~With~~ ~~it~~ *used it to* she ~~could~~ pull up the dark green Black Watch shawl she had brought from Scotland. She lost her sense of time, ~~and would~~ ask*ing* for lunch just after we cleared the *luncheon* dishes away, ~~and~~ she talked more often ~~with Morison and~~ with God. ~~But still she was~~ ~~in charge.~~

~~I always checked in with her first after school or work or church. She told my spinster uncle when to marry. And each week there were visits from each of the uncles. My father always stayed at a distance. His father and mother had both~~

I sense this is beginning to run long. I should get to the end faster.

What is editing? Putting in. Taking out. Re-ordering. That's all.

I'm reading these three paragraphs to see if they can be cut.

~~worked in a mill and never owned or lost~~
→ But   forties   in
~~one. And~~ my mother, in her ~~40's~~ and her
fifties,   daily   from Grandma
~~50's~~ still took instruction on how to make

           or
tea and never felt she did it right.

I went away summers to get tans
                              At home
Grandma could no longer scrub off. ~~More~~

~~and more my life was lived in my room,~~

~~where~~ I had a ceiling of maps—Arabia,
                    and thought that I would leave home.
Antarctica, Africa, China and Japan— ~~or~~

~~where I worked after school on week-ends,~~

~~or on streetcorners or in gas stations,~~

~~hanging out. I thought I was escaping this~~

~~tight Scottish family that lived so in fear.~~
                              No one in
I hung out with the Irish. ~~I smoked~~
the family smoked, so
~~two packs of cigarettes a day,~~ I learned to

let a cigarette hang from the corner of my
         taught myself
mouth, and ~~learned~~ to squint my eyes

against the smoke. I took that first drink,

and then I took more. I ate strange Med-

iterranean food—spaghetti and ravioli. I
   the   the   we never served at home,
ate pepper and salads. ~~I flunked out of high~~

~~school to show them there was a Scot who~~   True, but it doesn't
                                                              add to this story.
~~could betray the heritage,~~ and I went off
                  to think I had left Grandma and my
to college to play football and ~~never re-~~ family forever.

~~turned home.~~

The last time I saw Grandmother I

was ~~in the army~~ a paratrooper going over-

This may have to be cut more—does it add to the point I'm making: I can't leave home? Yes, it does.

seas to fight Hitler. ~~It was a hot, muggy August in Boston, and I was in my itching-woolen winter uniform on a bus going from camp to a Red Sox game. I'd won the chance by luck.~~

~~When I saw that the bus was going to pass ten blocks from my home I told the lieutenant that my grandmother was dying. I didn't mention that I had been watching for the sheets to move since I was a child. He told me he would slow down the bus, but if I weren't on this corner when they passed by on their way back to camp I would be a deserter, because we were going overseas, and I would face a general court martial. I nodded, swung off the bus, and even in my woolens ran the 10 blocks home.~~

A good story, but not necessary here.

~~My mother shook my hand. We were Scots, and we did not show emotion. We~~ —I stood ~~went to stand~~ by my grandmother's bed. ~~She was delighted to see me.~~ and She smiled her crooked smile and held my hand with her good/ right hand, terribly weak now She knew ~~what I was doing,~~ I was going off to war, but as we talked I realized I was not this Donald going off to World War II, or Donald, her son, ~~for whom~~ . . . .

I hope this gives the reader the sense of history I felt—and makes them feel the bonds of this family that can be fled but not escaped.

~~I was named and~~ was in the Navy in the

first World War, or Donald, her ~~brother,~~ father,

or Donald, her ~~father,~~ brothers but Donald, her great-

uncle who had sat around the fire when

she was a girl in the 1860's, and ~~had~~ shown off

~~her~~ the bent leg that had taken a ball ~~when~~

~~he fought with the Black Watch~~ at Water-

loo. And with that ~~great~~ bringing together

that the elderly can do, spanning centu-

ries in a sentence, ~~she was talking to that~~

~~uncle long before she was born, and~~ I be-

came ~~him when he was a boy~~ the lad going off to

fight Napoleon.

I thought this end stunk; now I think it may work. We'll see after it is typed, re-read and shown to some test readers.

Grandma died in a letter ~~that~~ I re-

ceived when I was ~~living~~ hiding ~~out of~~ from shellfire in the rubble of

a German city, ~~But I think~~ I knew by then

~~that although I would only for a few weeks~~

~~return home,~~ I would never really leave home,

and I would never live without the sense

of death nearby. Now I have, like Grandma,

buried my father, my mother, and a

daughter. I live to more of her standards than I like to admit, And when I wake early or come

home late it is first with a sense of dread.

I stand in the shadows of the upstairs hall, watching the ~~am still waiting in the shadows~~ to see if ones I love,

the sheets ~~will~~ move.

I have taken that marked up mess of copy and dictated a draft from it. It was hard to stick to the copy, and I made a few changes, marking them down by pen so I would know what I'd done. The piece still wanted to grow and change, and I had doubts about whether it was working or not.

Here is the draft—I still can't call it a final draft—after I had done the line-by-line editing. I hope that a draft rises from this scrawled-over one that reads as if it were spontaneous. The work must be there, but it shouldn't show and keep the reader from the message.

I returned to the essay two months after the book was completed and after that draft had been read by some readers. I reread it again and had to make some small but important changes. The changes in the text are left because they demonstrate the way a writer keeps refining a draft until it has gone to the printer and it is too late to do any more.

I Still Wait for the Sheets to Move

I woke in the black New England mornings to a family chore that came before my paper route, and stood in the pale orange of my grandmother's night-light to watch if the sheets rose and fell.

This tall authority of my childhood—a personal acquaintance of God—feared by all the uncles and her daughter, my mother, was now so frail her breathing barely moved the sheets. I tried not to look at the black hole of her mouth—her teeth grinned in a glass on the night table—and studied the top sheet. It did not move. This was the night Grandma died. Just before I decided to wake my parents, the sheet suddenly fluttered and fell.

I first remember Grandma as a great column of skirts and her face looking down, disapproving. Her hair was gathered in a topknot like the crown on Queen Mary, whose picture was in the living room with King George, the Bible, and the gilt-framed steel engravings crated from Scotland and always hung in the front room.

Grandma taught me her own legends. How when she was a schoolgirl in Islay, an island in the Hebrides off Scotland, she had led her friends through the shortcut across the forbidden pasture. I should never disobey as she had disobeyed. Grandma had looked for the bull, but hadn't seen him, and had taken the chance he was not there, as if she had known better than her parents. Then the bull charged.

She shoved her friends behind her, pulled her huge sewing scissors from her schoolbag, and rammed them up the nostrils of the bull.

At the end of the story, she always reminded me to obey my parents, but, of course, I started looking for shortcuts, hoping for bulls.

When I was a child, still living in a single-family house, there was a great porcelain jar in the front hall and, in it, a bouquet of umbrellas and canes. It reminded me of what happened to the robber. It was after Grandmother sailed to America from Scotland for the first time, and when the grandfather I never knew still owned the mill. The payroll was in the safe at the house, and Grandfather was away on business, when Grandma heard someone downstairs.

She found the robber in the kitchen, and he pointed a six-gun at her. She said, "Wait right there." Anyone who knew Grandmother knew he waited. She went to the front hall, selected a heavy cane from the same porcelain jar, returned to the kitchen, broke the robber's wrist with one stroke. Then Grandmother called my Uncle Alec, her oldest son, and told him to fetch the constable.

I never really began to understand why the uncles and my mother were so tied to Grandmother for direction and approval. She certainly gave them direction, but precious little approval. Scots felt duty, obligation, and guilt were better motivators than praise and earthly reward.

While researching this paper I found that Grandma's husband, Morison Smith, whose faced looked so sure of itself in the brown photograph on the wall of Grandma's bedroom, had died a failure. Mother and Grandma never let on about that. I was told he had been a mill owner, and he was held up to me as a standard of achievement and proof I belonged in the middle class. But Grandfather, it turns out, lost the mill and lost many other positions. Grandma baked bread to keep the family going. The farm girl from Islay had been a servant girl in London on the command of the absentee landlord, but she escaped that life a decade later by marrying a widower as he left for America to manage a linen mill. Eventually he started his own mill, and she had servants of her own as a mill owner's wife. But he had a "fiddle foot." He was always looking for a better position, a quicker way to become rich. Once he made Grandma cook chocolates on a kitchen stove and he sold them door to door, dreaming he was a Cadbury. Their children saw it was Mother who kept them together as Father failed in America, in England, in Scotland, and then back in America again, where he died, his youngest son still in school.

I despised her pretensions when I was young. We lived in a working-class neighborhood and I could not understand how important it was that we believed we were middle class. She was obsessed with what the neighbors thought. The shades had to be drawn just so, and she changed her clothes every afternoon. We never ate in the kitchen until she was paralyzed and didn't know. Her Sunday dinners were ceremonies, and the family came back for every holiday. She sat at the head of the table.

My mother, my father, my uncle, and I all lived in Grandmother's house, all children always. My mother did not cook, for it was Grandma's kitchen and Grandma's special wood stove; my father, who wore his salesman's smile to work or church, always kept his distance from my grandmother, as if he were still my mother's suitor; my spinster uncle, the accountant, ate his meals quickly, then returned to his account books on the oak desk in the corner of his bedroom; and I took to the streets.

They feared Grandma too much to leave. Our home seemed glued together by fear: fear of God, whose lightning-fast rod was held by Grandma; fear of the neighbors, especially those who were Irish Catholic; fear of Drink, the curse of Scotland; fear of Roosevelt; fear of smoking; fear of sex; fear of failure; fear of having dirty underwear when they take you to the hospital after the accident; fear of being hit by lightning; fear of irregularity and perpetual constipation; fear of food that might poison; fear of the flu that had killed Aunt Helen in 1917; fear of rust that could cause the blood poisoning that left Uncle Alec with a bent finger; fear of the bruise that would become the lump that would become cancer; fear of what you might say and fear of what you might not say; and the greatest fear of all, Grandma.

But she did not entirely terrify me and I don't know why. When I said "darn" she scrubbed out my mouth with laundry soap, and when I tanned in the summer she took the same brown soap and the scrubbing brush she used on the linoleum in the kitchen to scrub the tan away. She believed that "to spare the rod was to harm the child." I was not harmed; her rod was not spared. I was spanked with a shaving strap, with the back of a hairbrush soaked to make it hurt the more, and with my father's hand on my grandmother's command. But I also knew her in a way that her own children did not seem to know her.

When I was young my mother, not allowed to cook or clean in Grandma's house, spent her days with friends, shopping in Boston as if my father owned a mill instead of selling ladies' hosiery. I was alone with Grandma, I sang hymns with her as she did the housework and kept quiet when I heard her talking, casually, with God.

Grandmother was the only one who knew my friends who lived in the walls. She did not talk at them, smiling knowingly and winking over my head; she visited with them. She always remembered the imaginary cake in the invisible pan, and when I painted and repainted the back steps with water, she always knew to step over the wood where the paint had not yet dried. When I tipped over the woven cane living room chairs and covered them with a blanket, she would visit me in the igloo, the cave, the tent. When I lined up the dining room chairs she would sit in the bow and paddle the war canoe, and when I put the fan in front she would fly with me to Paris, as Lindbergh had just done. At the end of the day, when all her chores were done and it was too early to light the lamps and start supper yet too dark to read, she would let me sit with her in the gloaming, sharing her quiet.

Then one Saturday night I rushed up to bed, leaping two steps at a time, and found Grandmother collapsed on the stairs. Her dress moved at last, but she only grunted and could not seem to make sounds with her mouth, now strangely lopsided, and I can still hear myself scream for help.

Late that night, after they had told me time and time again to go to bed and I had paid no attention, long after Dr. Bartlett had gone, we all stood around her bed, where she lay propped halfway up on pillows. I was closest to her on her right side, and when she grew agitated, trying to speak with a terrible animal sound and flailing wildly with her one good arm, I brought her a pad of paper, and I translated the meaning that lay between the scrawled note and the face that was so terribly pulled down on one side. It was I who laughed, and I remember Grandma nodding when I said, "She's telling you when to put the leg of lamb in the oven for Sunday dinner."

Grandma might have suffered a stroke—a shock she would call it—but she would survive, and she would tell us what to do. She lived until she was eighty-nine, another eleven years, and she never got out of bed except when we carried her in a special canvas sling to the couch in the living room for a few awkward holiday dinners that never went right without Grandma in the kitchen.

She grew thin, and her auburn hair that had been gray turned white. Her left arm, which had always been so busy making bread or grape jelly or the thick kidney soup I loved, lay curled and useless outside of the covers, unless we put it in. The skin on that hand grew soft; it was almost transparent, and it had the shiny pale colors I saw on the inside of seashells.

In the early mornings when I went out on my paper route, when I returned for breakfast, when I came home from school, when I came in from playing street hockey, I always checked to see if the sheets still moved. I gave my Victorian grandmother the bedpan when it was needed, I wiped her afterwards, I helped lift her up in the bed, I put salve on her bedsores, and I fed her who had once fed me.

Her physical world shrank to as far as she could reach with her bamboo back-scratcher. She used it to pull up the dark green Black Watch shawl she had brought from Scotland. That back-scratcher is still on my desk. She talked more often with God and lost her sense of time, asking for lunch just after we cleared the luncheon dishes away. But my mother, in her forties and in her fifties, still took daily instruction from Grandma on how to make tea and never felt she did it right.

I went away summers to get tans Grandma could no longer scrub off. At home I had a ceiling of maps—Arabia, Antarctica, Africa, China and Japan—and thought I would leave home. I hung out with the Irish. No one in the family smoked, so I learned to let a cigarette hang from the corner of my mouth, and taught myself to squint my eyes against the smoke. I took that first drink, and then I took more. I ate strange Mediterranean food—spaghetti and ravioli. I ate the pepper and the salads we never served at home, and went off to college to play football and to think I had left Grandma and my family forever.

The last time I saw Grandmother I was a paratrooper going overseas to fight Hitler. I stood by my grandmother's bed and she smiled her crooked smile and held my hand with her good right hand, terribly weak now. She knew I was going off to war, but as we talked I realized I was not this Donald going off to World War II or Donald, her son, who was in the Navy in the First World War, or Donald her father, or Donald her brother, but Donald her great-uncle who had sat around the fire when she was a girl in the 1860s, and shown off the bent leg that had taken a ball at Waterloo. And with that bringing together that the elderly can do, spanning centuries in a second, I became the lad going off to fight Napoleon.

Grandma died in a letter I received when I was hiding from shellfire in the rubble of a German city, but I knew by then I would never really leave home, that I would never live without the sense of death nearby. Now I have, like Grandma, buried my father, my mother, and a daughter. I live to more of her standards than I like to admit, and when I wake early or come home late it is first with a sense of dread. I stand in the shadows of the upstairs hall, watching the ones I love, to see if the sheets will move.

I've read the piece through, making a few changes, and feeling, I must confess, a sense of elation. I've captured something of my grandmother and my childhood. I've taken it out of my head and put it down where I can look at it and try to understand it. I hope it will mean something to others, but that's less important than the fact it means something to me.

You should play Monday morning quarterback. You have my notes and my drafts. Edit it yourself; see what you would make of it. Second-guess me; after all, there isn't a right or wrong way in writing. There are many ways to make a piece of writing work or fail. That's the fun—and the challenge.

Reading as a Writer

The woman who plays basketball watches the game differently than the people around her in the bleachers. And in the same way, the person who writes reads differently than other readers.

The biggest difference for the writing reader is that every text is dynamic, capable of change, full of possibility. The writer sees choice on every page, in every line. The writer appreciates and applauds when the text represents a good choice, hisses and boos when it doesn't. The reader who writes becomes involved in the text.

Read Fragments

The effective writer—and the effective editor or teacher—has to learn to read unwritten texts. This means that the writer has to be able to sift through random words, phrases, sentences that half work, scribbled outlines, telegraphic notes, incomplete paragraphs, false starts, the way an archeologist has to sift through the excavated refuse of an ancient civilization. The archeologist has to be able to read these fragments to recreate what was; the writer has to read the fragments to recreate what may be.

It's easy to read a text after it has been drafted, but the writer has to develop the skill to read a text when there is no text. The writer has to see which words are code words, words that have special meaning for the writer when they appear in the notebook. The writer has to pick the phrase that gives the hint of a special meaning or an effective voice. The writer has to see how a fragment can be developed and to spot the meaningful connections that may be made between specific details.

The writer reads texts that haven't yet been written. This is a strange form of misty reading in which the reader has to spot meaning before it is clear. It is anything but careful reading. The writer squints ahead to see or hear what may become a draft. The writer can train himself or herself to this form of reading by looking always for the potential in the notes that keep appearing on the notebook page or on the pages of predrafts: fragmentary drafts, aborted drafts, drafts that seem to go nowhere, drafts that fall apart, drafts that turn around and destroy themselves, drafts that trail off—all drafts that can have possibility within them.

Read What Is

One of the hardest tasks of the writer is to read what *is* on the page, not what the writer hoped would be on the page. We all, in reading our text, hear what we intended to say when we see the words on our own pages. The difficulty is to read those words without our intent getting in the way.

To do this I have to give myself a bit of time—sometimes only ten minutes—and I usually have to move to a different chair or place or table, and often I have to arm myself with a different-colored pen. Then I am ready to look at the words on the page to discover what I have actually said, what those words I chose with hope and with imagination actually say when my intentions are removed from them.

This is reading with a cold eye, but it is necessary and it is fun. It fascinates me to see what language has done on its own. Sometimes it has done less than I intended, but other times it has done more. Words can conceive their own meanings when placed together on the page. It is my job to make sure I know what is there so I can decide what should be there.

Read What Isn't

It is just as important to recognize what isn't on the page as what is. Most of us underwrite; since we know the context and the connotation of what we have written, we think the reader will too. This is understandable. We spend most of our time speaking to those who are familiar with us and with whom we share a common world. Science fiction fans talk about science fiction to others who read it. Scientists talk about their experiments to those who work in the lab with them. Soldiers discuss tactics with other soldiers. Writing takes us out of our world and allows us to speak to those who need to know much more than those with whom we usually converse.

We have to know what isn't on the page; we have to define terms. We have to put details in context. We have to make the significance clear. We have to spell out connections and implications. We have to be able to stand back and see how the text needs to be developed. It is normal for my writing and the writing of my students to increase in length by a third between the first and second drafts. We read what isn't there, and then make sure it is.

Read for a Reader

The writer has to become the representative of the reader. This usually means role-playing a specific reader, and therefore coming to the text as a stranger.

The reader will read the text fast. The text must be clear in a relatively superficial reading. The text must carry the reader along: it must be slow enough so the reader can absorb each point, but fast enough so the reader will not put it down. The text must answer the reader's questions—when they are asked. The text must have the music of an individual voice, so that the prose moves pleasingly and gracefully in the reader's ear and eye.

How do you do all those things? Follow the golden rule: Write as you would have others write unto you.

Read Writers

Writers know they do not write alone. They work in a tradition of writers from the past, and they work beside contemporary writers. The writers of past and present are all trying to solve similar problems as they try to make their meanings clear with language.

Writers read other writers to learn, to enjoy, to share, to steal, to feel superior, to appreciate the choices writers make as they develop their texts.

By reading you will understand the traditions and limits of each genre— what people are doing and not doing in the short story or the magazine article— so that you can challenge, with your own text, those limits and traditions. By reading you will hear other voices that make language dance in ways you never thought possible. And this may help you hear voices within your own head you never heard before. By reading you will see subject matter you never thought had value made significant by another writer, and you'll see in your own world things that need to be written. By writing you will see how other writers make the ordinary extraordinary, switch the point of view from which you usually look at the world, turn the world inside out before your eyes, put you in places you did not know exist, give you ideas you never thought of, place you inside the skin of other people.

Reading, always an extending experience, is even more so for the writer, who begins to understand through his or her own writing how reading can be made.

Using Test Readers

First we write, then we step back and read as a reader. But before we know whether to present our manuscript for publication we need test readers. And it may be easier to choose a husband or a wife than to choose a test reader. At the moment in the writing process when we have completed a draft we are especially vulnerable.

We fear criticism, for it may confirm our worst secret anxieties that we have little that is worth saying and that we have said it badly. The writer is exposed by the writing, and none of us wants to be exposed to a critical eye. But we do have defenses against criticism. As John Osborne says, "Asking a working writer what he thinks about critics is like asking a lamp-post what it feels about dogs." The reader is a bad reader; the reader is stupid; the reader is prejudiced; the reader is vicious.

We may know how to protect ourselves against criticism, but many of us never survive praise. We need it, want it, love it, and never get enough of it, and the person who praises our work is wise, fair, just, insightful, understanding, and perceptive. But we have to protect ourselves against the "like wow" critics who give us bland, general, delightful, but meaningless praise. Those readers do not help us resee our text; in fact they may even prevent us from seeing it at an effective distance.

Qualities of Good Test Readers

The writer has to search for those few special readers with whom we can share work in progress, and from whom we can receive reactions that help us when the helping really counts—before publication, when the text can be improved. These test readers may be teachers, editors, or colleagues, but they usually share similar qualities:

▶ ***They Write Themselves***   They know the territory emotionally and mentally and can have an appreciation of how we are thinking and how we are feeling. They understand where we are in the writing process.

▶ ***They Listen to What the Text Is Saying Without Preconception of What We Should Say and How We Should Say It***   I once had a well-known poet read my short poems and tell me that since I was a big guy I should write big poems. He didn't seem to understand that the poet in me is a short, secretive little guy. The criticism wasn't helpful. The effective test reader is a colleague who helps you, the writer, see what is evolving which is unexpected and worth keeping. This reader delights in surprises, in variation, in diversity, and helps evaluate the text on its own terms.

▶ ***The Reader Is Honest***   The effective test reader is able, because of the reader's own accomplishments, to admit to envy and admiration and to deliver disagreement and doubt. The critic does not withhold comments from both ends of the spectrum, but tries to deal not so much in praise or criticism as in specific comments on what works, and why; what doesn't work, and why; what may work, and why.

▶ ***Most Important, the Test Reader Makes You Want to Write***   The test reader may deliver bad news, but you should always leave the effective test reader eager to get back to the writing desk, to attack and solve the writing problems. Cultivate this kind of test reader.

How do you find such readers? By sticking your neck out. You show your drafts to those who you think will help you, and you return to those who do.

But you say you have to deal with a teacher—or an editor—who isn't helpful. Of course you do; of course I do. So now you know how the world works. But I also have a few test readers from whom I learn. They are my secret editors and teachers. I turn to them to find out how to deal with the others. And some of them actually are editors and teachers, for if you are a writer you never stop going to school.

Questions about Clarifying

My classmates don't edit my copy the way I would. Who's right?

Many times no one's right. Except for the most explicit rules of usage it isn't a question of right or wrong; it's a question of what works—what makes the meaning clear. Your classmates edit with their language, as they should. You should listen to them, because they may have some good suggestions, but you shouldn't follow them blindly. It's your voice that should appear on the page, not theirs.

How will reading aloud help me? I don't talk too good.

You probably talk better than you write, but you should watch out for the slang, the clichés, and the local dialect which may be appropriate in casual talk, but may not be appropriate in the writing you're doing in school.

Won't editing ruin my spontaneity?

Not in my experience. I've heard of editing making a piece of writing go stale, but I've never actually seen it happen. The most spontaneous one-liners by Johnny Carson, hook shots by Kareem, and pistol shots by Billy the Kid came after long practice. John Kenneth Galbraith says, "When I'm greatly inspired, only four revisions are needed before, as I've often said, I put in that note of spontaneity which even my meanest critics concede." I agree.

But if your first draft is clean and clear and does the job, don't mess with it. We don't mess with our copy just to be messing, but to make it work.

Do you have to do three readings?

No, sometimes you have to do seven or thirteen, or one. As I said, when you get experience you may be able to read in the three ways at the same time, but in the beginning you usually have to read separately for meaning, order, and voice. And that may not be enough to make your meaning clear.

Doesn't it get bo-o-o-o-o-o-ring to edit so much?

It seems boring when you look at it from a distance, but it's actually fun when you are in there messing around with meaning and language. Each change— what is taken out, what is put in, what is reordered—is a new experiment in meaning. You keep running into surprises, finding out things that you didn't know you knew, making connections and building new meanings.

"Nothing is more satisfying than to write a good sentence," says Barbara Tuchman. "It is no fun to write lumpishly, dully, in prose the reader must plod through like wet sand. But it is a pleasure to achieve, if one can, a clear running prose that is simple yet full of surprises. This does not just happen. It requires skill, hard work, a good ear and continued practice, as much as it takes Heifetz to play the violin." There's nothing quite so satisfying as making a sentence run clear, carrying a meaning to the reader in a well-crafted way that seems spontaneous.

Can't you learn to write so you don't have to edit?

You can't learn to write; that's one of the great things about being a writer, and one of the not-so-great things. You keep on learning to write. There are always new opportunities and new challenges. Each morning when you sit at your writing desk you start at zero point. You have to prove you can write, and the fact you have written, published, or even won awards doesn't seem to help.

I seem to be reading published writers differently. I like some of them better than I did before, but some of them are trying to row without an oar. Does this make sense?

It certainly does. You are a writer now, and you have an insider's view of the game of writing. You will begin to understand how some easy writing wasn't so easy to make, and how some other writing doesn't work at all. The person who is writing becomes a far different and better reader than the person who does not write.

When do I know when I am done editing?

When you're on deadline. I once took a survey of all the people in my department at the university who had written books. They had all revised or edited their books *after* their books had been accepted. There is no natural end to the editing process. As Paul Valery said, "Writing is never finished, only abandoned."

Clarifying Activities

1. Read your draft as fast as you can without making notes. Write down what works best and anything that might need to be added or cut. Then use the checklist on pages 168–169. Do the same thing with several classmates' papers and have them do yours.
2. Read your draft again, more slowly, to see if there are any sections of the piece that need to be cut or expanded and any new ones that need to be added. Then use the checklist on page 175. Do the same thing with several classmates' papers and have them do yours.

3. Read your draft line by line, making the changes necessary to make your meaning come clear. Make the changes right on the text. If you can't read the text after you've made a number of changes, retype it, incorporating the editing you've done, and then attack it again. Use the checklist on pages 181–182. Have some of your classmates edit your paper while you edit theirs.

4. Proofread your final text, using the checklist on pages 182–183. Ask some classmates to check your proofing while you check theirs.

5. Take a published piece of writing and give it the three readings. It may be helpful to photocopy the text so that there are wide margins you can use for editing.

6. Make your own editing checklist of the problems you see in your writing. Go back through your writing folder and identify those writing habits that interfere with communication. Ask your teacher and the classmates who have been editing your copy to suggest other items for your checklist. Keep your checklist where you can use it when you're editing.

7. Take a paragraph or a page by a successful writer and edit it from a different point of view, for a different audience or publication, from a different set of facts or assumptions, to make it have a different voice. Play with it, editing it five, ten, or fifteen different ways. Do the same thing to one of your own paragraphs or pages.

8. Take a piece of your writing, or someone else's, and paste it on the right-hand side of the page; then on the left-hand side of the page write down what each paragraph did to contribute to the overall success of the piece.

9. Take a piece of your writing, or someone else's, and cut it by 75 percent.

10. Take an example of bad writing, your own or someone else's (perhaps a textbook; perhaps this textbook)—writing that is obscure, confused, unclear, in bad taste, pompous, clumsy, silly, trite, vague, jargony, overwritten, any or all of the above—and edit it so it is clear and graceful.

The Writing Process At Work

You have seen a writing process at work—*a* writing process, not *the* writing process. You have observed one writer doing one piece of writing. When other writers write they may use a different process, and when an individual writer moves from one project to another the process may change.

I do not do all of the things I demonstrated on the piece about my grandmother every time I go through a writing project. They are all tools I use at one time or another. But my purpose in writing is not to follow a particular process, but to communicate a meaning as efficiently and gracefully as possible.

Sometimes you will find yourself writing so easily and effectively that you will not be aware of any process at all. Those are the golden days. They are the days which are possible because you have internalized a writing process and made it your own.

Other days you will start the writing process in a different place than with collecting. Often you will have an assignment or a hint of a subject that will give you a focus, and you will begin with that focus. If you have your facts in hand you will move ahead, or you may find that you have to go back and collect information so that you can develop the focus.

Poets see the world as poems; novelists as novels; journalists as news stories. And you too may have times when you see the form or order of a piece of writing right away. You may want to go with it and move ahead to drafting, or move back to collect more material and then skip focusing.

The experienced writer often hears writing in his or her head; language leads the writer to a piece of writing. Sometimes a phrase ignites a draft. This morning my wife, just returned from the small city in Kentucky that she left when she was a teenager, said she felt she had visited an "alien homeland." That might be enough for her to plunge into a piece of writing. There's a nice tension between the comfortable, rooted belonging of "homeland" and the detached unbelonging of "alien." Many of us in a mobile society feel such tensions. And once she has that indication of voice she may be able to write a draft.

If she starts that draft she may be able to complete it and move ahead, or she may find that the draft runs dry and she has to go back to collect, focus, order, and then draft again.

It may be that the piece of writing will begin during the editing process, when you decide to polish an earlier draft and find that it has a new potential.

All of these approaches are correct. There is no one right way to write. Writing starts in the middle or the end or the beginning of the process. It starts where it starts. And you use the process in whatever way it can help you make an effective piece of writing.

It is perfectly appropriate to jump around in the process, like a kangaroo with a typewriter, drafting, collecting, and fitting in what you've collected during the editing process. You may write a draft to discover the focus or discover what you have to collect.

And the dividing lines between the stages of the process will become blurred. Most of the time you will not be aware that you have passed from collecting to focusing, or focusing to ordering. You may edit as you draft. The parts of the process are not separate nations kept apart by barbed wire, soldiers, and guard dogs. The parts of the process overlap.

As I have indicated, the writing process is recursive. You do not march through it as much as keep circling back through it, taking a step or two back whenever you need to make the writing go.

I hope, however, that you have discovered that writing is a craft before it is an art, that it may appear to be magic when it is finished, but that the most magical writing was built in a logical, understandable fashion.

I have two and a half bookshelves filled with interviews with writers. These interviews allow me to converse with writers, living and dead, to hear what they have to say about what they went through as they wrote. I also have writers' diaries and journals, writers' letters, autobiographies by writers and biographies about writers, and I have books on writing, most often by nonwriters. But I keep turning back to the interviews. Some of my favorites are:

> Writers at Work: The Paris Review Interviews, First Series, edited, and with an introduction, by Malcolm Cowley, Penguin Books, New York (Viking 1958).

> Writers at Work: The Paris Review Interviews, Second Series, edited by George Plimpton and introduced by Van Wyck Brooks, Penguin Books, New York (Viking 1963).

> Writers at Work: The Paris Review Interviews, Third Series, edited by George Plimpton and introduced by Alfred Kazin, Penguin Books, New York (Viking 1967).

> Writers at Work: The Paris Review Interviews, Fourth Series, edited by George Plimpton and introduced by Wilfrid Sheed, Penguin Books, New York (Viking 1976).

> Writers at Work: The Paris Review Interviews, Fifth Series, edited by George Plimpton and introduced by Francine du Plessix Gray, Penguin Books, New York (Viking 1981).

> Afterwords—Novelists on Their Novels, edited by Thomas McCormack, Harper & Row, New York, 1969.

> Writers on Writing, compiled and edited by Walter Allen, E. P. Dutton & Co., New York, 1959.

> The Writer on Her Work, edited and with an introduction by Janet Sternburg, W. W. Norton, New York, 1980.

> Woman as Writer, Jeanette L. Webber and Joan Grumman, Houghton Mifflin Co., Boston, 1978.

> The Writer's Craft, edited by John Hersey, Alfred A. Knopf, New York, 1974.

You should certainly study the processes of other arts—composing and performing, music, writing plays—and the processes of other creative activities, such as science and engineering, merchandising and advertising, administering and governing, to see what can be adapted from those processes and applied to the process of writing.

A better source, however, will be those writers, your classmates and your teacher, whose drafts you see in process. When you see a piece of writing that you particularly like you should ask the writer how he or she wrote it. We are not always aware of what we are doing when we write, and we may forget some of the decisions we made, but we do remember the process well.

You should try some of their tricks to see if they work for you, and you should try some of my tricks to see if they make it possible for you to write better. Some you will try will not work now, but may work later, as you get more experience and face new writing tasks.

Common Writing Problems—and Solutions

Your most important source, however, is yourself. You should be aware of how you write after you have written. You can't be too self-conscious at the moment of writing or you may choke up, but you should keep some record of how the writing is going so you can look back when the writing has gone well to see the conditions, the attitudes, and the processes that allowed you to produce effective writing. You should develop your own writing process with all its variations, so that you have a resource to fall back on and make use of all your writing life.

You should make your own list in your process log of the writing problems that occur on your own pages and list the ways you have solved them, the ways others have solved them, and the ways you may try to solve them in the future. Not every one of us has the same writing problems. Some writers shovel in so much extra documentation that the reader loses track of what is being documented; others expect to be taken on faith and rarely provide documentation.

We also have different problems at different stages of our writing development. When I first started writing, my prose was disorganized, and I had to work hard to limit and direct it. After decades of working at organization I organize instinctively, and my writing is sometimes too organized; I have to work hard to let my writing run free. Now I work on flow and think less about organization. I know it will be there.

Here are some of the most common writing problems I see in student papers, professionals' copy, and my own pages, and some of the most effective solutions to those problems. If you have followed the process approach many of these problems will be solved by the process itself, but you will still find that you will face most of these problems at one time or another. Add your ways of dealing with these problems so that you will have a range of solutions when the problems occur.

What's It Mean?

Many times a draft will remind me of mystery meat in the college dining hall. It's something, but what? An effective piece of writing has a single dominant meaning. Excellent writing usually has density, a number of additional meanings or levels of meaning. But all must add up to the principal meaning.

Of course, in writing there are always exceptions, but I don't know of an example of a piece of writing that has two or three equal meanings. And I certainly don't know of effective writing that has no meaning at all. Writing is thinking.

When you face a piece of writing without a single dominant meaning you may:

▶ Decide on a dominant meaning that can be stated in a sentence. Relate every part of the piece, explicitly or implicitly, to that meaning. Sections that can't be related to the meaning are cut.

▶ Try the piece of writing out on a few test readers. Ask them what they think the meaning is, or could be. If one suggestion makes sense to you, rework the piece to make that meaning clear.

▶ Put the text aside—hide it in a drawer or turn it over—and write out the meaning you think it should have; then rewrite or edit the piece so it does.

▶ Read through the piece and underline what interests or surprises you the most. See if that is the meaning the piece should focus on.

▶ Role-play a reader. Decide what information or meaning is most important to that reader. Fix the piece so it reveals and documents that point.

▶ Think back to the meaning you thought the piece would have when you started, and write it down. Then write the meaning you think the piece has now—what has been discovered through the writing—and write that down. See if you can blend the two into a single meaning.

Who Says?

The reader needs to have a feeling of authority in a piece of writing. The writer should sound familiar with the subject. Good writing is not hesitant or tentative. Here are some of the ways a piece can increase its authority:

▶ Write with specific details. The reader is impressed—often overly impressed—with concrete details. "Expensive cars drove up to the house" becomes much more convincing when it reads, "A Mercedes, two Cadillacs, a Lincoln, a Porsche, and another Mercedes drove up . . ."

▶ Write with verbs and nouns, in that order. Avoid adverbs and adjectives. Use simple active verbs and proper nouns. You will sound as if you speak with authority.

▶ Use quotations and attribute them to authorities. Cite other specialists, documents, reports, institutions. The reader will be helped by these examples of research within the text.

▶ Show as much as you tell, or more. Get out of the way and let the reader see the evidence firsthand—put the reader at the scene of the accident, let the reader sit in the back of the courtroom, let the reader watch the operation, make it possible for the reader to hear the politician.

▶ Use the first person—"I"—if it will help the reader believe the piece of writing. Do not use the abstract "one"; use the more direct "I" for documentation that will let the reader know the writer was on the scene.

Come On, Let's Get This Show on the Road.

Readers are impatient. Sometimes teachers will require introductions, and if so you will have to write them. But most readers don't want warm-ups, explanations, prologues. They want you to get right to it. Here are some ways you can:

▶ Read through your text in a hurry and identify the point nearest the end at which you can start. Start there. Sometimes it will be on page 4, other times it may be on page 11 or 14.

▶ Read through the text until you come to the first piece of hard evidence or the first scene, or the first anecdote, or the first good quote. Start there and weave in the information you had before that that the reader really needs. You may find a page—or three pages or seven—shrinking to a few sentences or paragraphs that can be worked into the text at the point the reader really needs the information.

▶ Take a piece of paper and cover up the first paragraph. Read the piece quickly—just the first page or so—and see if you miss that paragraph. If you don't, move on to the next one. I've made pages of my prose disappear this way.

The Ending Just Trails Off and Fades Away.

Reverse all of the above, working backwards from the end.

The Text Staggers over the Countryside, Circling Back and Crisscrossing Its Own Trail.

The reader will rarely be charmed by a wandering text. The reader expects to be presented with information that moves forward in an orderly fashion towards meaning. Sometimes the writer has to write a wandering text to discover meaning, but it is the responsibility of the writer to clarify and direct that meaning. Here are some of the ways a wandering text can get back on track:

▶ Write a sentence that contains all of the forces within the piece. For example, "This is a profile of a special forces commander who was arrested at a peace rally." When you have that focus on the piece you know that you'll be able to leave out or minimize the information about his hobbies of mountain climbing and wild boar hunting, his formal education and military experience, unless they relate to his present change of heart about military activity.

▶ Reoutline. This is one of the places where it is especially helpful to outline. When you outline you may be able to pick out precisely where you want to end, and then map a course that will get you there.

My Piece Doesn't Wander So Much as Go Off on Tangents.

It's hard for many writers to leave out a piece of information they have researched. Some of the information is very interesting, but it can't stay in unless it advances the meaning. The reader will simply follow the first or second tangent and continue on, never returning to the main piece at all.

▶ Cut the piece apart by paragraphs, and spread them out. As you move the paragraphs around it's usually easy to see which go off on tangents, which repeat what has already been said, and which were in wrong order in the piece.

▶ Cut the paragraphs or pages you have devoted to each tangent out of the text and put them in separate folders, one per tangent. Mark the subject on the tab of each folder and tell yourself you will do those articles later.

▶ Reoutline the piece to see if the material in the tangents can be fitted into the text in another place. Perhaps it needs to be moved closer to the front— or to the end. If it doesn't fit, cut it.

▶ Write the material in the tangent as a side bar. That's a magazine term for a short article published beside a longer one on the same subject. Sometimes the profile of a person mentioned in the article, or a complex definition of scientific terms, or the description of an engineering process, or suggestions for how the reader can take political action, cannot be fitted into the main piece but can be published alongside for interested readers.

Aw Come On, Who's Going to Believe That?

The reader should be skeptical. The writer, in most cases, is not the authority on the subject. The writer is reporting what other authorities have said. Who those authorities are has to be spelled out so that the reader can decide to accept them or not and knows where to investigate the source of significant information, if the reader wants to make that effort.

▶ Footnotes provide authority in scholarly writing. Each discipline has its own standard for footnoting, but the purpose and the effect are the same— they let the reader know where the information came from so the reader can go to that information.

▶ A bibliography gives a list of the principal sources used in a piece of writing, and it helps the reader know where the writer got the information, and also allows the reader to know where to go to pursue further information.

▶ Attribution is usually woven into the text in nonscholarly writing. This takes a bit of skill, for the way the reader is given the attribution depends on the flow of the text, its voice, its purpose, and the kind of information the reader needs. Much information is left out, but there should be enough so that the reader knows, either explicitly or implicitly, where the writer got the information.

▶ Analogy is another way to make the reader believe. A subject the reader does not know about is described in terms with which the reader is familiar. A computer microchip might be described as a road map. This is a powerful device, but a dangerous one. It can be patronizing and oversimplifying. Worst of all, it can be inaccurate—a microchip is not a road map.

Where Are You Coming from, Anyway?

One of the hardest things for the writer to guard against is building a piece on a totally unjustified assumption. Every piece of writing is built on a foundation of common assumptions that come from the heritage, the way of thinking, the experience, the language, the knowledge we share. It's fairly easy to guard against the assumptions that are clear prejudice or stereotypes—men aren't sensitive, women aren't tough, Greeks run restaurants, Vermonters don't talk. It's much harder to protect yourself against those beliefs that may be true for you, your family, and the people you've grown up with, but may not be true for your readers. Everyone, for example, may not think that America is a militaristic nation, or that it is not; everyone may not think abortion is murder, or is a normal matter of choice; everyone may not think that marijuana is harmful, or not harmful. Here are some of the ways you can guard against building your piece of writing on unjustified assumptions:

▶ Role-play a reader from a different part of the country, a different racial background, a different sex, a different religion, a different political persuasion, and look for the assumptions that lie behind the information in the piece and the tone with which it is conveyed.

▶ Select a reader from one of the categories above, or ask a fellow writer to role-play the appropriate category, and have this person tell you what assumptions you've used. Don't get mad—pay attention to those that surprise you. Your writing may reveal that you are more of a sexist or a racist than you realize. Pay attention. One of the reasons you are in college is to be confronted with the prejudices you do not realize you have, and writing is revealing. That's one reason it's so scary. And it's also a reason that it's important to write, for writing holds a mirror up to your own thinking.

Okay, You May Know What You Mean, But I Don't.

Most beginning writers underwrite. They are so familiar with their subject that they cannot understand how much information the reader needs. An example of this is the student who writes about Saturday night in this way:

> I didn't expect it to happen. I suppose I should have seen it coming, but I just didn't expect it. I do know, however, that as long as I live I will never forget Saturday night. It was the kind of experience that changes you and you are never the same again.

The writer could have been writing about a first kiss, a first baby, a tornado that killed seven people, an automobile wreck that killed three, an automobile accident that almost happened but didn't, the death of a parent, the eating of fried clams for the first time. That text is a blank check for the reader to fill in.

Readers read for information, specific, concrete information, and it is the writer's job to provide an abundance of that information. Here are some things to do to make sure you have:

▶ Read the piece as a stranger and note what information you would need if you didn't know the subject firsthand.

▶ Ask a test reader to tell you what additional information is needed.

▶ Go through the text and make every general or vague statement specific.

▶ Turn away from the text and brainstorm concrete details that you know about the subject, then weave the most interesting and significant ones into the text. As you do this, new ones will appear in your mind. Use them.

▶ Make a box outline described on page 103, indicating the amount of text you have for each point. Once when I did this while working on a novel I found I'd allowed only one paragraph for one of the most important scenes in the book. You're writing about an accident, and yet you may find that you've kissed off the accident in a sentence, when it may take a page, or pages, to make the reader experience it. Pay attention to the dimensions of each part of the piece you're writing and the proportions between those parts.

▶ Take the most important part of your draft and limit the whole article to that. Then use the space to develop that part of the article appropriately. In writing narrative, for example, most beginning writers give equal attention to every part of the trip from New Hampshire to Wyoming. In that case the article has to be general, with very little information on any one part of the trip. The experienced writer will focus on one part of the trip and develop it in such a way that the reader has the key experience of the trip. The same thing is true of writing an argument or a scientific report. A piece of writing that is fifteen pages long, for example, might be limited, in a rewrite, to the information that was given in two paragraphs in the first draft. Now the writer has fifteen pages in which to develop the most important part of the original text.

I Like To Read about People. Where Are They?

People like to read about people, and academics often scorn this. They want to write about ideas or theories apart from people. That may be appropriate, but if you want to make your writing more lively and have it appeal to a larger audience, then you should populate your pages. Here are some of the ways you can do that:

▶ Tell your story through the people who caused it or who are affected by it. Reveal them in action. Let the reader see them, watch them work and move, hear them speak. It's better to use a few people and develop them in detail than to crowd your pages with too many characters.

▶ Make your point with a quotation or an anecdote, so that other people speak from your pages or act on your pages.

▶ Put specific people into the text when possible. For example, in writing a report to persuade the management of a supermarket to stay open on a holiday you might say, "The store across the street was crowded," or you might say, "Before Thanksgiving dinner grandmothers, harried housewives, husbands and children sent on emergency errands rushed in for single purchases—sausage for the stuffing or a can of cranberry sauce. But in the afternoon the store filled up with families who were bored with television and needed something to do together. They strolled the aisles, filling their carriages with impulse, high-profit items—the first boxes of Christmas candy, ice-cream specialties, fruit baskets—and almost every carriage seemed to have paperback books or magazines in it." Which approach do you think would convince the management of a supermarket chain to change its policy of closing on holidays?

But What About . . .?

We've all gotten mad at a teacher or a speaker who talks over our head or under our feet. And we respond well to speakers who know exactly where we are and talk directly to us. This is a skill the writer has to develop to be effective. The writer may have good reason to ignore the reader and concentrate on other elements in writing a first draft, but during the revision process the writer must make sure that the text anticipates a reader's needs.

▶ Put the text aside and list the questions a reader will ask about the subject. You may also wish to ask another student what questions he or she would ask about the subject. Make sure the questions are answered in the text.

▶ Go through the text to make sure the information the reader needs is at the place in the text where the reader needs it. It won't work to tell the reader about the play that won the game before the reader knows who won.

▶ Read the text to make sure that none of the language is inflated or insulting or patronizing. Don't use terms that are more complicated than they need to be, or more simple than they need to be. Don't use language—or examples—that are sexist, racist, or offensive to any readers.

Hey, Slow Down—Or Speed Up.

The effective writer must also be aware of the pace at which the reader will read the text. If the writer moves too slowly the reader will fall asleep; if the writer moves too quickly the reader will become confused, for he or she will not have the time to absorb one point before becoming involved in the point that is built on it. Here are some ways to become aware of pace:

▶ Read the text the way the reader will. Whenever your mind wanders, put a mark in the margin. Go back later and do some cutting to speed that territory up. Also put a mark in the margin where you got confused. Go back and slow the text down by providing the reader with additional documentation of each point.

▶ Identify those points in the text that are important to the reader's understanding of the text, but that are likely to give the reader difficulty because they are complicated, or because the reader does not expect that point to be made. Make sure the reader has a number of examples for each of those points so the reader will be able to absorb the point being made.

▶ Read aloud as a way of judging the pace at which the language moves. Note where the text could be sped up or slowed down.

I Don't Want To Know This Much about Penguins.

Many pieces of writing run on and on and on. Most pieces of writing are improved by being cut. This is, of course, a matter of judgment. (Someone supposedly told Mozart that *Don Giovanni* had too many notes. He roared back that it had *exactly* the right number.) If you have to cut a piece of writing, here are some tricks:

▶ Select those parts of the text that are absolutely essential and make sure they are developed properly. Brevity is not achieved by the garbage compactor approach, in which everything is compressed, but by a process of selection, in which the most important points are developed to the appropriate length but everything else is cut away.

▶ Cut the pieces of documentation that are repetitive—use one anecdote instead of three, two quotes instead of five. But make sure that each is developed completely.

▶ Go through the text line by line and cut any paragraphs, sentences, or words that can be cut. But read aloud as you do this so that you keep the flavor of the text. The reader should hear an individual writer speaking to an individual reader. The text should not be a series of abrupt headlines or a mere catalogue listing, but that can happen with excessive and unskillful cutting.

Why Should I Keep Reading This?

Effective writing is almost always a story, and we all love to read a story to find how it comes out. Even written arguments, expository essays, and analytical pieces have an imbedded narrative that keeps the reader moving forward. The ability to write narrative is one of those qualities, such as voice, that seems instinctive. But it is a craft that can be studied and learned. Here are some of the ways a narrative can be imbedded in a piece of writing:

▶ Start with specific information that will catch the reader's attention and make the reader want to read on. Do not start with background information, introductions, exclamations, or the reasons you wrote the piece.

▶ Structure the article so that each section answers one question but asks another until you get to the end of the piece. For example, you tell the reader the effect that the chemical dump is having on the children in a playground nearby. But then the reader, naturally, wants to know why a dump was allowed near a playground. You answer that question, and the reader wants to know . . . You can fill it in. The narrative is drawing you along.

▶ Anticipate the reader's questions so the reader gets into the rhythm of having a dialogue with you and is carried forward by knowing you will anticipate his or her needs.

▶ Use any natural action that will carry the reader through the piece of writing. Use chronology and let the reader know that time is passing; use a series of problems and solutions so the reader will see the problems and the solutions as they are solved; hang the piece on a description of a process so the reader will want to follow that process to see how it works out; let the reader walk through the story so the reader takes a visit, let's say, to the state hospital, or goes along as a tug nudges a tanker into a tricky harbor. Use any device that will carry the reader forward in this way. And note that such a device can be the natural progress of thinking, of moving logically from one point to another. The most provocative intellectual essays are built on an imbedded narrative.

All the Stuff Is Jumbled Up; I Can't See What's Important.

If we bring the reader in too close to the subject or keep the reader too far away the result is the same: the elements in the subject blur, and the reader can't see what is important. Here are some tricks for establishing the appropriate distance the reader should stand from the subject:

▶ Focus on the most important element in the subject. Write and rewrite it until you get the focus clear. It may be a paragraph or a cluster of paragraphs, but it will be clear when the reader has enough information to understand it and not so much information that the reader is confused. You may have to use a test reader or two to check your impressions. When you have that section done, then you can write the rest of the piece at the same distance, or with the same degree of detachment or involvement.

▶ Stand back and see if you can include everything that must be included within the length of the piece. If, for example, you're writing a five-page essay you may have to limit your subject more than if you're writing a ten-page essay. You can't simply crowd everything into five pages that you would include in ten.

I Know a Lot about You, But What about the Subject?

The inexperienced writer is often too personal, just as the academic writer is often too impersonal. The biggest problem for most beginners, however, is to learn how to get out of the way so they do not stand between the reader and the subject. Here are some of the tricks of getting out of the way:

▶ Write in the third person—"he" or "she"—except when the "I" is absolutely necessary for the reader to care about or believe the information. To write successfully in the first person you have to achieve a detached "I"; the reader has to see that "I" as a person apart from the author. That's a tricky piece of business, and it's better, in general, to stick with "he" or "she."

▶ Show instead of tell. Reveal the information directly to the reader. Don't preach. Don't tell the reader how to think or feel. Just give the reader the information that will make the reader think or feel that way.

▶ Let other people tell your story. Let the reader hear them report, speak, give evidence.

I've Heard that Song Before.

A great deal of forgettable writing is the result of authors who deal in trite expressions ("It was gross"); clichés ("First the good news . . ."), and stereotypes (the villain wears a black hat). The writer should watch out to make sure that he or she does not view the world through stereotypes—all welfare mothers are . . ., every Scot is . . ., police always . . . It is the responsibility of the writer to go through a draft and eliminate those habits of vision and writing that make prose predictable, dishonest, and lazy.

▶ Read the piece as a whole to see if any of the people, the situations, the arguments, the thought sequences are tired, expected, and probably not true. Rethink the piece.

▶ Look at the examples and make sure they are not the examples the reader expects. Come up with some examples that are unexpected.

▶ Read the piece aloud and avoid expressions that are blank checks you are leaving for the reader to fill in. Eliminate the trite phrase, the dated popular expression, the combination of words that may once have been bright but is now worn with use.

Ho Hum.

Most writing is dull, and this is inexcusable, because it's one of the simplest problems to solve. Some of the tricks to make writing lively are:

▶ Be specific.
▶ Use active verbs.
▶ Use proper nouns.
▶ Put people on the page.
▶ Use direct quotes.
▶ Let the reader see.
▶ Vary sentence length.
▶ Vary paragraph length.
▶ Reveal your feelings about the subject.
▶ Give examples.
▶ Use analogies.
▶ Document with anecdotes.
▶ Change the pace.
▶ Let the reader hear a voice.

Which Computer Wrote This?

Much unread writing is written without a human voice. The writing that is read creates the illusion of a human being speaking to another human being. To put voice in your writing:

▶ Read the text aloud. Writing is not speech written down, but it should be able to be read easily. Edit those constructions that cannot be read gracefully.

▶ Listen to the music of the writing, the rhythm, the pace, the beat, the emphasis. The reader will hear what is being written more than see it. The eye brings a voice to our mind, and that voice should have the music of good speech.

▶ Work hard to make the writing flow easily, conversationally. We are uncomfortable when we hear someone struggle to speak, and for the same reason the reader will not pursue a text if the struggle of the writer is apparent.

So What?

Readers are too busy to be bothered with writing which is not significant and about which the writer didn't care when it was written. It is the responsibility of the writer to show the reader the subject's importance and to put the piece of writing in context. Here are some of the ways this can be done:

▶ If the significance of the subject is not clear to the reader there should be a third or fourth paragraph of the piece that makes the reader aware of the importance of the piece. An article about a cure for diabetes would have to have a context paragraph that showed how common a disease it is and how many people would be helped by the cure.

▶ Make sure that the lead touches on the importance of the subject, and that the ending also implies or explicitly states its importance.

▶ Remind the reader two or three times during the piece of its significance, using different devices, such as quotes or statistics or anecdotes or references to the context paragraph, so the reader knows why he or she is expected to read the piece.

Notes from One Writer's Log

But writing is not all problems. As you write and observe yourself writing, you will discover your own principles of craft, the insights and lessons that you will have to keep relearning during a lifetime of writing. Come into my workroom and listen to this one writer talking to himself at his desk.

> "It takes a great deal of experience to become natural."
> *Willa Cather*

Go out and watch the seagull or the hawk. Make your writing ride lightly on its subject. Make it look easy, as if it were written without effort.

Don't let them put you down because you write simply. It's hard to be simple, the hardest thing there is.

It takes courage to cut, to simplify, to reveal meaning. It's easy to obscure meaning in a swamp of language, but to cut everything away reveals the meaning and exposes the author.

Everything that is cut out of the piece of writing is still there; all the details and information that you have the courage to leave out support what is left in.

Don't forget to read aloud. Good writing must flow, like good talk. How rarely, however, good talk flows like good writing. We come to write better than we speak; we write what we wish we had said at the party, not what we, fumblingly, said.

Say something true and it will become true. You will make something up at your desk—a reason a person is married, or a house you have never seen. That night you will enter that house and have dinner with that marriage.

I write fiction and poetry because I can only tell facts and small truths in nonfiction. If I want to tell—no, if I want to discover Truth, I have to tell stories, make believe, and deal in the lies we call fiction and poetry. A funny business, having to lie to find Truth.

"I guess I work from a combination of curiosity and distance. It seems to me often that I'm looking from a window at something at a great distance and wondering what it is. But I'm not willing to actually go into it. I would rather sit behind the windowsill and write about it. So all my curiosity has to be answered within myself instead of by crossing the street and asking what's going on."
Anne Tyler

When the writing comes I have to remind myself to get out of the way. The writing has its own demands. It is in charge and it will tell me what to do if I pay attention to it.

Never write to impress—to impress others, or worst of all to impress yourself. Write to reveal. Writing is a way of cutting away the surface of things, of exploring, of understanding.

Be suspicious if you know what you want to say. Value those times when you write without notes, without need, from emptiness, thinking nothing is there. Accept the fear and ignore it. Let the writing come, and you will hear yourself say what you did not expect to hear.

Remember that much of the praise for published writing is as irrelevant and silly as editors' reasons for rejecting writing.

Writing for money is cleaner than writing for fame.

There are no publication-day parties.

Humility: the day I bought a used copy of my novel in a dry cleaner's for ten cents.

"If I write what you know, I bore you; if I write what I know, I bore myself; therefore I write what I don't know."
Robert Duncan

"*Nulla dies sine linea*": Pliny, Horace, Trollope, Updike, and others. Never a day without a line, the basic discipline. Nothing may happen if you write every day, but there won't be any writing if you don't have the writing muscle ready when the writing comes.

The comedian always wants to play Shakespeare. The hardest thing is to accept what you are, to write of what you know with your own voice. But that's the only way.

Don't talk about what you're going to write. Tell the story and it will have been told.

Where does the writing come from? From silence. Beware busyness, noise, mental clutter. Just sit; a rocking chair is fine; a back step will do. Wait, the writing will come.

"I started off with the desire to use language experimentally. Then I saw that the right way was the way of simplicity. Straight sentences, no involutions, no ambiguities. Not much description, description isn't my line. Get on with the story. Present the outside world economically and exactly."
    Graham Greene

Don't take yourself seriously, or your writing, or your subject, or your editors, or your teachers, or your friends. Writing is far too important a matter to be taken seriously.

Craft is what you do; art is what somebody else says you have done, usually after you're dead. Practice your craft, forget about art.

Let others do your work for you. Use quotes, anecdotes, information from other authorities; let them carry your message across.

Be arrogant. Don't express your opinion, don't tell people the meaning or what to think. Be much more arrogant than that. Present them with information. Let them believe they have done the thinking and the feeling on their own.

Think how boring it would be if you didn't look at the world with a writer's eye, making up stories, guessing reasons, finishing conversations, making blurred visions come clear.

Such delight in finding two simple words that rub against each other and leave a complicated meaning behind.

Underact. Underwrite.

Artists make me see what I can write. Reflected light, stillness captured, one simple curved line that leaves out and keeps in. When the writing doesn't come I look at paintings, and especially drawings. If I could draw I wouldn't have to write.

Free writing is never free.

"As an artist and scholar I prefer the specific detail to the generalization, images to ideas, obscure facts to clear symbols, and the discovered wild fruit to the synthetic jam."
    Vladimir Nabokov

Don't be objective. Be fair.

Delay the judging. You can't smell garlic when you're eating it.

Don't overlook the obvious. When I've revealed the obvious, readers have responded. I helped them see what they already knew.

"I have drawn things since I was six. All that I made before the age of sixty-five is not worth counting. At seventy-three I began to understand the true construction of animals, plants, trees, birds, fishes, and insects. At ninety I will enter into the secret of things. At one hundred and ten, everything—every dot, every dash—will live.''

> *Hokusai*

If you have to count, count words or pages or hours. No writer can tell if the writing went well today—or if it will go at all tomorrow.

It never gets easier. The longer you write, the higher your standards. The more you know about your craft, the greater the choices. That's what's good about writing: it can't be learned. I can't imagine having a job that can be learned. I want to start each day scared.

Get it down. Write. You have to write badly to write well. Inspiration comes from the chair and that part of the anatomy that belongs there.

"I must keep to my own style, and go on in my own way; and though I may never succeed *again* in that, I am convinced that I should totally fail in any other."

> *Jane Austen*

Write to Learn

The more you write the more you will discover about your subject, your world, and your self. I hope that through your writing and mine you have found out that we do not write what we know as much as *to* know. Writing is exploration. We use language to combine experience and feelings and thoughts into a meaning which we may share with a reader.

Why write? I write, above all, to learn. I hope you have learned that you learn by writing. I write to find out what I have lived, what I have felt, what I have thought. I use language as a tool of seeing and understanding, and I will continue to write, for writing increases my living. I hope you will join me as a writer because I am never bored, and I always have new things that will be taught me by my own words appearing on my page. As long as I write I will continue to learn.

But I will not know how to write. The great crafts are never learned. I take great comfort in that. I continue to learn to write each morning at my writing desk.

I sit down empty, drained, without purpose or possibility, and—if I wait and listen—words start to come. They arrive in awkward clumps. Often I'm not sure what they mean, but if I'm patient and prepared, if I do not try to force the writing, some of the clumps may connect, the fragments may start to flow, and soon I'm not even aware I'm writing.

When I read what I have written, I am often surprised. If I am lucky and have let language lead me toward meaning, it is not what I intended to write. At my desk I keep learning new tricks of my trade, new ways to allow language to extend my world, new ways to surprise myself with my writing.

I hope your writing has surprised you while you have written. I hope that you, like me, will never know how to write, but that we will share the challenge, surprise, and excitement of learning to write and being surprised by what we do not expect to write, write to learn.

Have fun.